LIGHT AND LEAN

CUISINE

**More than 200 Simple
and Delicious Recipes**

LIGHT AND LEAN CUISINE

More than 200 Simple
and Delicious Recipes

Anne Sheasby and Christine McFadden

CLB

5053 Light and Lean Cuisine
This edition published in 1998 by CLB
Copyright © 1998 Quadrillion Publishing Ltd.
Godalming Business Centre, Woolsack Way
Godalming, Surrey, England GU7 1XW

Distributed in the USA by Quadrillion Publishing Inc.
230 Fifth Avenue, New York, NY 10001

Printed in Italy
ISBN 1-85833-873-5

NUTRITIONAL CONSULTANCY by Jill Scott
PROJECT MANAGEMENT by Jo Richardson
PRODUCED by Anthology
ORIGINAL DESIGN CONCEPT by Roger Hyde
DESIGN MANAGEMENT by Rhoda Nottridge
PAGE MAKE-UP by Vanessa Good
PHOTOGRAPHY by Don Last and Sheila Terry
HOME ECONOMY by Christine McFadden,
Joy Parker and Christine France
PRODUCTION DIRECTOR Gerald Hughes
PRODUCTION by Ruth Arthur, Karen Staff,
Neil Randles and Paul Randles

ACKNOWLEDGEMENTS
Christine McFadden, the co-author, would like
to thank Pat Bacon, Katey Balfrey, Don Last
and Jo Richardson

This edition edited by Jillian Stewart

Introduction 10

Light, Lean, & Low-fat 16
Breakfasts & Brunches 20
Soups & Appetizers 26
Light Dishes & Snacks 32
Entrées 42
Salads & Vegetables 56
Desserts 62

Virtually Fat-free 72
Vegetables 78
Poultry, Meat, & Game 92
Fish & Seafood 102
Grains & Beans 112
Fruits & Desserts 122

High Energy 130
Breads 134
Cereals 140
Pasta 148
Rice & Grains 158
Potatoes 164
Beans & Lentils 172
Fruit & Vegetables 182

Index 188

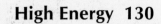

INTRODUCTION

Nutritional recommendations come and go with the regularity of the seasons, but a constant theme with which all commentators seem to agree is the need to cut down on dietary fat. Too much of our energy comes from fat and we need to reduce our intake (and make sensible choices about the types of fat we eat) if we are to reduce our risks of heart disease and other such problems. Unfortunately all the talk of arteries and cholesterol has lead some people to believe that reducing their fat intake must be difficult; in fact, much like giving up smoking. Thankfully this couldn't be further from the truth. The Light and Lean Cuisine *cookbook makes reducing your fat intake easy with delicious, appetising recipes that fall within dietary guidelines that recommend no more than 30-35% of dietary energy comes from fat. This cookbook is aimed at anyone who wants to improve their diet and is split into three sections to cater for some of the most popular areas of healthy eating. 'Light, Lean, and Low-fat' is for anyone who wants to make positive changes regarding their eating habits, and to feel more healthy. If you enjoy what you eat but would like to make general improvements to your diet then this section will prove invaluable. The section on 'Virtually Fat-free' cooking is suitable for those who would like to reduce their fat consumption to lose weight, to minimise fat in their diet for medical reasons, or those who simply want the occasional very low-fat dish as part of their programme of healthy eating. 'High-energy' cooking is about choosing the right balance of foods to help us feel healthier and more energetic. Obviously this aim is relevant to everyone, but is particularly suited to those who have demanding occupations, those engaged in sport and those who work long hours.*

THE BALANCE OF GOOD HEALTH

Diet has long been recognized as an important contributor to health and to the prevention of life-threatening diseases, particularly coronary heart disease and stroke. Eating the right types, combinations, and amounts of foods is important for health for a variety of reasons, including

● less risk of becoming overweight
● less risk of developing heart disease and some cancers
● fewer bowel disorders

Within each food group, it is not only the quantity of foods eaten but also the type of foods chosen that is important for good health. The table opposite indicates the nutrients provided by the different food groups, the healthier options, and an indication of how much you need from each group.

The recipes in this book are specifically designed to fit within these guidelines, so that the choices you make are healthy ones.

One practical way to ensure you are obtaining all the nutrients your body needs is to choose a variety of foods from the major food groups every day. No single food contains all nutrients; different foods are rich in different nutrients. It is the total diet that is either healthy or unhealthy rather than specific foods, although some foods contribute more to healthy eating than others.

FOOD GROUPS

FOOD GROUP AND ITS MAIN NUTRIENTS	TYPES OF FOODS TO CHOOSE MOST OFTEN	HOW MUCH TO CHOOSE
FRUITS AND VEGETABLES *Provide: vitamins, e.g. vitamin C; carotenes; folates; some minerals; and dietary fiber.*	*All types. Eat a wide variety of fresh, frozen, and canned; dried fruits and fruit juices.*	*Aim for at least five servings daily, e.g. orange juice at breakfast; salad in a sandwich at lunch; banana to follow; 2 servings of vegetables with evening meal.*
BREAD, PASTA, RICE, OTHER GRAINS, AND POTATOES *Provide: energy; some protein, calcium, and iron; B vitamins. Whole-grain varieties are higher in fiber.*	*Whole-grain varieties of bread, pasta, rice, pita bread, breakfast cereals; Boiled, baked, or mashed potato.*	*Should be the entrée in every meal. Eat lots!*
MILK AND DAIRY FOODS *Includes milk, yogurt, yellow cheese, and cottage cheese. Provide: calcium, protein, vitamins A & D; vitamin B 12.*	*Lower fat varieties, e.g. skim, 2%, or low-fat milk; low-fat yogurts or low-fat cheeses.*	*Eat or dink moderate amounts: as a guide — 2-3 servings daily (e.g. 1 carton yogurt, 1 cup milk, 1 ounce cheese).*
MEAT, FISH, AND ALTERNATIVES *Includes meat, poultry, fish, eggs, nuts, beans, and legumes. Provide: iron, protein, B vitamins; minerals including zinc and magnesium.*	*Lean cuts of meat; all types of fish (not coated); beans, peas, and lentils are low in fat, high in fiber: use in stews, chili, and casseroles.*	*Eat moderate amounts: as a guide — 2-3 servings daily (e.g. 2-3 ounces meat, 4-5 ounces fish, 1 cup beans/legumes; 2 ounces cheese).*
FOODS CONTAINING FAT; FOODS CONTAINING SUGAR *Includes: fat spreads, i.e. butter, margarine, low-fat spreads; oils; dressings; cream; mayonnaise; cookies; savory snacks; sweets and sugar. Provides: energy and some vitamins and essential fatty acids. Also contain a lot of fat, sugar, and salt.*	*Low-fat spreads, or small amounts of other sour spreads. Use unsaturated oil in cooking, e.g. pure vegetable oils, olive, sunflower, safflower, etc.*	*Small amounts of spreading/cooking fats daily. Savory snacks, cakes, cream, etc. only occasionally.*

FOODS FOR GOOD HEALTH

A number of foods, including fruits and vegetables, are particularly important for good health, since they are known to protect people from chronic illness such as coronary disease and some cancers. Here we explain why these "superfoods" are so good for you. Turn to page 70 and the beginning of Chapter Seven for some delicious recipes using a variety of fruits and vegetables.

ANTIOXIDANTS AND HEALTH

The antioxidant vitamins are beta-carotene, sometimes known as provitamin A because it can be converted to vitamin A in the body, vitamins C, and E (often referred to as the "ACE" vitamins). Certain minerals have antioxidant properties — selenium, zinc, manganese, and copper. They work together to destroy the so-called "free radicals," and thus protect body cells from damage. Compounds called flavenoids, which can be found in red wine, tea, and onions, may also have antioxidant properties.

Free radicals are produced in the body as the by-product of normal metabolism. They can also be taken into the body, for instance through cigarette smoke, and other environmental pollutants such as exhaust fumes or radiation.

Free radicals are highly reactive, unstable compounds which can cause damage to the genetic make-up (DNA) of cells if left unchecked. In order to protect cells against free radical attacks, the body has developed a series of protective mechanisms which involve the "ACE" vitamins.

Beta-carotene or Provitamin A can be converted to vitamin A in the body. However, beta-carotene is also a powerful antioxidant in its own right. It is fat soluble and appears to help protect fatty parts of cells.

Vitamin C is a water-soluble vitamin. It "mops up" free radicals, and is also able to help regenerate vitamin E.

Vitamin E is thought to be the first line of defense against damage to the fatty parts of the cell. Populations with low blood levels of vitamin E have been shown to have a higher risk of heart disease.

The antioxidant minerals described above (selenium, zinc, etc.) are found in a wide range of foods, particularly whole-grain cereals, nuts, meat, milk, and other dairy products.

FOOD SOURCES OF ANTIOXIDANT VITAMINS

Beta-carotene/Provitamin A Bright yellow and orange fruits and green vegetables; carrots; apricots; peaches; tomatoes; red and yellow bell peppers; green leaf vegetables.

Vitamin C Citrus fruits and juices; kiwi fruits; blueberries; acerola; strawberries; green bell peppers; tomatoes; green leaf vegetables; new potatoes.

Vitamin E Vegetable oils (particularly sunflower); almonds; hazelnuts; whole-grain breakfast cereals and bread; green leaf vegetables; avocados; eggs; cheese and other dairy products; margarine.

FIVE-A-DAY FOR HEALTH

Eating a healthy, well-balanced diet that is low in fat, with plenty of fruits and vegetables, is one of the best ways to help protect you and your family from coronary heart disease and cancer. The research evidence that fruits and vegetables have an important protective effect on a wide range of cancers is strong, consistent, and universally accepted.

Leading health organizations recommend consuming at least five servings of different fruits and vegetables every day. For many people, this represents about a 50% increase from current intakes.

One serving of fruit is equivalent to: one piece of fruit, e.g. a large slice of melon, or an apple; a wineglass of fruit juice (about 1/2 cup); 1 tbsp of dried fruits, or 1/2 cup stewed or canned fruits.

One serving of vegetables is equivalent to: two heaped tbsp (approximately 3 ounces) of green or root vegetables, three serving spoons of peas or corn, or a bowl of green salad.

Nature packages a range of different nutrients into fruits and vegetables, so it is important to eat a variety every day in order to maximize your intake of vitamins, minerals, and fiber.

TIPS FOR RETAINING VITAMINS AND MINERALS

- Wash/scrub vegetables rather than peel, where possible.
- Prepare vegetables just before cooking; do not soak them in water prior to cooking.
- Add prepared vegetables to the minimum of boiling water and cook briefly, so that they sill have "crunch."
- Never add baking soda to cooking water.
- Eat raw, steamed, microwaved, or stir-fried vegetables whenever possible, to minimize vitamin losses.
- Serve cooked vegetables immediately — keeping them warm rapidly destroys the vitamin C.
- Frozen fruits and vegetables are as nutritious as fresh, and many even contain more vitamin C.

THE IMPORTANCE OF DIETARY FIBER

There are two types of dietary fiber: insoluble and soluble.

Insoluble fiber is generally found in whole-grain cereals, such as wheat and rye, and is not absorbed or digested by the human body. This form of fiber is important for healthy bowels, and can help protect you from constipation and other bowel problems.

Soluble fiber is found mainly in fruits and vegetables, as well as in oatmeal, and some forms of this fiber can be absorbed into the digestive system. Recent evidence suggests that soluble fiber can help lower blood cholesterol levels, and therefore is useful in protecting the body against heart disease.

We need to consume around 12-18g (about half an ounce) of fiber a day for good health. This dietary fiber should consist of a mixture of cereal fiber, oat bran fiber, beans, and legumes, as well as a variety of fruits and vegetables. Check the nutrition panels on each recipe in the book to monitor your daily fiber intake.

FATS AND HEALTH

A small amount of fat in the diet is important for good health and makes food tastier. Consuming too much fat, however, is associated with obesity, heart disease, and the development of some cancers. Throughout The High-Energy Cookbook, the levels of fat in each recipe are within the international recommended guidelines of no more than 30-35% dietary energy from fat.

Achieving a healthy balance of both the total amount of fat intake in your diet, as well as the type of fat, is an important part of healthy eating. There are three main types of fat: saturated, monounsaturated, and polyunsaturated fats.

SATURATED FATS: These are not essential in the diet, and a high intake is associated with a higher risk of developing heart disease. Saturated fats can raise blood cholesterol levels, so it is a good idea to keep your intake of these fats low.

DIETARY SOURCES OF SATURATED FATS:
● full-fat dairy products (whole milk, cream, sour cream, hard, and soft cheese)
● fatty cuts of red meat and red meat products, such as ground meats and hamburgers, sausages, and sausage patties
● butter and other spreading fats
● foods containing "hidden" fats, including cakes, cookies, snacks, ice cream, and candy

MONOUNSATURATED FATS: Recent studies have shown that monounsaturated fats are effective at lowering blood cholesterol, so they can help protect against the development of heart disease. In the countries of the Mediterranean, such as southern Italy and Greece, where the diet is fairly high in fat (mainly from olive oil, which is rich in monounsaturates) but low in saturated fat, the inhabitants have a very low incidence of heart disease. It is thought that a diet rich in monounsaturates, combined with a high intake of fruits and vegetables, may protect these populations from heart disease.

DIETARY SOURCES OF MONOUNSATURATED FATS:
● Olive oil, peanut oil, canola oil, and fat spreads made from these oils
● nuts (brazils, pecans, and pistachios)
● seeds (sesame)
● meat (lamb, beef, and chicken)

POLYUNSATURATED FATS: Small amounts of these fats are essential for good health. Some can also be helpful at lowering blood cholesterol levels.

Dietary sources of polyunsaturated fats:
● vegetable oils, especially safflower, sunflower, soya, and corn oil
● margarines and spreads labeled "high in polyunsaturates"
● some nuts (pine nuts, walnuts, and brazil nuts) and seeds (sesame)

THE HEALTHY FAT PLAN
● Choose a low-fat spread or a spread high in unsaturated fats, instead of butter.
● Use skim, low-fat, or 2% milk instead of full cream milk.
● Buy the leanest cuts of red meat you can afford; cut away any visible fat.
● Eat fish more often, including oil-rich fish. Broil, microwave, steam, or bake it rather than sautéing or frying it.
● When you use oil for cooking, use it sparingly, and choose one high in unsaturates, such as olive oil, canola, sunflower, or corn oil.
● Choose healthy snacks, such as fresh fruits, corn tortillas, or English muffins, instead of cakes, cookies, and pastries.

PREPARING FOODS

● Choose leaner cuts of meat and cut any visible fat off the meat before cooking. Buy smaller amounts of meat and replace it with vegetables, beans, or lentils.

● Try using low-fat alternatives to meat such as tofu in recipes.

● When using reduced-fat hard cheese such as Cheddar, Monterey jack, or Colby in recipes, use full-flavored varieties so that you are able to use less and retain the flavor.

● Grate or shred cheese finely rather than coarsely — the quantity will go a lot further so that you use less cheese.

● Use water from vegetables, broth cubes, and herbs to make gravies rather than using the meat juices.

● When using oil in a recipe, measure out the oil accurately using measuring spoons rather than pouring the oil straight from the bottle and guessing the amount.

● Use mashed potatoes or a mixture of cooked, mashed root vegetables such as potatoes, carrots, and rutabaga, to top savory dishes instead of pastry.

● Thicken sauces with cornstarch or arrowroot rather than using a butter and flour "roux."

● If using pastry for a pie, make a pie with one crust rather than two crusts, and use whole-wheat pastry made with poly or monounsaturated margarine.

● Use low-fat yogurt, reduced-fat mayonnaise, or low-fat curd cheese as the basis for low-fat or reduced-fat salad dressings.

● Extend reduced-fat mayonnaise with low-fat natural yogurt or curd cheese. Alternatively, thin it down using skim milk or tomato juice and add lots of fat-free or low-fat flavorings such as herbs, spices, mustard, honey, etc. for delicious low-calorie, low-fat salad dressings.

● Use tomato juice or tomato paste mixed with liquid as the basis for a salad dressing.

COOKING FOODS

● Grill, broil, poach, microwave, steam, or boil food whenever possible.

● Choose oven-baked french fries, or if making your own french fries, make thick-cut fries and fry them in unsaturated oil such as sunflower or corn oil.

● When cooking food in a wok, use only a small amount of oil or wine, fruit juice, or low-fat or fat-free broth in place of oil.

● Avoid frying foods as much as possible, but if you do fry foods, use an oil that is high in unsaturates such as sunflower, olive, or canola oil, and use as little as possible.

● "Sweat" or cook vegetables in a covered pan in their own juices, rather than frying or sautéing them, or soften in a little low-fat broth, wine, or water.

● Baste foods with fruit juice or a fat-free marinade instead of adding fat when broiling, grilling, or barbecuing.

● Roast meats on a rack so that some of the fat will drain away from the meat collected under the roast.

● When stewing tougher cuts of meat, skim off and discard any fat that rises to the surface during cooking.

● Dry-fry ground meats and other meats, and drain off excess fat before adding vegetables and other ingredients for casseroles, etc.

SERVING FOODS

● When serving cooked vegetables, toss them in chopped fresh mixed herbs and/or a splash of lemon juice for added flavor and color, rather than dotting with butter to serve.

● Garnish savory dishes with chopped fresh herbs, watercress, or a sprinkling of seeds such as cumin or sesame, to add flavor, colour, and texture to the food.

● Choose baked or boiled potatoes in place of french fries, roasted, or fried potatoes.

● Mash potatoes with skim milk or yogurt and seasoning instead of using butter and whole milk.

● Spread toasted muffins, coffeecake, and bagels with low-fat or very low-fat spread or with fat-free products such as reduced-sugar jam or jelly.

● In sandwiches, spread the bread with low-fat or fat-free dressing or mayonnaise instead of using full-fat spreads.

PREPARING AND SERVING DESSERTS

● Choose fruit canned in fruit juice rather than in syrup.

● Use skim milk to make sauces, baked desserts, scones, and batter mixtures, etc.

● Use dried or fresh fruit purées in place of all or some of the fat in suitable baking recipes (see the feature on page 64).

● Reduce the quantity of sugar in a recipe and replace it with dried fruit such as apricots or yellow raisins, or fresh fruit such as bananas.

● Decorate desserts with fresh herb sprigs such as mint sprigs, edible flowers, or slices or twists of fruit in place of piped cream or chocolate.

LOW-FAT SPREADS

A wide range of low-fat and very low-fat spreads are widely available, and some are suitable for using in cooking as well as for spreading. Very low-fat spreads, which have a fat content of about 20%, are only suitable for spreading and are not suitable for cooking due to their high water content.

Low-fat spreads, which have a fat content of about 40%, are suitable for some cooking methods. They can be used for some all-in-one cake and cookie recipes, all-in-one sauces, choux pastry, for gently cooking or sautéing vegetables, and for some cake icings. They are not suitable for deep-fat or shallow frying, clarifying, pastry-making, some types of cookie, shortbread, rich fruit cakes, or preserves such as lemon curd or lemon cheese.

When heating low-fat spreads for a recipe, always melt the spread over a gentle heat and do not allow it to boil, since this may cause the product to spit, burn, or spoil. All-in-one sauces should be whisked continuously during cooking over a low heat. Low-fat spreads may in cooking behave slightly differently than full-fat products such as butter, but the results will be just as acceptable and you won't even notice the difference.

Some cooked products made with half or low-fat spreads may be slightly different in texture, but again they are just as delicious. For example, choux pastry made using low-fat spread may be slightly more crisp and light in texture than choux pastry made using butter or margarine. Sponge cakes tend to have a slightly lighter texture, and uncooked graham cracker cheesecake bases may not be quite so crisp. The shelf-life of cooked products made using low-fat spreads may be reduced due to the lower fat content, but you can be sure that these goodies will have gone before the food becomes stale!

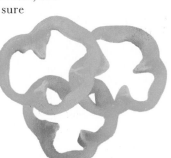

NUTRITIONAL ANALYSES

Nutritional information for each recipe in the book is provided in easy-reference panels. The nutritional figures are per serving of the recipe in each case, and do not include any serving suggestions that may be included in the introduction or at the end of a recipe. These analyses have been compiled as accurately as possible, but the nutritional content of foods will vary depending on their source.

As well as specifying the number of calories per serving, the nutritional analysis also gives the overall fat content, which is then broken down into the three main types of fat: saturates, monounsaturates, and polyunsaturates.

The recommended daily intake of dietary fiber is betwen 12 and 18 g. The figures given in the nutritional analyses indicate how much fiber each recipe contributes to your daily total.

Figures for the sodium content of each recipe are also included. This figure does not include any seasoning (i.e. salt) that is added to the recipe during preparation and cooking.

The nutritional analyses detail the percentage of total calories from fat, and the percentage of calories from saturated fat is also given — in a healthy diet, this should provide no more than 10% of calories.

Where a nutritional analysis states that a recipe is a good source of a particular vitamin, mineral, or another nutrient, this indicates that a serving of the recipe will make a significant contribution to the recommended daily allowance (RDA) of the nutrients.

A GUIDE TO THE RECIPES

● All spoon measurements refer to American Standard measuring spoons, and all measurements given are for level spoons unless otherwise stated.

● The cooking times for all the recipes in this book are based on the oven or broiler being preheated.

● All eggs used in the recipes are medium (weighing 21 ounces per dozen) eggs.

KEY TO SYMBOLS

 Suitable for freezing.

 Suitable for cooking in a microwave oven.

 Suitable for vegetarians.

Please note that the term vegetarian applies to lacto-ovo vegetarians, i.e. people who eat eggs and dairy products but not meat, fish, and poultry, nor any products derived from these foods.

LIGHT, LEAN, AND LOW-FAT

A low-fat diet is a recognized part of a healthy lifestyle but, contrary to what many people believe, this does not mean abstaining from many of the pleasures of good food. If you enjoy what you eat, but would like to reduce your calorie and fat intake to healthier levels, then the recipes in this section are for you.

Reducing the amount of fat in the diet does not necessarily mean opting for all those expensive low-calorie sandwiches and diet meals in the supermarkets (many of which are stuffed with additives and not very many vitamins and minerals), but eating fresh, healthy foods, along with a small proportion of unsaturated fats and a minimum of saturated fats. In this section you will find a wealth of recipes that illustrate this principle, alongside invaluable tips on how to incorporate low-fat methods into your own everyday cooking. As these recipes illustrate, producing light, low-fat recipes that everyone will enjoy is simply a matter of thinking a little about your ingredients and cooking methods.

REDUCING FAT AND CALORIES
IN EVERYDAY MEALS

There are many ways in which you can reduce the fat content of everyday meals and eat a more healthy balance of foods, which can help to improve your general health and well-being. One simple way to reduce your fat intake is to replace full-fat ingredients such as butter, cheese, and sour or heavy cream with reduced-fat ingredients.

By replacing one full-fat ingredient such as cream for a similar, "lighter" ingredient, you will also be able to reduce the fat and therefore calorie content of a meal without affecting the flavor.

Three fairly typical meals have been chosen here and featured in pairs. Each pair of meals consists of an "original" recipe, which is made using more traditional ingredients, and a "lighter" version of the same recipe, which uses alternative fat-reduced ingredients or healthier cooking methods.

As you can see, the recipes within each pair do not differ very much in appearance, but the fat contents and therefore the calorie contents are surprisingly different. The lighter recipe in each case illustrates just how easy it is to make a few simple changes when preparing recipes or cooking food, resulting in quite remarkable fat and calorie savings.

For each pair of meals, there is a panel of points summarizing the ways in which fat and calories have been saved or reduced with only relatively minor changes to the original recipe. Sometimes you will even get a larger portion of food with the lighter recipe, which can't be a bad option!

APPETIZER: AVOCADO & SHRIMP COCKTAIL

(original recipe)

Slices of avocado and shrimp have been dressed with a flavored mayonnaise and served on a bed of shredded lettuce.

Avocado pears are high in calories and high in fat, but the fats are predominantly monounsaturates.

AVOCADO & SHRIMP COCKTAIL

(lighter recipe)

(full recipe on page 31)

Half the amount of avocado has been used for this recipe. It has been diced and mixed with some cucumber, green onions (scallions), and green bell pepper together with the shrimp.

A low-fat yogurt dressing replaces the mayonnaise dressing.

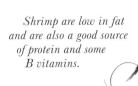

Shrimp are low in fat and are also a good source of protein and some B vitamins.

HOW WE REDUCED CALORIES AND FAT

● replaced some of the avocado with a tasty mixture of sliced cucumber, chopped green onions (scallions), and diced green bell pepper

● made a delicious dressing using low-fat yogurt combined with a little tomato ketchup, honey, chopped fresh coriander (cilantro), and a dash of Tabasco sauce. Chili, ground coriander (cilantro), cumin, or crushed fresh garlic may be added to vary the flavor of the dressing

Calories saved = 217 calories per serving

Fat saved = 25.7 g fat per serving

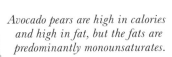

These baby carrots have been boiled, then glazed with a mixture of melted butter and sugar.

The new potatoes have been roasted whole in oil, then tossed in chopped, fresh herbs.

SPICY ROAST CHICKEN

(lighter recipe)

(full recipe on page 44)

A skinless, boneless chicken breast has been lightly brushed with a mixture of lemon juice, garlic, and spices, then oven-roasted in a parchment paper parcel with no added fat.

These baby carrots have been braised in the oven in broth, dried mixed herbs, and seasoning. They are served and garnished with cumin seeds for added flavor and color.

These new potatoes have been brushed with oil, roasted, then tossed in chopped fresh herbs.

PROFITEROLES

(lighter recipe)

(full recipe on page 69)

These profiteroles have been filled with low-fat vanilla ice cream and served with a "lighter" chocolate sauce.

Serve the profiteroles with fresh, ripe strawberries and decorate with strawberry leaves or mint sprigs.

ENTRÉE: SPICY ROAST CHICKEN MEAL

(original recipe)
A boneless chicken breast with the skin left on has been brushed with olive oil flavored with lemon juice, garlic, and spices, then roasted in the oven with some butter.

Steamed broccoli is low in calories and fat, and is a good source of vitamin C.

DESSERT: PROFITEROLES

(original recipe)
These profiteroles have been filled with whipped cream and served with a rich chocolate sauce.

HOW WE REDUCED CALORIES AND FAT

- removed skin from the chicken breast
- roasted the chicken breast in a parchment paper parcel rather than roasting it with the addition of butter
- brushed the potatoes lightly with a small amount of oil rather than letting them sit in a larger amount of oil
- braised the carrots in broth and herbs, rather than glazing them in a mixture of melted butter and sugar

Calories saved = 435 calories per serving

Fat saved = 46.1 g fat per serving

- used low-fat spread in place of butter or margarine to make the choux pastry
- omitted the butter and cream traditionally added to the chocolate sauce
- reduced the quantity of chocolate used to make the chocolate sauce, and therefore slightly reduced the amount of chocolate sauce served with the profiteroles
- filled the profiteroles with reduced-fat ice cream in place of whipped cream

Calories saved = 138 calories per serving

Fat saved = 21.3 g fat per serving

BREAKFASTS & BRUNCHES

W̲hether you're an early riser or a late sleeper, breakfast is a critical part of your day. Make your mornings both healthy and memorable with nutritious and delicious dishes. Here is a selection of quick and easy breakfast and brunch recipes, some sweetly fruity and others satisfyingly savory, but all as appetizing as they are nourishing, to ensure a positive start to your day.

BROILED FRUIT
KABOBS

Serve these delectable warm kabobs with low-fat plain or fruit-flavored yogurt for an appetizing and refreshing start to the day. Alternatively, they can be served with low-fat ice cream or reduced-fat cream for a delightful dessert.

Preparation time: 15 minutes

Cooking time: 5-10 minutes

Serves 4

*2 small bananas
juice of 1 lemon
8 canned pineapple cubes in fruit juice, drained
1 pink grapefruit, peeled and segmented
8 ready-to-eat dried pitted prunes
8 ready-to-eat dried apricots
2 tbsp unsweetened orange juice
1 tbsp clear honey
¹/₂ tsp ground mixed spice*

1 Peel and slice the bananas into chunks and toss them in lemon juice, to prevent browning.

2 Thread the fresh and dried fruit onto 4 long skewers, dividing the ingredients equally between the kabobs.

3 Mix together the orange juice, honey, and mixed spice, and brush over the kabobs.

4 Barbecue the kabobs or broil under a preheated broiler for 5-10 minutes, turning frequently. Brush the kabobs with any remaining orange juice mixture while they are cooking, to prevent them from drying out.

5 Serve the warm kabobs with low-fat plain yogurt.

VARIATIONS
● Use other fresh, canned, and dried fruits of your choice, such as oranges, peaches, kiwi fruits, pears, and raisins.
● Use pineapple or apple juice in place of the orange juice.
● Use ground cinnamon or nutmeg in place of the mixed spice.

BRAN FRUIT
CEREAL

This tasty and nutritious whole-grain cereal mixed with fruits is ideal for breakfast or as a filling dish for brunch.

Preparation time: 15 minutes
Serves 6

4 tbsp rolled oats
4 tbsp bran flakes
2 tbsp wheat flakes
2 tbsp barley flakes
2 tbsp sunflower seeds
$^1/_2$ cup yellow raisins
2 tbsp dried pears, chopped
2 tbsp dried apples, chopped
2 tbsp dried peaches, chopped
2 cups small strawberries, hulled and halved
1 cup raspberries

1 Place the rolled oats, bran flakes, wheat flakes, barley flakes, sunflower seeds, and dried fruits in a large bowl and mix well. Spoon the cereal into 6 serving bowls.

2 Combine the strawberries and raspberries, and scatter them over the cereal, dividing them equally between the bowls.

3 Serve immediately with skim milk or low-fat plain yogurt.

VARIATIONS
● Use rye flakes and jumbo oats in place of the wheat flakes and rolled oats.
● Use other dried fruits such as raisins, apricots, and pineapple in place of the yellow raisins, apples, and pears.
● Use chopped nuts such as almonds, pecans, or brazil nuts in place of the sunflower seeds.
● Top the cereal with fresh fruit of your choice such as sliced kiwi fruit and peaches.

COOK'S TIP
● Make up a large batch of this whole-grain cereal and store it in an airtight container. Add the fresh fruit just before serving.

SAVORY
RICE

Smoked fish and rice are a delicious combination, and ensure an energy-packed start to the day.

Preparation time: 15 minutes

Cooking time: 40 minutes

Serves 4

³/₄ cup long-grain brown rice
12 ounces skinless, smoked fish fillets, such as finnan haddie, smoked cod, or smoked white fish
1 small onion, minced
¹/₂ cup button mushrooms, sliced
2 eggs, hard-boiled
3 tbsp low-fat or 2% milk
2 tbsp minced fresh parsley
salt and freshly ground black pepper
juice of 1 lime (optional)
fresh lime slices and fresh herb sprigs, to garnish

1 Cook the rice in a saucepan of lightly salted, boiling water for about 30-35 minutes, until just cooked and tender. Drain thoroughly and keep hot.

2 Meanwhile, place the fish fillets, onion, and mushrooms in a large nonstick skillet with a lid, and cover with water. Cover, bring to the boil, and simmer gently for 10-15 minutes, until the fish is just cooked and tender.

3 Drain, reserving the fish, onion, and mushrooms and discarding the remaining liquid. Flake the fish and set aside. Peel the eggs, discard the shells, and chop the eggs coarsely.

4 Place the milk in a nonstick saucepan. Add the cooked rice, fish, vegetables, eggs, parsley, and seasoning and stir to mix.

5 Cook gently, stirring frequently, for about 5 minutes, until piping hot. Sprinkle with the lime juice, if using, and stir to mix.

6 Garnish with lime slices and fresh herb sprigs and serve on its own or with some fresh crusty bread.

NUTRITIONAL ANALYSIS
(figures are per serving)

Calories = 297

Fat = 5.3g

of which saturates = 1.5g

    monounsaturates = 1.8g

    polyunsaturates = 1.1g

Protein = 24.4g

Carbohydrate = 40.5 g

Dietary fiber = 1.6g

Sodium = 0.7g

Percentage of total calories from fat = 16%

of which saturates = 5%

Good source of vitamin B12

VARIATIONS
● Use smoked oysters or marinated salmon in place of smoked white fish.
● Use lemon juice in place of the lime juice.
● Use long-grain white rice in place of the brown rice.

COOK'S TIP
● Reserve the fish cooking liquid and use as broth for another recipe. Freeze for later use when it has cooled.

SAUTÉED POTATOES WITH
BACON & HERBS

*This recipe makes a great start to the day.
Serve it with toast for breakfast or with poached eggs for
a more substantial brunch.*

Preparation time: 10 minutes

Cooking time: 15-20 minutes

Serves 4

*2 tsp sunflower oil
1 pound (4 cups) boiled potatoes, cooled and diced
4 shallots, minced
4 slices smoked lean bacon, trimmed and diced
2-3 tbsp chopped fresh mixed herbs or
1-2 tsp dried herbs
salt and freshly ground black pepper*

1 Heat the oil in a nonstick skillet and add the potatoes, shallots, and bacon.

2 Cook over a medium heat, stirring frequently, until the potatoes are browned and the bacon is cooked.

3 Add the herbs and seasoning, mix well, and serve immediately with fresh crusty bread or toast.

NUTRITIONAL ANALYSIS

(figures are per serving)

Calories = 129

Fat = 3.1g

of which saturates = 0.8g

monounsaturates = 1.7g

polyunsaturates = 0.4g

Protein = 6.4g

Carbohydrate = 20.0g

Dietary fiber = 1.7g

Sodium = 0.4g

Percentage of total calories from fat = 22%, of which saturates = 5%

APPLE & CINNAMON
COFFEECAKE

Serve this deliciously moist, yeastless coffeecake warm or cold, on its own or with a thin scraping of low-fat spread or reduced-sugar jam or jelly.

Preparation time: 20 minutes
Cooking time: 25-30 minutes
Makes 8 wedges

1 cup self-rising flour
1 cup whole-wheat flour
$^1/_2$ tsp double-acting baking powder
pinch of salt
1 tsp baking soda
4 tbsp soft margarine
4 tbsp light soft brown sugar
1 tsp ground cinnamon
1 medium-size tart apple, peeled,
cored, and coarsely grated
3-4 tbsp skim milk,
plus extra for glazing
1 tbsp light brown sugar

1 Sieve the flours, baking powder, salt, and baking soda into a bowl. Rub in the margarine until the mixture resembles bread crumbs.

2 Stir in the soft brown sugar and cinnamon, then add the grated apples and mix well. Stir in enough milk to give a soft but not sticky dough.

3 Turn the dough onto a floured surface, knead lightly, and form into a 7-inch round.

4 Place the cake on a lightly floured cookie sheet, brush the top with milk, and sprinkle with the light brown sugar. Mark the cake into 8 even wedges.

5 Bake in a preheated oven at 400° for 25-30 minutes, until risen and golden brown.

6 Transfer to a wire rack to cool and break into wedges to serve. Serve warm or cold on its own, or with a thin scraping of low-fat spread or reduced-sugar jam or jelly.

VARIATIONS

- Use all whole-wheat flour, graham flour, or all white flour in place of a mixture.
- Replace the cinnamon with ground mixed spice.
- Use white or golden granulated sugar in place of the soft brown sugar.

COOK'S TIP

- When making this kind of yeastless dough and mixing the ingredients together, never over-mix or knead the mixture too heavily, since this may result in a heavy, uneven cake.

NUTRITIONAL ANALYSIS

(figures are per wedge)

Calories = 190
Fat = 6.2g
of which saturates = 1.3g
     monounsaturates = 1.9g
     polyunsaturates = 2.7g
Protein = 3.5g
Carbohydrate = 32.5g
Dietary fiber = 2.2g
Sodium = 0.2g

Percentage of total calories from fat = 29%
of which saturates = 6%

❄ APRICOT & DATE 🌿
BREAKFAST LOAF

This tasty treat is an excellent choice for breakfast or brunch, and also makes a great snack for any time of the day.

Preparation time: 15 minutes, plus soaking time for the fruits

Cooking time: 1 hour

Makes one 2-pound loaf (12 slices)

1 cup ready-to-eat dried apricots, chopped
1 cup dried pitted dates, chopped
¹/₂ cup yellow raisins
¹/₂ cup light soft brown sugar
²/₃ cup cold tea
2 eggs, beaten
2 cups whole-wheat flour
1 tsp baking powder
2 tsp ground mixed spice

1 Place the fruit and sugar in a bowl and stir to mix. Add the tea and mix well. Cover and leave to soak for at least 4 hours or overnight, until most of the tea has been absorbed and the fruit is plumped up.

2 Stir in the eggs, then add the flour, baking powder, and mixed spice, and mix thoroughly.

3 Turn the mixture into a lightly greased 2-pound loaf pan and level the surface.

4 Bake in a preheated oven at 350° for about 1 hour, or until firm to the touch. Cool in the pan for a few minutes, then unmold onto a wire rack to cool completely.

5 Serve warm or cold in slices, on its own or with a thin scraping of low-fat spread or reduced-sugar jam or jelly.

VARIATIONS

- Use a mixture of dried fruits of your choice such as papaya and raisins.
- Use ground cinnamon in place of the mixed spice.

NUTRITIONAL ANALYSIS

(figures are per slice)

Calories = 196
Fat = 1.6g
of which saturates = 0.4g
     monounsaturates = 0.5g
     polyunsaturates = 0.3g
Protein = 4.9g
Carbohydrate = 43.6g
Dietary fiber = 3.4g
Sodium = 0.02g

Percentage of total calories from fat = 7%
of which saturates = 2%

SOUPS & APPETIZERS

*I*n taking the time and effort to make your own soups, you will be rewarded both
by quality flavor and a high level of nutrients. Here are hearty hot soups as
well as refreshing chilled soups, all of which are quick and easy to prepare.
Your choice of appetizer should relate to the composition of the meal as a whole.
A good appetizer will complement rather than copy the taste and appearance
of the entrée. Choose accordingly from this delicious selection, ranging from
dips and cocktails to classics such as Macaroni and Cheese.

FRESH TOMATO & BASIL
SOUP

*This is a light, fresh-tasting soup ideal served with thick slices of fresh
crusty bread or bread rolls.*

Preparation time: 15 minutes

Cooking time: 30 minutes

Serves 4

2 pounds tomatoes, roughly chopped
2 onions, chopped
8 ounces carrots, sliced
3³/₄ cups vegetable broth
1 tbsp tomato paste
pinch of sugar
salt and freshly ground black pepper
3 tbsp chopped fresh basil

1 Place all the ingredients,
except the basil, in a large
saucepan and mix well.

2 Cover, bring to the boil, and
simmer for about 30 minutes,
stirring occasionally, until the
vegetables are tender.

3 Cool the mixture slightly, then
transfer it to a blender or food
processor and blend until smooth.

4 Strain the soup through a sieve and
discard the pulp.

5 Return the mixture to the saucepan and stir in the basil. Reheat gently and adjust the seasoning before serving. Serve with fresh crusty bread rolls.

VARIATIONS

● Use other chopped fresh herbs such as coriander (cilantro), parsley, or mixed fresh herbs in place of the basil.

● Use two 14-ounce cans chopped tomatoes in place of the fresh tomatoes.

● Use 2 trimmed and sliced leeks in place of the onions.

Try creating your own delicious light soups with other simple mixtures of vegetables such as leek and potato, carrot and coriander (cilantro), cauliflower and broccoli (flavored with chili powder), spinach and nutmeg, tomato, lentil, and onion, watercress and onion, or celery and parsley.

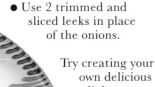

NUTRITIONAL ANALYSIS

(figures are per serving)

Calories = 98
Fat = 1.5g
of which saturates = 0.3g
    monounsaturates = 0.2g
    polyunsaturates = 0.6g
Protein = 3.4g
Carbohydrate = 18.8g
Dietary fiber = 4.8g
Sodium = 0.5g

Percentage of total calories from fat = 14%
of which saturates = 3%
Good source of vitamins A, C, & E

CHILLED CUCUMBER & MINT
SOUP

An elegant, refreshing soup that would bring a cooling note to a balmy summer evening.

Preparation time: 15 minutes, plus 20 minutes standing time for the cucumber, plus chilling time

Serves 4

2 cucumbers, peeled and cut into large cubes
1 small onion, chopped
1 clove garlic, crushed
2 cups low-fat plain yogurt
$2/3$ cup vegetable broth, cooled
2 tbsp chopped fresh mint
salt and freshly ground black pepper
fresh mint sprigs, to garnish

1 Place the cucumber in a bowl, sprinkle with salt, and set aside for 20 minutes. Rinse thoroughly and pat dry with paper towels.

2 Place the cucumber, onion, garlic, yogurt, broth, mint, and seasoning in a blender or food processor and blend until relatively smooth and well mixed. Taste and add more seasoning, if needed.

3 Pour into a bowl, cover, and chill before serving. Garnish with fresh mint sprigs and serve with thick slices of fresh whole-wheat bread or toast.

VARIATIONS

● Use other herbs such as tarragon, parsley, coriander (cilantro), or mixed herbs in place of the mint.

● Use 4 shallots in place of the onion.

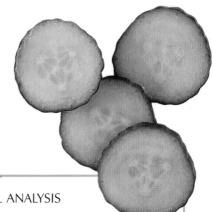

NUTRITIONAL ANALYSIS

(figures are per serving)

Calories = 89
Fat = 1.3g
of which saturates = 0.6g
    monounsaturates = 0.2g
    polyunsaturates = 0g

Protein = 7.4g
Carbohydrate = 12.3g
Dietary fiber = 0.9g
Sodium = 0.2g

Percentage of total calories from fat = 13%, of which saturates = 6%

HERBED MUSHROOM
PÂTÉ

A light pâté that is excellent spread on thick slices
of toast or fresh bread for an appetizer.

Preparation time: 30 minutes, plus cooling and chilling time

Cooking time: 1 hour

Serves 8

4 tbsp vegetable broth
1 onion, minced
2 cloves garlic, crushed
2 sticks celery, chopped
12 ounces (about 2 cups) closed cup mushrooms,
sliced
12 ounces (about 2 cups) brown cap mushrooms,
sliced
3-4 tbsp chopped fresh mixed herbs
3 tbsp port wine
salt and freshly ground black pepper
6 tbsp fresh whole-wheat bread crumbs
2 eggs, beaten
fresh herb sprigs and tomato slices, to garnish

1 Place the broth, onion, garlic, and celery
in a saucepan, cover, and cook gently for
10 minutes, stirring occasionally.

2 Stir in the mushrooms, cover, and cook
gently for 10 minutes, stirring occasionally.

3 Remove the pan from the heat, add
the herbs, port wine, and seasoning and
mix well.

4 Set aside to cool slightly, then place
the mixture in a liquidizer or food
processor and blend until smooth.
Transfer the mixture to a bowl, add the
bread crumbs and eggs, and mix well.

5 Adjust the seasoning, transfer to a
lightly greased and lined 2-pound loaf
pan, and level the surface.

6 Bake in a preheated oven at 350° for
about 1 hour, until lightly browned and
set on top.

7 Set aside to cool completely in the pan.
Once cool, cover and refrigerate for
several hours before serving.

8 To serve, turn carefully out of the pan
and garnish with fresh herb sprigs and
tomato slices. Serve in slices with fresh
crusty bread or toast.

VARIATIONS
● Use fresh parsley in place of the fresh
mixed herbs.
● Use sherry or brandy in place of the
port wine.
● Use white or brown bread crumbs in
place of the whole-wheat bread crumbs
● Use 2 leeks in place of the onion.
● Use button mushrooms in place of the
closed cap mushrooms.

TUNA & WATERCRESS
DIP

This is a delicious and refreshing dip that is best served with a good selection of nutritious and colorful raw vegetables.

Preparation time: 10 minutes, plus chilling time
Serves 8

14-ounce can tuna in water, drained and flaked
1 pound canned pinto beans, rinsed and drained
1 cup small-curd cottage cheese
small bunch watercress, roughly chopped
2 tbsp reduced-calorie mayonnaise
2 tbsp low-fat plain yogurt
finely grated rind of 1 lime
salt and freshly ground black pepper

1 Place the tuna, beans, cottage cheese, watercress, mayonnaise, yogurt, lime rind, and seasoning in a liquidizer or food processor. Blend until the mixture is smooth and thoroughly mixed.

2 Transfer the tuna mixture to a serving dish, cover, and chill before serving.

3 Serve the dip with a selection of raw vegetables such as sticks of bell pepper, cucumber, and carrots, green onions (scallions), and baby corn cobs.

VARIATIONS
● Use canned or barbecued salmon in place of the tuna.
● Add 1-2 tbsp chopped fresh mixed herbs or fresh parsley to the mixture before serving.
● Add 1 small onion or 4 green onions (scallions), the green parts included, to the mixture before blending.

NUTRITIONAL ANALYSIS
(figures are per serving)

Calories = 112
Fat = 2.8g
of which saturates = 0.8g
      monounsaturates = 0.4g
      polyunsaturates = 0.2g
Protein = 15.6g
Carbohydrate = 6.6g
Dietary fiber = 2.0g
Sodium = 0.4g

Percentage of total calories from fat = 23%
of which saturates = 6%
Good source of vitamins B12 & D

SEAFOOD
COCKTAIL

This combination of mixed seafood and fresh salad ingredients, tossed together in a tangy horseradish dressing, makes a sumptuous appetizer for a special occasion meal.

Preparation time: 15 minutes

Serves 6

4 tbsp reduced-calorie mayonnaise
2 tbsp low-fat plain yogurt
2 tbsp hot horseradish sauce or grated fresh horseradish
salt and freshly ground black pepper
2 tbsp chopped fresh mixed herbs (optional)
$^1/_2$ cup cooked, peeled jumbo shrimp
1 cup cooked, shelled mussels
1 cup cooked, shelled scallops
1 cup cherry (salad) tomatoes, halved
$^1/_2$ cucumber, diced
1 bunch green onions (scallions), chopped
mixed green salad leaves
fresh herb sprigs, to garnish

1 To make the dressing, place the mayonnaise, yogurt, horseradish sauce, seasoning, and herbs, if using, in a bowl and mix together thoroughly. Set aside.

2 Place the shrimp, mussels, and scallops in a bowl, add the tomatoes, cucumber, and green onions (scallions) and stir to mix. Add the dressing and toss together.

3 Arrange a bed of green salad leaves in 4 serving dishes and spoon the seafood mixture over the top.

4 Garnish with fresh herb sprigs and serve immediately with warm bread rolls.

VARIATIONS
● Use your own choice of cooked seafood for this recipe.
● Use salad ingredients of your choice such as radishes, sugar-snap peas, and mushrooms.
● Use whole-grain mustard in place of the horseradish.

NUTRITIONAL ANALYSIS
(figures are per serving)

Calories = 144
Fat = 4.9g
of which saturates = 0.8g
    monounsaturates = 1.0g
    polyunsaturates = 2.5g

Protein = 19.4g
Carbohydrate = 3.9g
Dietary fiber = 0.8g
Sodium = 0.8g

Percentage of total calories from fat = 31%, of which saturates = 5%
Good source of vitamin B12

AVOCADO & SHRIMP
COCKTAIL

In this light version of an old favorite, diced avocado and plump shrimp are brought together in a tasty yogurt dressing.

Preparation time: 15 minutes
Serves 4

FOR THE DRESSING
2/3 cup low-fat plain yogurt
1 tsp honey
1 tbsp tomato ketchup
1 tbsp chopped fresh coriander (cilantro)
dash of Tabasco sauce
salt and freshly ground black pepper

FOR THE COCKTAIL
1 small avocado
lemon juice, for sprinkling
4 green onions (scallions), chopped
1/2 cucumber, peeled and sliced
1 small green bell pepper, seeded and diced
8 cooked jumbo shrimp
shredded lettuce
fresh coriander (cilantro) leaves, to garnish

1 Place all the dressing ingredients in a bowl and mix well. Set aside.

2 Peel, pit, and dice the avocado and sprinkle with lemon juice to prevent discoloration.

3 Place the diced avocado, green onions (scallions), cucumber, bell pepper, and shrimp in a bowl and stir to mix.

4 Arrange a bed of shredded lettuce in 4 serving dishes. Top with the avocado-and-shrimp mixture.

5 Spoon some dressing over each portion, garnish with fresh coriander (cilantro) leaves, and serve immediately with thick slices of fresh crusty whole-wheat bread.

VARIATIONS
● Add 1 tsp chili powder, ground coriander (cilantro), or cumin to the mayonnaise mixture.
● Use cooked, shelled clams, scallops, or mussels in place of the shrimp.
● Add 1 crushed clove of garlic to the dressing for added piquancy, if preferred.

NUTRITIONAL ANALYSIS

(figures are per serving)

Calories = 151
Fat = 6.0g
of which saturates = 1.4g
⠀⠀⠀⠀monounsaturates = 3.2g
⠀⠀⠀⠀polyunsaturates = 0.8g
Protein = 17.3g
Carbohydrate = 7.3g
Dietary fiber = 1.5g
Sodium = 1.1g

Percentage of total calories from fat = 35%
of which saturates = 8%
Good source of vitamin B12

PEARS WITH
BLUE CHEESE

A creamy blue cheese sauce complements perfectly the luscious fruity flavor of pears in this dish. Try serving the sauce as a baked potato topping for a delicious entrée.

Preparation time: 15 minutes
Serves 6

1/2 cup low-fat soft cheese with garlic and herbs
1/3 cup whole milk plain yogurt
2 tbsp crumbled mature blue cheese
6 large ripe pears
juice of 1 lemon

1 Place the soft cheese, yogurt, and blue cheese in a small bowl and blend together until smooth and well mixed.

2 Peel, core, and slice the pears and toss them in lemon juice.

3 Arrange the pear slices on serving plates and spoon the blue cheese sauce alongside the pears. Serve immediately.

VARIATION
● Any variety of strongly flavored soft cheese, such as Stilton or Gorgonzola, can be used for the sauce.

NUTRITIONAL ANALYSIS

(figures are per serving)

Calories = 155
Fat = 4.3g
of which saturates = 1.8g
⠀⠀⠀⠀monounsaturates = 0.9g
⠀⠀⠀⠀polyunsaturates = 0.1g
Protein = 6.0g
Carbohydrate = 24.5g
Dietary fiber = 3.7g
Sodium = 0.1g

Percentage of total calories from fat = 25%
of which saturates = 10%

LIGHT DISHES & SNACKS

*B*e it lunchtime or dinner, eating alone or feasting with friends, this selection
of delicious light dishes and snacks will impress your tastebuds every time.
Try the tempting Spiced Chicken and Pepper Rolls or the filling and nutritious Roast
Pepper and Mushroom Pizza, and don't miss an old favorite, Chili con Carne. They are all
light choices, whether vegetarian or otherwise, full of flavor and nutrients, and are sure to
satisfy even the most persistent hunger pangs.

TUNA & ZUCCHINI
OMELET

*The addition of potatoes to this omelet recipe makes the
dish more filling without piling on the fat or calories.*

Preparation time: 20 minutes

Cooking time: 20 minutes

Serves 4

1 tsp sunflower oil
1 onion, minced
1 clove garlic, crushed
3 zucchini, thinly sliced
1 cup diced, boiled potatoes
3 eggs, plus 2 egg whites
7-ounce can tuna in water, drained and flaked
1 tbsp chopped fresh tarragon
salt and freshly ground black pepper
3 tbsp finely grated reduced-fat sharp cheese
fresh herb sprigs, to garnish

1 Heat the oil in a large nonstick skillet.
Add the onion, garlic, and zucchini and
cook for 5 minutes, stirring.

2 Add the potatoes and cook for 2-3
minutes, stirring.

3 Beat the eggs, egg whites, and 2 tbsp
water together. Add the tuna, tarragon,
and seasoning, and mix well.

4 Pour the egg mixture into the skillet
and cook over a medium heat until the
eggs are beginning to set and the omelet
is golden brown underneath.

5 Sprinkle the cheese over the
top of the tortilla and place
under a preheated medium
broiler. Cook until the
cheese has melted and
the top is golden brown.

6 Garnish with fresh
herb sprigs and
serve in wedges
with a crisp mixed
side salad.

VARIATIONS
● Use other
vegetables such
as blanched
broccoli
flowerets or
peas in place
of the zucchini.
● Use other
fish canned in
water such
as salmon in
place of
the tuna.

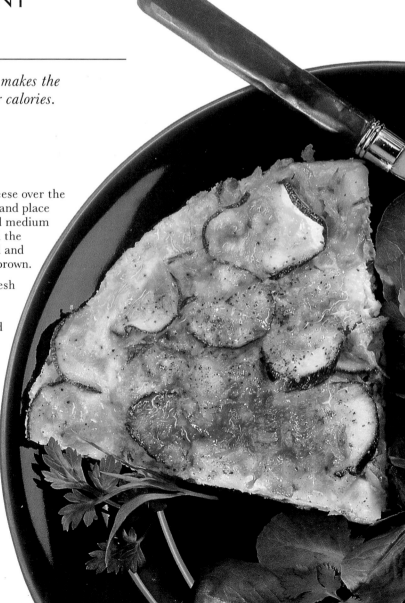

SPICED
CHICKEN & PEPPER ROLLS

*These flavorsome filled soft rolls make an excellent lunchtime snack
or a quick and easy light supper. Try serving the spiced chicken
in warmed pita pockets for a change.*

Preparation time: 10 minutes

Cooking time: 6 minutes

Serves 4

1 tbsp dry sherry

1 tbsp light soy sauce

1 tsp paprika

$^1/_2$ tsp ground cumin

$^1/_2$ tsp ground coriander (cilantro)

$^1/_2$ tsp chili powder

salt and freshly ground black pepper

2 tsp sunflower oil

1 clove garlic, crushed

*1-inch piece fresh root ginger, peeled,
grated, or minced*

1 bunch green onions (scallions), chopped

*12 ounces skinless, boneless chicken breast, cut
into thin strips*

1 red bell pepper, seeded and diced

4 whole-wheat soft rolls

very low-fat spread, for spreading

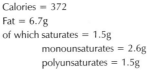

1 Place the sherry, soy sauce, spices, and seasoning in a bowl and mix well. Set aside.

2 Heat the oil in a large nonstick skillet or wok. Add the garlic, ginger, and green onions (scallions) and stir-fry over a high heat for 30 seconds.

3 Add the chicken and stir-fry for 2 minutes. Add the bell pepper and stir fry for a further 2 minutes. Add the sherry mixture and stir-fry for 1 minute.

4 Split the rolls in half and spread each with a thin scraping of low-fat spread. Spoon some spicy chicken into each one. Top with tomato and cucumber slices, season, and serve immediately with a green side salad or low-calorie coleslaw.

VARIATION

● Experiment with different types of whole-grain bread rolls.

CHILI CON CARNE

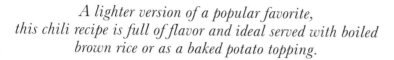

*A lighter version of a popular favorite,
this chili recipe is full of flavor and ideal served with boiled
brown rice or as a baked potato topping.*

Preparation time: 10 minutes

Cooking time: 1 hour, 5 minutes

Serves 4

10 ounces (1¼ cups) extra-lean ground beef
2 onions, minced
1 clove garlic, crushed
2 fresh red chilies, seeded and finely chopped
1 tbsp all-purpose flour
1 tsp ground cumin
1 tsp ground coriander (cilantro)
2 tbsp tomato paste
14-ounce can peeled, chopped tomatoes
1¼ cups beef broth
salt and freshly ground black pepper
14-ounce can red kidney beans, rinsed and drained
1 large red bell pepper, seeded and diced
1¼ cups sliced mushrooms

1 Place the ground beef, onions, garlic, and chilies in a large, nonstick saucepan, and cook gently until browned all over, stirring frequently.

2 Add the flour, spices, tomato paste, tomatoes, broth, and seasoning and mix.

3 Bring to the boil, stirring, then cover and simmer for 30 minutes, stirring occasionally.

4 Add the kidney beans, bell pepper, and mushrooms, and stir to mix. Cover and simmer for a further 30 minutes, stirring occasionally.

5 Serve with boiled brown rice.

VARIATIONS

● Use other lean ground meats such as pork, lamb, turkey, or chicken in place of the beef. For a vegetarian option, use ground soya.
● Use other canned beans such as pinto beans or chick-peas (garbanzo beans) in place of the kidney beans.
● Use 1-2 tsp hot chili powder in place of the fresh chilies.

NUTRITIONAL ANALYSIS

(figures are per serving)

Calories = 283
Fat = 8.1g
of which saturates = 3.1g
     monounsaturates = 2.9g
     polyunsaturates = 0.9g
Protein = 25.0g
Carbohydrate = 29.9g
Dietary fiber = 8.1g
Sodium = 0.6g

Percentage of total calories from fat = 26%
of which saturates = 10%
Good source of vitamins A, C, & B vitamins

ZUCCHINI, CHEESE, & ONION
POTATO BAKE

A scrumptious combination of potatoes, zucchini, and onions in a creamy cheese sauce makes a healthy but satisfying choice for a family meal.

Preparation time: 20 minutes
Cooking time: 1½-2 hours
Serves 6

2 tbsp low-fat spread (suitable for cooking)
2 tbsp all-purpose flour
2½ cups skim milk
½ cup finely grated reduced-fat mature yellow cheese
salt and freshly ground black pepper
350 g (12 oz) zucchini, sliced
2 onions, sliced
3 tbsp chopped fresh chives
3 tbsp chopped fresh parsley
1¾ pounds potatoes, washed and thinly sliced
fresh parsley sprigs, to garnish

1 Place the low-fat spread, flour, and milk in a saucepan and heat gently, whisking continuously, until the sauce comes to the boil and thickens. Simmer gently for 3 minutes, stirring.

2 Remove the pan from the heat, add the cheese and seasoning, and stir until the cheese has melted.

3 Mix together the zucchini, onions, herbs, and seasoning.

4 Spread a layer of the zucchini mixture over the base of a lightly greased ovenproof casserole dish. Top with some potato slices. Continue layering the vegetables, ending with a layer of potatoes.

5 Pour the cheese sauce over the vegetables and cover the dish with foil.

6 Bake in a preheated oven at 350° for 1½-2 hours, until the vegetables are cooked and tender. Remove the foil for the last 30 minutes of the cooking time, to brown the potato topping.

7 Garnish with fresh parsley sprigs and serve on its own or with steamed fresh seasonal vegetables such as green beans and baby carrots. For a more substantial meal, serve with broiled fish such as cod or red snapper, and seasonal fresh vegetables.

VARIATIONS
● Use sweet potatoes or a mixture of sweet and standard potatoes.
● Use chopped fresh mixed herbs in place of the chives and parsley.

NUTRITIONAL ANALYSIS
(figures are per serving)

Calories = 231
Fat = 5.3g
of which saturates = 2.4g
    monounsaturates = 0.9g
    polyunsaturates = 0.9g

Protein = 14.3g
Carbohydrate = 33.6g
Dietary fiber = 2.9g
Sodium = 0.2g

Percentage of total calories from fat = 21%, of which saturates = 9%

SPICY SEAFOOD
PIZZA

*This Mediterranean-style pizza has a light, whole-wheat base and a spicy
seafood topping with melted mozzarella cheese and a scattering of black olives.*

Preparation time: 30 minutes, plus kneading and rising time for the pizza dough
Cooking time: 25-35 minutes

Serves 6

1 recipe pizza dough (see opposite)
1 tsp olive oil
1 red onion, sliced
1 yellow bell pepper, seeded and diced
1 clove garlic, crushed
1 recipe tomato sauce (see opposite)
1¹/₂ cups shelled mixed seafood
1 tsp ground coriander (cilantro)
1 tsp ground cumin
1 tsp chili powder
1 tsp ground ginger
¹/₃ cup shredded mozzarella cheese
16 black olives
fresh herb sprigs, to garnish

1 Prepare and shape the pizza dough as
instructed opposite.

2 Heat the oil in a saucepan, add the
onion, bell pepper, and garlic and cook
gently for 5-10 minutes, stirring occasionally, until the vegetables begin to soften.

3 Spread the tomato sauce evenly over
the pizza base, then the onion mixture.

4 Place the seafood and spices in a bowl
and mix well. Spoon over the pizza.

5 Sprinkle the cheese over the pizza
and scatter the olives over the top.

6 Bake in a preheated oven at
425°, for 25-35 minutes, until
the dough is risen and the pizza
is golden brown.

7 Garnish with fresh herb
sprigs and serve hot or cold in
slices with a tossed green
salad or homemade low-
calorie coleslaw.

VARIATIONS
● Use a flavored oil such as
chili or herb oil in place of
the olive oil.
● Use jumbo shrimp in place
of the mixed seafood.
● Use reduced-fat yellow
cheese such as Cheddar in
place of the mozzarella.

NUTRITIONAL ANALYSIS
(figures are per serving)

Calories = 294
Fat = 8.3g
of which   saturates = 2.6g
    monounsaturates = 3.3g
    polyunsaturates = 1.0g

Protein = 22.7g
Carbohydrate = 34.0g
Dietary fiber = 4.0g
Sodium = 1.0g

Percentage of calories from fat = 25%, of which saturates = 8%
Good source of vitamins B12 & C

TOMATO SAUCE

14-ounce can peeled, chopped tomatoes
1 small onion, minced
1 clove garlic, crushed
1 tbsp tomato paste
1 tbsp chopped fresh mixed herbs
or 1 tsp dried herbs
pinch of sugar
salt and freshly ground black pepper

Place all the ingredients in a saucepan. Bring to the boil, then simmer, uncovered, for 15-20 minutes, until the sauce becomes fairly thick. Adjust the seasoning and use as a base topping for your pizza.

BASIC PIZZA DOUGH

¹/₂ oz fresh yeast or 1 package active dry yeast
¹/₂ tsp sugar
²/₃ cup warm water
1 cup all-purpose flour
1 cup whole-wheat flour
¹/₂ tsp salt
1 tbsp olive oil

1 Blend the fresh yeast with the sugar and water and set aside until frothy. For dried yeast, mix the sugar with the water, sprinkle the yeast over the water, then set aside until frothy.

2 In a bowl, stir together the flours and salt. Make a well in the center and add the yeast liquid and oil. Mix the flour into the liquid to make a firm dough.

3 Turn the dough out onto a lightly floured surface and knead for about 10 minutes, until the dough feels smooth and elastic and no longer sticky.

4 Place the dough in a clean bowl, cover with plastic wrap or a damp kitchen towel, and leave in a warm place until doubled in size — about 45 minutes.

5 Turn the dough out onto a lightly floured surface and knead again for 2-3 minutes.

6 Roll the dough out to a circle roughly 10 inches in diameter. Place on a baking sheet, making the edges of the dough slightly thicker than the center. The pizza dough is now ready to complete and bake with a delicious topping.

VARIATION
● Stir 3-4 tbsp chopped fresh herbs or 2-3 tsp dried mixed herbs into the flour before making the dough.

ROAST PEPPER & MUSHROOM
PIZZA

Preparation time: 30 minutes, plus kneading and rising time for the pizza dough

Cooking time: 25-35 minutes

Serves 6

1 quantity pizza dough (see page 37)
1 red bell pepper
1 green bell pepper
1 yellow bell pepper
1 tsp olive oil
1 small onion, sliced
1¹/₂ cups mushrooms, sliced
1 recipe tomato sauce (see page 37)
2 tbsp chopped fresh mixed herbs or 2 tsp dried herbs
¹/₄ cup shredded mozzarella cheese
2 tbsp finely grated Parmesan cheese
fresh herb sprigs, to garnish

1 Prepare and shape the pizza dough as explained in the recipe on page 37.

2 Place the bell peppers under a hot broiler and cook for 10-15 minutes, until the skin is charred and black. Plunge the bell peppers into cold water — the skins will rub off between your fingers. Pat dry. Core, seed, and slice the bell peppers.

3 Meanwhile, heat the oil in a saucepan, add the onion and mushrooms, and cook gently for 5-10 minutes, stirring occasionally, until the vegetables are beginning to soften.

4 Spread the tomato sauce evenly over the pizza base, then sprinkle the mixed herbs over the top.

5 Arrange the bell peppers, onions, and mushrooms over the tomato sauce.

6 Sprinkle the mozzarella cheese over the pizza, then sprinkle the Parmesan cheese over the top.

7 Bake in a preheated oven at 425°, for 25-35 minutes, until the dough is risen and the pizza is golden brown.

8 Garnish with fresh herb sprigs and serve hot or cold in slices with a mixed side salad.

NUTRITIONAL ANALYSIS

(figures are per serving)

Calories = 241
Fat = 6.9g
of which saturates = 2.6g
      monounsaturates = 2.7g
      polyunsaturates = 0.9g
Protein = 11.7g
Carbohydrate = 35.4g
Dietary fiber = 5.0g
Sodium = 0.3g

Percentage of total calories from fat = 26%
of which saturates = 9%
Good source of vitamin C

VARIATIONS
● Use other vegetables such as zucchini in place of the mushrooms.
● Use reduced-fat hard cheese such as Cheddar or Monterey jack cheese in place of the mozzarella.
● Use 4 shallots, 1 red onion, or 1 leek in place of the onion.

SMOKED HAM, TOMATO, &
BASIL PIZZA

Preparation time: 25 minutes, plus kneading and rising time for the pizza dough

Cooking time: 25-35 minutes

Serves 6

1 quantity pizza dough (see page 37)
1 quantity tomato sauce (see page 37)
2-3 tbsp chopped fresh basil
1 cup diced cooked, lean, smoked ham
4 tomatoes, sliced
¹/₄ cup finely grated
reduced-fat mature
Cheddar cheese
¹/₄ cup finely shredded
mozzarella cheese
fresh basil leaves,
to garnish

1 Prepare and shape the pizza dough as instructed on page 37.

2 Spread the tomato sauce evenly over the pizza base, then sprinkle the basil over the top.

3 Scatter the ham over the sauce and top with the tomato slices.

4 Mix the yellow cheese and mozzarella together and sprinkle over the pizza.

5 Bake the pizza in a preheated oven at 425° for 25-35 minutes, until the dough is risen and the pizza is golden-brown in color.

6 Garnish with fresh basil leaves and serve hot or cold in slices with seasonal fresh vegetables.

VARIATIONS

● Use any kind of lean smoked meat in place of the smoked ham.
● Use mixed herbs in place of the basil.
● Use other reduced-fat yellow cheese in place of the Cheddar.

NUTRITIONAL ANALYSIS

(figures are per serving)

Calories = 263
Fat = 6.8g
of which saturates = 2.7g
      monounsaturates = 2.4g
      polyunsaturates = 0.8g
Protein = 18.7g
Carbohydrate = 33.4g
Dietary fiber = 3.6g
Sodium = 0.3g

Percentage of total calories from fat = 23%
of which saturates = 9%

ORIENTAL VEGETABLE STIR-FRY

This colorful mixture of fresh, crispy vegetables tossed in a light sweet-and-sour sauce makes a nutritious yet quick and easy stir-fry dinner or snack.

Preparation time: 20 minutes

Cooking time: 8-10 minutes

Serves 4

1 tbsp white wine or rice wine
1 tsp grated ginger root
2 tsp cornstarch
4 tbsp unsweetened apple juice
2 tbsp light soft brown sugar
2 tbsp light soy sauce
1 tbsp tomato ketchup
1 tbsp white wine or rice vinegar
2 tsp sunflower oil
2 cloves garlic, crushed
2 leeks (trimmed weight), thinly sliced
1 red bell pepper, seeded and sliced
1 green bell pepper, seeded and sliced
3 carrots, cut into matchstick strips
1 cup mushrooms, sliced
1/2 cup snow-peas, trimmed
1/2 cup bean sprouts
14-ounce can corn, drained

1 Combine the wine and ginger root and leave to steep for at least 30 minutes. In a small bowl, blend the cornstarch with the apple juice until smooth. Add the wine and ginger mixture, sugar, soy sauce, tomato ketchup, and vinegar and mix well. Set aside.

2 Heat the oil in a large nonstick skillet or wok. Add the garlic and stir-fry over a high heat for 30 seconds.

3 Add the leeks, peppers, and carrots and stir-fry for 2-3 minutes. Add the remaining vegetables and stir-fry for 2-3 minutes.

4 Reduce the heat a little and add the sauce to the vegetables. Stir-fry until the

sauce comes to the boil and thickens, then cook for a further 1-2 minutes, stirring frequently.

5 Serve immediately on its own or with baked potatoes or a cooked mixture of brown and wild or pecan rice.

VARIATIONS
● Use your own choice of fresh vegetables.
● For the sauce, use unsweetened pineapple juice and sherry in place of the apple juice and wine.
● Sprinkle the stir-fry with toasted sesame seeds or shelled sunflower seeds just before serving.

40

CHEESE-TOPPED VEGETABLES
PROVENÇAL

This combination of braised fresh vegetables with a crispy, cheese topping is ideal served with boiled pasta, baked potatoes, or thick slices of fresh bread. Try serving it as an accompaniment to broiled lean meat or fish as an entrée.

Preparation time: 20 minutes

Cooking time: 20-25 minutes

Serves 6

4 cups tomatoes, skinned and chopped
4 zucchini, sliced
3 leeks trimmed and sliced
1¹/₄ cups button mushrooms
1 onion, sliced
1 red bell pepper, seeded and sliced
1 yellow bell pepper, seeded and sliced
1 clove garlic, crushed
14-ounce can chick-peas (garbanzo beans), rinsed and drained
²/₃ cup tomato juice
1 tbsp tomato paste
1 tbsp tomato ketchup
1 tbsp chopped fresh rosemary
salt and freshly ground black pepper
¹/₂ cup finely grated reduced-fat mature yellow cheese
4 tbsp fresh whole-wheat bread crumbs
fresh herb sprigs, to garnish

1 Place all the ingredients, except the cheese, whole-wheat bread crumbs, and herb sprigs, in a saucepan and mix well.

2 Cover, bring to the boil, and cook gently for 15-20 minutes, until the vegetables are just tender, stirring occasionally.

3 Transfer the vegetable mixture to a shallow, ovenproof serving dish.

4 Mix together the cheese and bread crumbs and sprinkle over the vegetables. Cook under a preheated medium broiler until the cheese has melted and the topping is crispy.

5 Garnish with fresh herb sprigs, such as rosemary or thyme.

VARIATIONS
● Use your own choice of fresh vegetables.
● Use other canned beans such as kidney or lima beans in place of the chick-peas (garbanzo beans).
● Use fresh mixed herbs or fresh thyme in place of the rosemary.

NUTRITIONAL ANALYSIS

(figures are per serving)

Calories = 192
Fat = 5.5g
of which   saturates = 2.2g
     monounsaturates = 1.3g
     polyunsaturates = 1.3g

Protein = 14.0g
Carbohydrate = 23.2g
Dietary fiber = 6.2g
Sodium = 0.3g

Percentage of total calories from fat = 26%, of which saturates = 10%
Good source of vitamins A & C

ENTRÉES

*W*hether you eat your main meal at lunchtime, teatime, or in the evening,
*it will be, by definition, your most substantial meal of the day, and it is
therefore important to make it as appetizing and nutritious as possible.
Here are mouthwatering meals that are quick and easy both
to prepare and cook, and are ideal for everyday cooking, such as stir-fries
and casseroles. Additionally, there are grander dishes for special occasions and for
serving to guests, such as stuffed fish or a savory choux ring.
Also included are meals for out-of-doors cooking, such as kabobs, as well as
a selection of vegetarian meals that make an interesting and flavorful
change from meat- or fish-based meals.*

BAKED COD
WITH WATERCRESS SAUCE

*Fresh cod steaks are baked until just cooked and tender, and served with a
light watercress — an ideal dish for the family or for guests.*

Preparation time: 25 minutes

Cooking time: 20-30 minutes

Serves 4

*4 cod steaks, each weighing about 8 ounces
juice of 1 lemon
2 tbsp chopped fresh mixed herbs
salt and freshly ground black pepper
1 small onion, minced
1 clove garlic, crushed
¹/₃ cup chopped watercress
²/₃ cup vegetable broth
2 tbsp low-fat spread
2 tbsp all-purpose flour
1¹/₂ cups skim milk
2 tbsp finely grated reduced-fat mature Cheddar
or Monterey jack cheese*

1 Lightly grease 4 pieces of aluminum
foil large enough to hold each cod steak.
Place a cod steak on each piece of foil,
sprinkle with lemon juice, herbs, and
seasoning, and fold up loosely in the foil.

2 Place on a cookie sheet and bake
in a preheated oven at 350° for
20-30 minutes.

3 Meanwhile, make the watercress
sauce. Place the onion, garlic,
watercress, and broth in a saucepan and
stir to mix.

4 Cover and cook gently for 5 minutes.

5 Remove from the heat and allow to
cool slightly, then place in a blender or
food processor and blend until smooth.

6 Place the low-fat spread, flour, and
milk in a saucepan and heat gently,
whisking continuously, until the sauce
comes to the boil and thickens. Simmer
gently for 3 minutes, stirring.

7 Add the watercress purée and mix
well. Reheat gently, stirring.

8 Remove the pan from the heat, add
the cheese and seasoning, and stir until
well-blended.

9 Serve the cod steaks with the sauce
poured over.

SPICY SHRIMP & MUSHROOM
PHYLLO CLUSTERS

Serve these deliciously light and crispy phyllo clusters with baked potatoes and seasonal fresh vegetables such as cauliflower and broccoli flowerets.

Preparation time: 25 minutes
Cooking time: 25-30 minutes
Serves 4 (2 clusters per serving)

FOR THE FILLING
1 bunch green onions (scallions), chopped
³/₄ cup minced mushrooms
³/₄ cup small peeled bay shrimp
4 sun-dried tomatoes, soaked, drained, and finely chopped
¹/₂-inch piece fresh root ginger, peeled and minced or grated
1 clove garlic, crushed
¹/₂ tsp hot chili powder or 1 small red chili, seeded and finely chopped
1 tsp ground coriander (cilantro)
2 tbsp chopped fresh coriander (cilantro)
1 tbsp fresh Parmesan cheese, finely grated
salt and freshly ground black pepper

8 sheets phyllo dough
2 tbsp sunflower oil
fresh coriander (cilantro), to garnish

1 Place all the ingredients for the filling in a bowl and mix together thoroughly. Set aside.

2 To make each phyllo cluster, cut each sheet of phyllo dough in half crosswise to make two squares or rectangles (a total of 16 squares or rectangles), depending on the shape of the sheet.

3 Lightly brush 2 squares of dough with oil and place one on top of the other diagonally. Place some shrimp filling in the center of the dough.

4 Gather up the dough over the filling and secure with string. Place the cluster on a cookie sheet lined with nonstick baking paper and brush lightly with oil.

5 Repeat with the remaining dough squares and filling to make 8 clusters.

6 Bake in a preheated oven at 400° for 25-30 minutes, until golden brown and crisp.

7 Carefully remove the string from each cluster before serving. Garnish with fresh coriander (cilantro) leaves.

VARIATIONS
● Use other cooked, shelled seafood such as mussels or clams in place of the shrimp.
● Use other spices such as curry powder or cumin in place of the chili powder or coriander (cilantro).
● Use other fresh herbs such as mixed herbs or parsley in place of the coriander (cilantro).

SPICY ROAST CHICKEN

An appetizing way of serving roast chicken that contains little fat but plenty of flavor and color.

Preparation time: 10 minutes
Cooking time: 30-45 minutes
Serves 4

*1 tbsp olive oil
juice of $\frac{1}{2}$ lemon or lime
1 clove garlic, crushed
1 tsp ground coriander (cilantro)
1 tsp ground cumin
1 tsp hot chili powder
salt and freshly ground black pepper
4 skinless, boneless chicken breasts
chopped fresh coriander (cilantro) sprigs,
to garnish*

1 Place the oil, lemon or lime juice, garlic, spices, and seasoning in a bowl and whisk together until thoroughly mixed.

2 Place each chicken breast on a piece of parchment paper large enough to hold each chicken breast in a package.

3 Slash each piece of chicken diagonally across the top and brush with some of the spicy mixture.

4 Fold the paper loosely over each chicken breast and twist the edges together to seal tightly, making a total of 4 packages. Place the packages on a baking sheet.

5 Bake in a preheated oven at 400° for 30-45 minutes, until cooked and tender.

6 Undo the packages and place the chicken breasts on warmed serving dishes. Pour any juices over the chicken and garnish with chopped coriander (cilantro).

7 Serve immediately with a crunchy, mixed vegetable stir-fry.

<small>VARIATION</small>
● Use flavored oil such as chili or herb oil in place of the olive oil.

NUTRITIONAL ANALYSIS
(figures are per serving)

Calories = 184
Fat = 4.6g
of which saturates = 0.8g
    monounsaturates = 2.8g
    polyunsaturates = 0.5g

Protein = 36.2g
Carbohydrate = 0.04g
Dietary fiber = 0g
Sodium = 0.1g

Percentage of total calories from fat = 23%
of which saturates = 4%

QUICK & EASY
SAUCES

CHEESE & CHIVE
Follow the Chicken & Mustard Sauce recipe but add 4 tbsp finely grated reduced-fat mature Cheddar cheese and 2-3 tbsp chopped fresh chives to the cooked sauce in place of the mustard.

PARSLEY OR TARRAGON
Follow the Chicken & Mustard Sauce recipe but add 2-3 tbsp chopped fresh parsley or fresh tarragon to the cooked sauce in place of the mustard.

SAGE & ONION
Follow the Chicken & Mustard Sauce recipe but add 1-2 tbsp chopped fresh sage and 1 blanced, minced onion to the cooked sauce in place of the mustard.

CAPER
Follow the Chicken & Mustard Sauce recipe but add 1-2 tbsp chopped capers and 1-2 tsp of the vinegar from the capers to the cooked sauce in place of the mustard.

MUSHROOM
Follow the Chicken & Mustard Sauce recipe but add $^3/_4$-1 cup mushrooms, chopped or sliced and blanched, to the cooked sauce in place of the mustard.

NUTRITIONAL ANALYSIS
(figures are per serving)

Calories = 233
Fat = 6.5g
of which saturates = 1.3g
    monounsaturates = 3g
    polyunsaturates = 1g

Protein = 38.4g
Carbohydrate = 5.5g
Dietary fiber = 0.3g
Sodium = 0.6g

Percentage of total calories from fat = 25%
of which saturates = 5%

CHICKEN &
MUSTARD SAUCE

Juicy, tender, oven-baked chicken breasts are spiced up in this recipe with a tangy mustard sauce.

Preparation time: 15 minutes
Cooking time: 30-45 minutes
Serves 4

1 tbsp olive oil
1 tbsp light soy sauce
juice of 1 lemon
2 tbsp chopped fresh mixed herbs
salt and freshly ground black pepper
4 skinless, boneless chicken breasts
1 tbsp low-fat spread
1 tbsp all-purpose flour
$^2/_3$ cup skim milk
$^2/_3$ cup chicken broth, cooled
1 tbsp whole-grain mustard
fresh herb sprigs, to garnish

1 Whisk together the oil, soy sauce, lemon juice, herbs, and seasoning. Place each chicken breast on a piece of parchment paper large enough to hold it in a package. Spoon some of the herb mixture over each piece of chicken.

2 Fold over the paper and twist the edges together to seal. Place on a cookie sheet and bake in a preheated oven at 400° for 30-45 minutes, until cooked and tender.

3 Meanwhile, make the mustard sauce. Place the low-fat spread, flour, milk, and broth in a saucepan and heat gently, whisking continuously, until the sauce comes to the boil and thickens. Simmer gently for 3 minutes, stirring.

4 Add the mustard and seasoning and mix well.

5 Serve the cooked chicken breasts with the mustard sauce poured over. Garnish with fresh herb sprigs.

VARIATIONS
● Use turkey breasts in place of the chicken breasts.
● Use lime in place of the lemon juice.

QUICK & EASY STIR-FRIES

Stir-frying is a very quick and easy method of cooking and combining many foods and ingredients, to create colorful and nutritious meals in just a few minutes. This method of cooking seals in the food's natural juices, and ensures that it stays crisp and keeps its flavor as well as its nutrients.

Extend your repertoire by stir-frying other complementary combinations of ingredients, such as peppered beef with snow-peas, crunchy cabbage and wild mushrooms, beef with garlic and ginger, stir-fried baby vegetables, oriental pork and vegetables, sweet-and-sour shrimp, or hot and spicy chicken.

LAMB & VEGETABLE STIR-FRY

Tender lamb and crispy vegetables are subtly flavored with an oriental spice mix in this tasty stir-fry.

Preparation time: 15 minutes
Cooking time: 9-12 minutes
Serves 4

2 tsp cornstarch
2 tbsp light soy sauce
2 tbsp dry sherry
1 tbsp tomato paste
$^2/_3$ cup vegetable or beef broth, cooled
1 tsp five-spice powder
salt and freshly ground black pepper
8 ounces lean lamb, cut into thin strips
1 bunch green onions (scallions), chopped
1 clove garlic, crushed
1 red bell pepper, seeded and sliced
1 yellow bell pepper, seeded and sliced
1 cup small broccoli flowerets
4 carrots, cut into matchstick strips
$1^1/_4$ cups sliced mushrooms
$^3/_4$ cup bean sprouts
$^3/_4$ cup snow-peas, trimmed

1 In a small bowl, blend the cornstarch with the soy sauce. Add the sherry, tomato paste, broth, five-spice powder, and seasoning and mix well. Set aside.

2 Heat a large nonstick skillet or wok. Add the lamb, green onions (scallions), and garlic, and stir-fry over a medium heat for 2-3 minutes.

3 Add the bell peppers, broccoli, and carrots and stir-fry for 3-4 minutes.

4 Add the remaining vegetables and stir-fry for a further 2-3 minutes. Lower the heat, add the cornstarch mixture, and stir-fry until the sauce is thickened and glossy. Simmer for 2 minutes, stirring frequently.

5 Serve immediately on a bed of boiled brown and pecan rice or bulghur wheat with a mixed green side salad.

VARIATIONS

● Use other lean meat such as beef, pork, chicken, or turkey in place of the lamb.
● Use your own choice of mixed vegetables.
● Use applejack, brandy, or unsweetened apple juice in place of the sherry.
● Use chili or curry powder in place of the five-spice powder.

NUTRITIONAL ANALYSIS

(figures are per serving)

Calories = 200
Fat = 6.2g
of which saturates = 2.4g
     monounsaturates = 1.9g
     polyunsaturates = 1g
Protein = 18.4g
Carbohydrate = 16.6g
Dietary fiber = 6.2g
Sodium = 0.7g

Percentage of total calories from fat = 28%
of which saturates = 10%

STIR-FRIED TURKEY WITH
SPRING VEGETABLES

Young, spring vegetables bring an array of contrasting textures to this stimulating stir-fry.

Preparation time: 15 minutes
Cooking time: 8-12 minutes
Serves 4

2 tbsp dry sherry
2 tbsp light soy sauce
4 tbsp fresh tomato juice
1 tbsp chili sauce
1 tsp chili powder (optional)
salt and freshly ground black pepper
2 tsp sunflower oil
1 clove garlic, crushed
12 ounces skinless, boneless turkey breast, cut into thin strips
1 bunch green onions (scallions), chopped
2 carrots, cut into matchstick strips
1 cup rutabaga, cut into matchstick strips
1 red bell pepper, seeded and diced
³/₄ cup green beans, trimmed and halved
4 zucchini, peeled and thinly sliced
³/₄ cup bean sprouts
³/₄ cup broccoli flowerets or collard greens, chopped
chopped fresh mixed herbs, to garnish

1 In a bowl, mix together the sherry, soy sauce, tomato juice, chili sauce, chili powder (if using), and seasoning. Set aside.

2 Heat the oil in a large nonstick skillet or wok. Add the garlic and stir-fry over a high heat for 10 seconds. Add the turkey and stir-fry for 2-3 minutes.

3 Add the green onions (scallions), carrots, rutabaga, bell pepper, and green beans, and stir-fry for 3-4 minutes.

4 Add the remaining vegetables and stir-fry for 2-3 minutes.

5 Add the sherry mixture and stir-fry for 1-2 minutes, until the sauce is hot and bubbling.

6 Garnish with chopped fresh herbs and serve immediately with cooked egg noodles or fresh, crusty bread.

VARIATIONS

● Use other lean meats such as chicken, pork, or beef or cooked, peeled shrimp in place of the turkey.
● Use mushrooms and cauliflower in place of the green beans and zucchini.
● Use curry sauce and curry powder in place of the chili sauce and chili powder, for a change.

NUTRITIONAL ANALYSIS

(figures are per serving)

Calories = 205
Fat = 3.5g
of which saturates = 0.8g
     monounsaturates = 1.4g
     polyunsaturates = 1g
Protein = 26.5g
Carbohydrate = 15.5g
Dietary fiber = 5.3g
Sodium = 0.7g

Percentage of total calories from fat = 15%
of which saturates = 3%
Good source of vitamins A, C, & B vitamins

COQ AU VIN

Preparation time: 25 minutes

Cooking time: 1½-2 hours

Serves 4

2 skinless chicken leg joints
2 skinless chicken breast joints
2 slices smoked lean bacon, trimmed and diced
1½ cups shallots or button onions, peeled
6 carrots, sliced
1¼ cups dry red wine
1¼ cups chicken broth
1 tbsp tomato paste
2 small cloves garlic, crushed
salt and freshly ground black pepper
1 bouquet garni (thyme, bay leaf,
and parsley tied together)
1¼ cups button mushrooms
1½ tbsp cornstarch

1 Place the chicken joints in a large, flameproof, ovenproof casserole dish

with the bacon, shallots or button onions, and carrots.

2 Mix together the wine, broth, tomato paste, garlic, and seasoning and pour over the chicken and vegetables. Add the bouquet garni and mix.

3 Cook in a preheated oven at 350° for 1 hour. Add the mushrooms and stir gently to mix.

4 Cook for a further 30-60 minutes.

5 Remove the chicken. Place on a serving platter, cover, and keep hot.

6 Discard the bouquet garni. Blend the cornstarch with 3 tbsp water and stir into the juices and vegetables in the casserole. Bring to the boil, stirring, until thickened, then simmer for 3 minutes, stirring.

7 Spoon the vegetables and sauce over the chicken and serve.

VARIATIONS
● Use white wine in place of the red.
● Use 1 large sliced onion in place of the shallots.

NUTRITIONAL ANALYSIS

(figures are per serving)

Calories = 279
Fat = 3.4g
of which saturates = 0.9g
       monounsaturates = 1g
       polyunsaturates = 0.8g
Protein = 36.1g
Carbohydrate = 14.3g
Dietary fiber = 4.1g
Sodium = 0.6g

Percentage of total calories from fat = 11%
of which saturates = 3%
Good source of vitamin A

BEEF & VEGETABLE
KABOBS

Cubes of lean beef and crispy fresh vegetables are broiled or barbecued to perfection for a memorable summer meal alfresco.

Preparation time: 20 minutes

Cooking time: 8-12 minutes

Serves 4 (2 kabobs per serving)

12 ounces lean topside, tenderloin,
or sirloin steak, trimmed of fat
1 small green bell pepper
1 small red bell pepper
1 small yellow bell pepper
1 zucchini
16 button onions, peeled
16 button mushrooms
16 cherry tomatoes
4 bay leaves (optional)
1 tbsp olive oil
juice of 1 orange
1 tsp dried thyme
salt and freshly ground black pepper

1 Cut the beef into 24 small cubes and set aside. Cut the bell peppers in half, and remove and discard the seeds. Cut each half into 4 squares (making a total of 8 squares per bell pepper). Slice the zucchini into 16 slices.

2 Thread the beef, bell peppers, zucchini, onions, mushrooms, and tomatoes onto 8 skewers, dividing the ingredients equally between the kabobs. Thread a bay leaf onto the end of 4 of the skewers, if using.

3 Beat together the oil, orange juice, thyme, and seasoning and brush the mixture over the kabobs.

4 Cook the kabobs over a barbecue or under a preheated broiler on medium heat for about 8-12 minutes, turning frequently, until the beef is cooked to your liking. Brush the kabobs with any remaining oil mixture while they are cooking, to prevent them from drying out.

5 Serve with slices of fresh crusty bread and a green side salad.

VARIATIONS
● Use other lean meats such as chicken, turkey, or pork in place of the beef.
● Use other vegetables or fruit such as baby corn or pineapple cubes.
● Use curry powder, ground cumin, or chili powder in place of the thyme.
● Twist sprigs of thyme around the kabobs.

NUTRITIONAL ANALYSIS
(figures are per serving)

Calories = 199
Fat = 7.1g
of which   saturates = 2.1g
    monounsaturates = 3.6g
    polyunsaturates = 0.9g

Protein = 22.3g
Carbohydrate = 12.3g
Dietary fiber = 3.3g
Sodium = 0.06g

Percentage of total calories from fat = 32%, of which saturates = 9%
Good source of B vitamins & vitamin C

MEDITERRANEAN VEGETABLE
LASAGNA

A nutritious vegetarian version of the traditional meat-based dish, this lasagna is packed with flavor and appetizing color.

Preparation time: 30 minutes

Cooking time: 45-60 minutes

Serves 6

1 Place the onions, garlic, bell peppers, zucchini, mushrooms, tomatoes, fresh tomato juice, and tomato paste in a large saucepan. Cover and cook for 10 minutes, stirring occasionally. Add the herbs and seasoning, and mix well.

2 Meanwhile, make the cheese sauce. Place the low-fat spread, flour, mustard, milk, and broth in a saucepan. Heat gently, whisking continuously, until the sauce comes to the boil and thickens. Simmer gently for 3 minutes, stirring.

3 Remove the pan from the heat, add half the cheese and seasoning, and mix well.

4 Assemble the lasagna. Spoon half the vegetable mixture in a shallow pie pan or ovenproof dish. Cover this with half the pasta and top with one third of the cheese sauce.

5 Repeat these layers, topping with the remaining cheese sauce to cover the pasta completely. Sprinkle the remaining cheese over the top.

6 Bake the lasagna in a preheated oven at 350° for 45-60 minutes, until cooked and golden brown on top.

7 Garnish with mixed salad leaves and serve with low-calorie coleslaw and fresh crusty bread.

VARIATIONS
● Use your own choice of mixed vegetables for this lasagna.
● Use white or whole-wheat lasagna in place of the green lasagna.
● Use other reduced-fat hard cheese such as Monterey jack in place of the Cheddar.
● Use one 14-ounce can peeled, chopped tomatoes in place of the fresh tomatoes.
● Use whole-grain mustard in place of the smooth mustard.

NUTRITIONAL ANALYSIS

(figures are per serving)

Calories = 263

Fat = 7.3g

of which saturates = 2.9g

monounsaturates = 1g

polyunsaturates = 1.7g

Protein = 15.6g

Carbohydrate = 35.9g

Dietary fiber = 4.7g

Sodium = 0.3g

Percentage of total calories from fat = 25%

of which saturates = 9%

Good source of calcium & vitamin A

EGGPLANT, TOMATO, & ZUCCHINI
PASTA BAKE

Preparation time: 30 minutes, plus standing time for the eggplant

Cooking time: 30 minutes

Serves 6

1¹/₂ cups sliced eggplant
salt and freshly ground black pepper
1 onion, sliced
2 leeks, washed and thinly sliced
1 clove garlic, crushed
1 cup sliced zucchini
1 cup sliced yellow zucchini or summer squash
14-ounce can peeled, chopped tomatoes
1 tbsp tomato paste
1 tbsp tomato ketchup
8 ounces short macaroni
2 tbsp low-fat spread
2 tbsp all-purpose flour
2¹/₂ cups skim milk
14-ounce can chick-peas (garbanzo beans), rinsed and drained
3 tbsp chopped fresh mixed herbs
6 tbsp finely grated reduced-fat Monterey jack cheese
2 tbsp fresh whole-wheat bread crumbs

1 Sprinkle the eggplant slices with salt and leave to stand for about 30 minutes, to extract the bitter juices. Rinse thoroughly under cold running water and pat dry with paper towels.

2 Place the eggplant, onion, leeks, garlic, zucchini, tomatoes, tomato paste, and tomato ketchup in a large saucepan and stir to mix.

3 Cover and cook gently for 20 minutes, stirring occasionally.

4 Meanwhile, cook the macaroni in a large saucepan of lightly salted, boiling water for 8 minutes, until just tender. Drain thoroughly and keep warm.

5 In the meantime, make the white sauce. Place the low-fat spread, flour, and milk in a saucepan. Heat gently, whisking continuously, until the sauce comes to the boil and thickens. Simmer gently for 3 minutes, stirring.

6 Add the chick-peas (garbanzo beans), herbs, and seasoning and stir to mix.

7 Stir the vegetable mixture, macaroni, and white sauce together and place in a large ovenproof casserole dish. Mix the cheese and bread crumbs together and sprinkle evenly over the top.

8 Bake in a preheated oven at 375° for about 30 minutes, until lightly browned and bubbling. Serve with a crisp green side salad.

VARIATIONS
● Use your own choice of mixed vegetables for this pasta bake.
● Use other shapes of pasta, such as twists or shell, in place of the macaroni.

NUTRITIONAL ANALYSIS
(figures are per serving)

Calories = 313
Fat = 6.8g
of which saturates = 2.3g
       monounsaturates = 1.1g
       polyunsaturates = 1.8g
Protein = 18.9g
Carbohydrate = 46.8g
Dietary fiber = 6.8g
Sodium = 0.4g

Percentage of total calories from fat = 20%
of which saturates = 7%

RATATOUILLE
RING

*In this recipe, a crispy, cheese-flavored choux pastry
ring surrounds a classic mixture of lightly braised vegetables.*

Preparation time: 25 minutes
Cooking time: 30-40 minutes
Serves 6

FOR THE PASTRY RING
*5 tbsp all-purpose flour
4 tbsp low-fat spread
2 eggs, beaten
2 tbsp finely grated reduced-fat mature Cheddar
cheese*

FOR THE RATATOUILLE
*2 onions, sliced
2 cloves garlic, crushed
1 red bell pepper, seeded and cut into large dice
1 green bell pepper, seeded and cut into large dice
1 yellow bell pepper, seeded and cut into large dice
4 small zucchini, cut into small chunks
1 cup button mushrooms
4 medium tomatoes, skinned and roughly chopped
2 tbsp dry red wine
1 tbsp tomato paste
2 tsp dried mixed herbs
salt and freshly ground black pepper*

fresh parsley sprigs, to garnish

1 To make the pastry ring, sift the flour
onto a plate. Place the low-fat spread
and ²/₃ cup water in a saucepan. Heat
gently until the fat has melted, then
bring to the boil.

2 Remove the pan from the heat and tip
the flour all at once into the hot liquid.
Beat thoroughly with a wooden spoon,
until the mixture forms a ball in the
center of the pan. Leave to cool slightly.

3 Beat the eggs in gradually, using a
wooden spoon or electric hand-whisk,
adding only enough to give the right
consistency for piping the mixture
through a forcing bag, beating the
mixture thoroughly after each addition.
Beat in the cheese.

4 Spoon or pipe the mixture in a ring
around the edges of a lightly greased
9-inch ovenproof dish.

5 Bake in a preheated oven at 425° for
30-40 minutes, until well-risen and
golden brown.

6 Meanwhile, make the ratatouille
filling. Place all the ratatouille
ingredients in a saucepan and stir to mix.

7 Cover, bring to the boil, and cook
gently for 20-30 minutes, stirring
occasionally, until the vegetables are
tender but not overcooked. Remove the
lid for the last 10 minutes of the cooking
time and increase the heat, to reduce the
liquid slightly, if the mixture is too liquid.

8 Spoon the ratatouille sauce into the
center of the ring. Garnish with fresh
parsley sprigs and serve with a crisp
side salad.

*The ratatouille sauce is suitable for cooking in
a microwave oven, and is also suitable for
freezing.*

VARIATIONS
● Use one 14-ounce can peeled, chopped
tomatoes in place of the fresh tomatoes.
● Use dry white wine or vermouth in
place of the red wine.
● Use other reduced-fat hard
cheese such as Monterey jack in place
of the Cheddar.

NUTRITIONAL ANALYSIS
(figures are per serving)

Calories = 177
Fat = 7g
of which saturates = 2.1g
      monounsaturates = 1.2g
      polyunsaturates = 1.7g
Protein = 8.6g
Carbohydrate = 20.3g
Dietary fiber = 4g
Sodium = 0.07g

Percentage of total calories
from fat = 35%
of which saturates = 10%
Good source of vitamins A & C

FARMHOUSE VEGETABLE
STEW

*Serve this stew of tender mixed vegetables with
a mixed green side salad and some crusty French bread.*

Preparation time: 15 minutes

Cooking time: 1¼-1½ hours

Serves 4

*1 onion, chopped
3 carrots, thinly sliced
3 leeks, washed and thinly sliced
1 turnip, thinly sliced
1 small rutabaga, finely diced
4 sticks celery, chopped
1¼ cups button mushrooms
14-ounce can peeled, chopped tomatoes
1 pound potatoes, washed and thinly sliced
1 tbsp olive oil
2 tbsp low-fat spread
2 tbsp all-purpose flour
⅔ cup vegetable broth, cooled
⅔ cup dry white wine
3 tbsp minced parsley
1 tbsp minced rosemary
salt and freshly ground black pepper
fresh herb sprigs, to garnish*

1 Place the onion, carrots, leeks, turnip, rutabaga, celery, mushrooms, and tomatoes in a saucepan and stir to mix.

2 Cover and cook gently for 25 minutes, stirring occasionally.

3 Parboil the potatoes in a saucepan of boiling water for 4 minutes. Drain thoroughly, then toss the potato slices in the oil. Set aside.

4 Meanwhile, make the sauce. Place the low-fat spread, flour, broth, and wine in a saucepan and heat gently, whisking continuously, until the sauce comes to the boil and thickens.

5 Simmer gently for 3 minutes, stirring. Add to the cooked vegetables with the chopped herbs and seasoning and mix well.

6 Place the vegetable mixture in an ovenproof casserole dish. Arrange the potato slices over the vegetable mixture, covering it completely.

7 Cover with foil and bake in a preheated oven at 400° for 45-60 minutes, until the potatoes are cooked, tender, and lightly browned on top. Remove the foil for the last 20 minutes of the cooking time.

8 Garnish with fresh herb sprigs and serve immediately.

VARIATIONS
● Use sweet potatoes in place of the standard potatoes.
● Use jicama in place of the turnip.
● Use red wine in place of the white wine, or use grape juice.

NUTRITIONAL ANALYSIS

(figures are per serving)

Calories = 299
Fat = 7.4g
of which saturates = 1.3g
       monounsaturates = 2.3g
       polyunsaturates = 1.8g
Protein = 8.7g
Carbohydrate = 46.3g
Dietary fiber = 9.9g
Sodium = 0.2g

Percentage of total calories from fat = 22%
of which saturates = 4%
Good source of vitamins A & C

MUSHROOM
RISOTTO

*Fresh chopped mixed herbs add vibrant flavor to this appetizing risotto,
which is ideal served with some fresh crusty bread and a green side salad.*

Preparation time: 15 minutes

Cooking time: 45 minutes

Serves 4

1 red onion, chopped
3 leeks, washed and thinly sliced
2 cloves garlic, crushed
1 red bell pepper, seeded and diced
4 sticks celery, chopped
1 cup long-grain brown rice
1¹/₄ cups sliced mushrooms,
1¹/₄ cups brown-cap mushrooms, sliced
2¹/₂ cups vegetable broth
1¹/₄ cups dry white wine
salt and freshly ground black pepper
7-ounce can corn kernels, drained
¹/₂ cup frozen peas
3-4 tbsp chopped fresh mixed herbs
4 tbsp fresh Parmesan cheese shavings (optional)
fresh herb sprigs, to garnish

● Use red kidney beans or chick-peas (garbanzo beans) in place of the corn.
● Use fava beans or lima beans in place of the peas.

1 Place the onion, leeks, garlic, bell pepper, celery, rice, mushrooms, broth, wine, and seasoning in a large saucepan and stir to mix.

2 Bring to the boil and simmer, uncovered, for 25-30 minutes, stirring occasionally, until almost all the liquid has been absorbed.

3 Stir in the corn and peas and cook gently for about 10 minutes, stirring occasionally.

4 Stir in the chopped herbs and stir again to mix. Sprinkle with Parmesan cheese shavings, if using, and garnish with fresh herb sprigs.

VARIATIONS
● Use a mixture of edible wild mushrooms such as shiitake and oyster mushrooms for a change.
● Use finely grated Cheddar cheese in place of the Parmesan cheese shavings.

COUNTRY VEGETABLE & BARLEY

CASSEROLE

A warming and satisfying casserole for a comforting winter's day meal.

Preparation time: 15 minutes

Cooking time: 2 hours

Serves 4

NUTRITIONAL ANALYSIS

(figures are per serving)

Calories = 448
Fat = 7.4g
of which saturates = 2.9g
    monounsaturates = 1.6g
    polyunsaturates = 1.8g
Protein = 15.5g
Carbohydrate = 72.5g
Dietary fiber = 7.3g
Sodium = 0.5g

Percentage of total calories from
fat = 15%
of which saturates = 6%
Good source of vitamin C

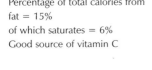

2 tsp sunflower oil
1 onion, sliced
3 leeks, washed and sliced
1 clove garlic, crushed
1 pound new potatoes, washed
1 celery root, diced
3 carrots, sliced
2 turnips, sliced
1 cup button mushrooms
2 tbsp pearl barley
14-ounce can peeled, chopped tomatoes
2 1/2 cups vegetable broth
2 tbsp tomato paste
1 bouquet garni
1 tsp ground coriander (cilantro)
salt and freshly ground black pepper
1-2 tbsp chopped fresh coriander (cilantro)
1-2 tbsp chopped fresh parsley

1 Heat the oil in a large ovenproof casserole dish. Add the onion, leeks, and garlic and cook for 5 minutes, stirring occasionally.

2 Add all the remaining ingredients, except the fresh herbs, and mix well.

3 Cover and bake in a preheated oven at 350° for about 2 hours, stirring occasionally, until the vegetables and barley are cooked and tender.

4 Stir in the chopped fresh herbs and serve with crusty whole-wheat bread and broiled lean meat or fish such as chicken or cod.

VARIATIONS

● Use jicama and diced sweet potatoes in place of the turnips and new potatoes.
● Use 4 skinned and chopped fresh tomatoes in place of the canned tomatoes.
● Use chopped fresh mixed herbs in place of the coriander (cilantro) and parsley.
● Use 2 tbsp long-grain brown rice in place of the barley.

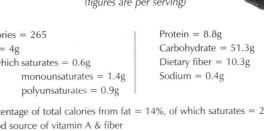

NUTRITIONAL ANALYSIS

(figures are per serving)

Calories = 265
Fat = 4g
of which saturates = 0.6g
    monounsaturates = 1.4g
    polyunsaturates = 0.9g

Protein = 8.8g
Carbohydrate = 51.3g
Dietary fiber = 10.3g
Sodium = 0.4g

Percentage of total calories from fat = 14%, of which saturates = 2%
Good source of vitamin A & fiber

SALADS & VEGETABLES

*S*alads and vegetables play an important part in meals, whether they
are served as the main part or as an accompaniment to another dish.
They also have a significant place in a healthy, well-balanced diet and
contain important nutrients such as vitamins, minerals, and some fiber.
Fresh vegetables and salad ingredients, as well as being nutritious,
offer an infinite variety of flavors, textures, and colors, perfect for
creating appetizing and delicious dishes for every occasion.

MIXED TOMATO &
PEPPER SALAD
WITH PARSLEY DRESSING

*This colorful salad comprises fresh bell peppers
and tomatoes tossed together in a light, herbed dressing.
Serve with broiled lean meat or fish kabobs and warm pita bread.*

Preparation time: 15 minutes

Serves 6

4 red plum tomatoes
4 yellow tomatoes
1 cup cherry tomatoes
1 red bell pepper, seeded and sliced into rings
1 yellow bell pepper, seeded and sliced into rings
1 large red onion, sliced into rings
*4 sun-dried tomatoes, soaked, drained, and finely
chopped*

FOR THE DRESSING
6 tbsp low-fat plain yogurt
4 tbsp reduced-calorie mayonnaise
2 tsp whole-grain mustard
3-4 tbsp chopped fresh parsley
salt and freshly ground black pepper
fresh parsley sprigs, to garnish

1 Slice the plum tomatoes and the yellow
tomatoes thinly, and halve the cherry
tomatoes.

2 Place the tomatoes, bell
peppers, and onion slices in a
serving bowl or on a serving
platter and toss together to mix.
Scatter the sun-dried tomatoes
over the top.

3 Place the yogurt, mayonnaise,
mustard, parsley, and seasoning
in a small bowl and mix
thoroughly.

4 Sprinkle the dressing over the
tomato-and-pepper salad and toss
lightly to mix. Garnish with fresh
parsley sprigs and serve with
broiled lean meat or fish kabobs and
warm pita bread.

VARIATION
● Use standard red tomatoes if yellow
tomatoes are not available.

NUTRITIONAL ANALYSIS

(figures are per serving)

Calories = 107
Fat = 3.9g
of which saturates = 0.6g
      monounsaturates = 0.9g
      polyunsaturates = 2.2g
Protein = 3.5g
Carbohydrate = 15.1g
Dietary fiber = 3.0g
Sodium = 0.2g

Percentage of total calories from fat = 33%
of which saturates = 2%
Good source of vitamins A, C, & E

CURRIED CHICK-PEA &
 BROWN RICE SALAD

A blend of aromatic spices brings exotic flavor to this rice salad. Serve with fresh multi-grain bread rolls and mixed salad leaves.

Preparation time: 15 minutes

Cooking time: 20 minutes

Serves 6

1 cup mixed brown and wild rice
1 tsp olive oil
1 clove garlic, crushed
1 tsp ground coriander (cilantro)
1 tsp ground cumin
1 tsp turmeric
$^1/_2$ tsp hot chili powder
$^2/_3$ cup fresh tomato juice
2 tbsp red wine vinegar
1 tbsp tomato ketchup
salt and freshly ground black pepper
1 cup broccoli flowerets
3 tbsp minced parsley
1 tbsp chopped fresh thyme
2 bunches green onions (scallions), chopped
2 x 14-ounce cans chick-peas (garbanzo beans), rinsed and drained
$^3/_4$ cup yellow raisins

1 Cook the rice in a large saucepan of lightly salted, boiling water for about 20 minutes, or according to the package instructions, until the rice is cooked and just tender. Drain thoroughly and keep hot.

2 Meanwhile, make the dressing. Heat the oil in a saucepan, add the garlic and spices, and cook gently for 2 minutes, stirring.

3 Add the passata, vinegar, tomato ketchup, and seasoning and mix well. Heat gently, stirring occasionally, until the mixture comes to the boil. Keep the dressing warm.

4 Cook the broccoli in a saucepan of lightly salted, boiling water for about 5 minutes, until just tender. Drain thoroughly.

5 Place the cooked rice in a bowl, add the spicy tomato dressing, and stir to mix. Add the cooked broccoli and the remaining ingredients and toss together to mix.

6 Serve the rice salad warm or cold.

VARIATIONS

● Use brown or white rice in place of the brown and wild rice mix.
● Use other canned beans such as kidney beans or pinto beans in place of the chick-peas (garbanzo beans).
● Use chopped ready-to-eat dried apricots, peaches, or pears in place of the yellow raisins.

NUTRITIONAL ANALYSIS

(figures are per serving)

Calories = 372
Fat = 5.2g
of which saturates = 0.8g
      monounsaturates = 1.5g
      polyunsaturates = 2g
Protein = 12.9g
Carbohydrate = 73g
Dietary fiber = 6.9g
Sodium = 0.3g

Percentage of total calories from fat = 13%
of which saturates = 2%

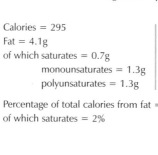

WARM
PASTA SALAD

This warm whole-wheat pasta salad, with zucchini and mushrooms tossed in a lightly spiced tomato dressing, makes an ideal dish for lunch or dinner.

Preparation time: 10 minutes
Cooking time: 10-12 minutes
Serves 4

12 ounces whole-wheat pasta shapes
2 tsp olive oil
1 clove garlic, crushed
1 bunch green onions (scallions), chopped
3 green zucchini, thinly sliced
3 yellow zucchini or summer squash, thinly sliced
2 cups sliced mushrooms
1 1/4 cups tomato juice or crushed tomatoes
1 tsp chili powder
salt and freshly ground black pepper
2 tbsp chopped fresh mixed herbs

1 Cook the pasta in a large saucepan of lightly salted, boiling water for 10-12 minutes, until just cooked or *al dente*.

2 Meanwhile, heat the oil in a large nonstick skillet or wok. Add the garlic and stir-fry over a medium heat for 30 seconds.

3 Add the green onions (scallions), zucchini, and mushrooms and stir-fry for about 5 minutes, until just cooked.

4 Add the tomato juice or crushed tomatoes, chili powder, and seasoning, and stir-fry until the tomato juice is hot and bubbling.

5 Drain the pasta thoroughly. Toss the pasta and zucchini mixture together until well mixed and sprinkle with the fresh herbs.

6 Serve immediately with slices of fresh, crusty bread.

NUTRITIONAL ANALYSIS
(figures are per serving)

Calories = 295
Fat = 4.1g
of which saturates = 0.7g
    monounsaturates = 1.3g
    polyunsaturates = 1.3g

Protein = 12.3g
Carbohydrate = 55.6g
Dietary fiber = 5.1g
Sodium = 0.01g

Percentage of total calories from fat = 12%
of which saturates = 2%

VARIATIONS
● Use other mixtures of vegetables such as carrots and bell peppers in place of the zucchini and mushrooms.
● Use white or flavored pasta in place of the whole-wheat pasta.
● Use ground cumin or curry powder in place of the chili powder.

MULTI-COLORED
MIXED-BEAN SALAD

A colorful salad that is equally appetizing served warm or cold.

Preparation time: 10 minutes

Cooking time: 10 minutes

Serves 4

1 cup green beans, trimmed and halved
14-ounce can black-eyed peas, rinsed and drained
14-ounce can red kidney beans, rinsed and drained
14-ounce can chick-peas (garbanzo beans), rinsed
and drained
1 sweet onion, chopped
1 yellow bell pepper, seeded and diced
2 tsp olive oil
2 cloves garlic, crushed
1 small red chili, seeded and finely chopped
²/₃ cup tomato juice
2 tbsp tomato ketchup
2 tbsp wine vinegar
2 tsp American mustard
few drops of Tabasco sauce
salt and freshly ground black pepper

1 Cook the green beans in a saucepan of lightly salted, boiling water for about 5 minutes, until just tender. Drain and cool.

2 Place the cooked green beans, black-eyed peas, red kidney beans, and chick-peas (garbanzo beans) in a bowl and stir together to mix. Add the onion and bell pepper and mix well.

3 Heat the oil in a saucepan, add the garlic and chili, and cook for 1 minute, stirring. Add all the remaining ingredients, mix well, and heat gently until boiling, stirring occasionally.

4 Pour the hot dressing over the beans and toss the ingredients together to mix.

5 Serve warm or cold with warmed pita bread or fresh crusty bread.

The dressing is suitable for cooking in a microwave oven.

VARIATIONS
● Use a different combination of beans such as pinto beans and lima beans.
● Use cider or tarragon vinegar in place of the wine vinegar.
● Use 1 red or orange bell pepper in place of the yellow bell pepper.
● Use 1 tsp chili powder in place of the fresh chili.
● Use whole-grain mustard in place of the American mustard.

NUTRITIONAL ANALYSIS
(figures are per serving)

Calories = 276

Fat = 5g

of which saturates = 0.6g

monounsaturates = 1.9g

polyunsaturates = 1.7g

Protein = 16.3g

Carbohydrate = 43.9g

Dietary fiber = 13.1g

Sodium = 1g

Percentage of total calories from fat = 16%, of which saturates = 2%

Good source of fiber & vitamin C

ROASTED
VEGETABLES

The flavors and colors of crisp Mediterranean-style vegetables are combined in this delicious and nutritious recipe, ideal for serving with broiled lean meat or fish and baked potatoes or pasta.

Preparation time: 10 minutes

Cooking time: 20-30 minutes

Serves 4

*1 red onion, sliced
1 white or yellow onion, sliced
4 zucchini, thickly sliced
8 ounces baby corn
1 eggplant, cut into chunks
1 red bell pepper, seeded and cut into large dice
1 yellow bell pepper, seeded and cut into large dice
2 cloves garlic, thinly sliced
4 tsp olive oil
salt and freshly ground black pepper
2-3 tbsp chopped fresh mixed herbs*

1 Place all the vegetables and garlic in a nonstick roasting pan and mix together.

2 Add the oil and seasoning and toss until the vegetables are lightly coated with oil.

3 Bake in a preheated oven at 425° for 20-30 minutes, until just tender and tinged brown at the edges, stirring once or twice.

4 Sprinkle with the herbs and toss to mix. Serve hot or cold with broiled lean meat or fish and baked potatoes.

VARIATIONS
● Use flavored olive oil such as chili oil or herb oil.
● Use other chopped fresh herbs such as parsley, chives, or rosemary in place of the mixed herbs.
● Sprinkle the vegetables with red wine vinegar or herb vinegar just before serving.

NUTRITIONAL ANALYSIS
(figures are per serving)

Calories = 116

Fat = 4.2g

of which saturates = 0.6g

monounsaturates = 2.2g

polyunsaturates = 0.7g

Protein = 5.6g

Carbohydrate = 14.6g

Dietary fiber = 5.3g

Sodium = 0.6g

Percentage of total calories from fat = 33%

of which saturates = 5%

Good source of vitamins A & C

SAUTÉED ROOT
VEGETABLES

Root vegetables are full of their own natural flavors and combine well with fresh rosemary and seasoning.

Preparation time: 20 minutes

Cooking time: 20 minutes

Serves 4

12 ounces potatoes
1 medium sweet potato
1 small jicama
1 small rutabaga
3 carrots
1 celery root
1 tbsp olive oil
1 onion, chopped
2 cloves garlic, crushed
1-2 tbsp finely chopped fresh rosemary
salt and freshly ground black pepper
fresh rosemary sprigs, to garnish

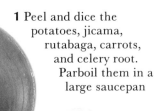

1 Peel and dice the potatoes, jicama, rutabaga, carrots, and celery root. Parboil them in a large saucepan of lightly salted, boiling water for 5 minutes. Drain thoroughly.

2 Heat the oil in a large nonstick skillet, add the onion and garlic, and cook for 1 minute, stirring.

3 Add the diced vegetables, chopped rosemary, and seasoning, and mix well. Cook over a medium heat, turning over frequently, until the vegetables are cooked, lightly browned, and crispy.

4 Garnish with fresh rosemary sprigs and serve hot with broiled fish such as salmon or rainbow trout and fresh seasonal vegetables such as broccoli flowerets and baby carrots.

VARIATION
● Use 1 red onion or 6 shallots in place of the onion, for a change.

NUTRITIONAL ANALYSIS

(figures are per serving)

Calories = 205
Fat = 4.1g
of which saturates = 0.6g
      monounsaturates = 2.2g
      polyunsaturates = 0.7g
Protein = 4.7g
Carbohydrate = 39.6g
Dietary fiber = 8.2g
Sodium = 0.09g

Percentage of total calories from fat = 18%
of which saturates = 3%
Good source of vitamin A

STIR-FRIED
JULIENNE
OF VEGETABLES

Preparation time: 10 minutes

Cooking time: 5 minutes

Serves 4

2 tsp olive oil
3 zucchini, cut into matchstick (julienne) strips
4 carrots, cut into matchstick strips
1 red bell pepper, seeded and sliced into strips
1 yellow bell pepper, seeded and sliced into strips
juice of 1 lemon
salt and freshly ground black pepper
2 tbsp chopped fresh mixed herbs

1 Heat the oil in a large nonstick skillet or wok. Add the zucchini, carrots, and bell peppers and stir-fry over a high heat for 4-5 minutes, until just tender.

2 Add the lemon juice and seasoning and stir-fry for 30-60 seconds.

3 Add the herbs, toss together to mix, and serve immediately.

VARIATION
● Use the juice of 1 lime or 1 orange in place of the lemon juice.

NUTRITIONAL ANALYSIS

(figures are per serving)

Calories = 84
Fat = 2.4g
of which saturates = 0.4g
      monounsaturates = 1.1g
      polyunsaturates = 0.6g
Protein = 3g
Carbohydrate = 13.3g
Dietary fiber = 4.3g
Sodium = 0.03g

Percentage of total calories from fat = 25%
of which saturates = 5%
Good source of vitamins A & C

DESSERTS

*D*esserts are often the part of a meal that people most look forward to. Even if you are watching your intake of calories and fat, there is no need to miss out. You can still indulge and enjoy something sweet without having to feel guilty about eating a calorie- and fat-laden dessert. Here is a tempting selection of mouthwatering desserts that exploit the full flavor potential of ripe, fresh fruits, as well as versatile dried fruits and convenient canned fruits. Enjoy these light desserts whenever you like as part of a healthy diet.

RED SUMMER FRUIT
ROULADE

In this sumptuous dessert, an airy sponge is filled with a creamy yogurt mixture and luscious fresh berries.

Preparation time: 25 minutes, plus cooling time

Cooking time: 10-12 minutes

Serves 8

3 eggs
²/₃ cup sugar
finely grated rind of 1 lemon
1 cup all-purpose flour
²/₃ cup reduced-fat sour cream
²/₃ cup low-fat plain yogurt
³/₄ cup sliced strawberries
³/₄ cup red or black raspberries

1 Lightly grease a 13 x 9-inch jellyroll pan and line it with nonstick baking paper.

2 Place the eggs and ¹/₂ cup of the sugar in a large bowl and stand the bowl over a saucepan of hot water.

3 Using an electric whisk, whisk the mixture until pale and creamy, and thick enough to leave a trail on the surface of the mixture when the whisk is lifted out.

4 Remove the bowl from the saucepan and whisk until cool. Add the lemon rind, sift the flour over the mixture, and gently fold them in using a metal spoon. Gently fold in 1 tbsp hot water.

5 Pour the mixture into the pan and tilt to spread the mixture evenly.

6 Bake in a preheated oven at 40° for 10-12 minutes, until well-risen, golden brown, and firm to the touch.

7 Meanwhile, sprinkle a sheet of nonstick baking paper or parchment paper with the remaining sugar. Quickly turn the cake out onto the paper, trim off the crusty edges, and roll the cake up loosely with the paper inside. Place, seam downward, on a wire rack to cool.

8 Fold together the yogurt and sour cream. When the cake is cool, unroll it and spread the yogurt mixture over the cake, not quite to the edges. Scatter the strawberries and raspberries over the top.

9 Roll up the roulade, place it on a serving plate, seam downward, slice, and serve immediately.

The baked jellyroll without the filling is suitable for freezing.

QUICK CHERRY
BRULÉE

A quick and light dessert that is sure to satisfy those sweet-loving tastebuds every time.

Preparation time: 10 minutes, plus chilling time

Serves 4

1¼ cups low-fat plain yogurt
⅔ cup reduced-fat sour cream
ince can cherries in syrup, drained
2 tbsp light soft brown sugar
fresh mint sprigs, to decorate
1 pound fresh cherries

1 Combine the yogurt and sour cream. Place half the canned cherries in a serving bowl.

2 Spread half the yogurt mixture over the cherries and sprinkle with half the sugar.

3 Repeat the layers with the remaining cherries, yogurt mixture, and sugar, ending with a layer of sugar.

4 Cover and chill for several hours before serving. Decorate with fresh mint sprigs and serve with fresh cherries.

VARIATIONS

● This dessert may be made and served in individual sundae glasses.
● Use other canned fruit in fruit juice such as peaches, apricots, or raspberries in place of the cherries.
● Use dark brown sugar in place of the light soft brown sugar.

NUTRITIONAL ANALYSIS

(figures are per serving)

Calories = 271
Fat = 6.7g
of which saturates = 3.8g
    monounsaturates = 1.9g
    polyunsaturates = 0.4g
Protein = 7.9g
Carbohydrate = 48.2g
Dietary fiber = 1.6g
Sodium = 0.04g

Percentage of total calories from fat = 23%
of which saturates = 10%

DRIED FRUIT PURÉES

An excellent way to reduce your fat intake yet still enjoy delicious, home-baked cakes is to use an easy-to-make natural sugar substitute in the form of a dried fruit purée. Dried fruit purées such as apricot or prune purée may even be used to replace the fat in some cake recipes. They are most suited to cakes which require a moist texture and a fruity flavor. Dried fruit purées are not suitable for replacing the fat in recipes such as sponge cakes, yellow cakes, or pastry.

By substituting dried fruit purée for butter, margarine, or oil, you are able to cut down the fat content of some cake recipes quite dramatically, as well as reducing the calories. Dried fruit purées also contribute additional nutrients to your diet, including dietary fiber, iron, and vitamin A.

Dried fruit purées are very simple to make and are easy to use. To make a fruit purée, roughly chop about ³/₄ cup ready-to-eat dried apricots. Place them in a liquidizer or food processor with 5 tbsp water and blend until fairly smooth — the consistency of cooked oatmeal.

To use the dried fruit purée in place of fat, simply substitute fruit purée for the same amount of butter, margarine, or oil in the original recipe. For example, if a recipe calls for ³/₄ cup butter or margarine, use ³/₄ cup ready-to-eat dried apricots or prunes, puréed with 5 tbsp water (as above), in place of the fat.

As an alternative, you may wish to use a combination of half dried fruit purée and half fat in place of the normal weight of fat in some recipes — this would still make a considerable reduction in the fat content.

Experiment with your own recipes at home and try using other dried fruit purées in place of the apricot and prune purées — you'll be pleasantly surprised at the results!

APRICOT & CINNAMON
RAISIN SQUARES

Apricot purée replaces the fat in this recipe but you won't miss out on anything! Enjoy these moist cakes on their own as a snack with a piece of fresh fruit, or with low-fat topping or ice cream for a delicious dessert.

Preparation time: 15 minutes

Cooking time: 30-35 minutes

Makes 16 squares

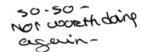

so-so – Not worth doing again –

³/₄ cup ready-to-eat dried apricots
1 cup self-rising flour, sifted
¹/₄ tsp baking powder
2 tsp ground cinnamon
³/₄ cup light soft brown sugar
2 eggs, beaten
¹/₂ cup yellow raisins
3 tbsp freshly squeezed orange juice
2 tbsp granulated sugar

1 Chop the apricots coarsely and place them in a liquidizer or food processor with 5 tbsp water. Blend until they are the consistency of cooked oatmeal.

2 Place the apricot purée, flour, baking powder, cinnamon, soft brown sugar, and eggs in a bowl and beat together until thoroughly mixed. Stir in the yellow raisins and mix well.

3 Turn the mixture into a lightly greased 7-inch square cake pan and level the surface.

4 Bake in a preheated oven at 350° for 30-35 minutes, until risen, golden brown, and firm to the touch.

5 Mix the orange juice and granulated sugar together and pour the mixture evenly over the hot cake.

6 Using a sharp knife, mark the cake into squares while it is still hot and allow to cool in the pan for 10 minutes. Cut the cake into squares and transfer to a wire rack to cool completely.

7 Once cool, store these cakes in an airtight container at room temperature.

VARIATIONS

● Add the finely grated rind of 1 small orange to the cake mixture before baking.
● Use other ground spices such as ginger or mixed spice in place of the cinnamon.
● Use lemon juice for the cake topping.
● If self-rising flour is not available, use all-purpose flour with double the quantity of double-acting baking powder and 1 tsp baking soda.

CHOCOLATE RAISIN SQUARES

Follow the recipe above but omit the cinnamon, use ³/₄ cup raisins in place of the yellow raisins, and add 2 ounces (2 squares) melted baking chocolate to the cake mixture in Step 2 before stirring in the raisins.

NUTRITIONAL ANALYSIS

(figures are per square)

Calories = 102
Fat = 0.9g
of which saturates = 0.2g
monounsaturates = 0.3g
polyunsaturates = 0.1g
Protein = 2g
Carbohydrate = 23.2g
Dietary fiber = 0.8g
Sodium = 0.04g

Percentage of total calories from fat = 8%
of which saturates = 2%

PINEAPPLE UPSIDE-DOWN
CAKE

*A reduced-fat version of an old favorite, this upside-down cake comprises a
light sponge topped with a layer of juicy fruit.*

Preparation time: 20 minutes

Cooking time: 45 minutes

Serves 6

6 tbsp dark corn syrup
8-ounce can pineapple rings in fruit juice, drained
9 ready-to-eat dried apricots
$^1/_2$ cup low-fat spread
$^1/_2$ cup sugar
2 eggs
$1^1/_2$ cups self-rising flour
1 tsp baking powder
1 tsp ground cinnamon
3 tbsp unsweetened pineapple juice

● Use other dried fruits such as prunes
or candied cherries in place of the
apricots, for added variety.
● Omit the cinnamon, if preferred.

NUTRITIONAL ANALYSIS

(figures are per serving)

Calories = 346
Fat = 10.2g
of which saturates = 2.8g
     monounsaturates = 4.3g
     polyunsaturates = 2.3g
Protein = 6.5g
Carbohydrate = 60.9g
Dietary fiber = 1.4g
Sodium = 0.3g

Percentage of total calories from fat = 27%
of which saturates = 7%

1 Lightly grease the base of a 7-inch
round cake pan and line it with nonstick
baking paper. Heat the syrup in a
saucepan and boil it until it is slightly
reduced. Pour it into the prepared pan to
cover the bottom.

2 Arrange the pineapple rings and
apricots in the syrup.

3 Place the low-fat spread, sugar, and
eggs in a bowl. Sift the flour, baking
powder, and cinnamon into the bowl and
then add the pineapple juice.

4 Beat the mixture thoroughly, using an
electric mixer or wooden spoon, until
smooth and creamy.

5 Spread the cake mixture evenly over
the fruit. Bake in a preheated oven at
350° for about 45 minutes until well-risen,
golden brown, and firm to the touch.

6 Unmold onto a warmed serving platter
and serve in slices with low-fat yogurt or
reduced-fat cream.

VARIATIONS
● Replace 2 tbsp of the flour with sifted
cocoa powder.
● Use other canned fruits such as pears
or apricots in place of the pineapple.

APPLE PUDDING

This chunky apple pudding, subtly flavored with cinnamon and served with low-fat topping, is sure to become a family favorite.

Preparation time: 15 minutes

Cooking time: 1-1¼ hours

Serves 6

½ cup low-fat spread
½ cup light soft brown sugar
2 eggs
1½ cups self-rising flour, sifted
1 tsp baking powder, sifted
1 tsp ground cinnamon
3 tbsp skim milk
3 tart dessert apples
2 tbsp yellow raisins
2 tbsp dark raisins

1 Place the low-fat spread, sugar, eggs, flour, baking powder, cinnamon, and milk in a bowl. Beat the mixture thoroughly, using an electric mixer or wooden spoon, until smooth.

2 Peel, core, and dice the apples, add to the cake mixture with the yellow and dark raisins, and mix well.

3 Transfer the mixture to a lightly greased ovenproof dish and bake in a preheated oven at 350° for 1-1¼ hours, until risen, golden brown, and firm to the touch.

4 Serve hot with low-fat topping or ice cream.

VARIATIONS
● Use peaches in place of the apples.
● Use white granulated sugar in place of the brown sugar.
● If self-rising flour is not available, use all-purpose flour, or half all-purpose and half whole-wheat flour, with double the quantity of double-acting baking powder and 1 tsp baking soda

NUTRITIONAL ANALYSIS

(figures are per serving)

Calories = 336
Fat = 10.3g
of which saturates = 2.8g
     monounsaturates = 4.3g
     polyunsaturates = 2.3g

Protein = 6.9g
Carbohydrate = 58.4g
Dietary fiber = 1.9g
Sodium = 0.3g

Percentage of total calories from fat = 28%
of which saturates = 7%

HONEY-BAKED FRUIT

Preparation time: 15 minutes

Cooking time: 30 minutes

Serves 4

8-ounce can pineapple chunks
in fruit juice
4 tbsp clear honey
½ tsp ground mixed spice
2 dessert apples, peeled, cored, and sliced
2 pears, peeled, cored, and sliced
2 peaches, peeled, pitted, and sliced
2 bananas, peeled and cut into chunks

1 Drain the pineapple, reserving the juice and fruit separately. Place the pineapple juice in a bowl with the honey and spice and mix well.

2 Place the prepared fresh fruits in an ovenproof dish and stir to mix.

3 Pour the honey mixture over the fruits and stir to mix. Cover and bake in a preheated oven at 350° for about 30 minutes, until the fruit is just beginning to soften.

4 Serve hot with low-fat ice cream or reduced-fat cream.

NUTRITIONAL ANALYSIS

(figures are per serving)

Calories = 211
Fat = 0.3g
of which saturates = 0g
     monounsaturates = 0g
     polyunsaturates = 0.1g
Protein = 1.8g
Carbohydrate = 53.4g
Dietary fiber = 3.9g
Sodium = 0g

Percentage of total calories from fat = 1%
of which saturates = 0%
Good source of vitamin C

NECTARINE
CHOUX RING

This light and crispy choux pastry ring, filled with a creamy combination of low-fat yogurt and topping and topped with fresh fruit, is sure to impress your family or guests.

Preparation time: 25 minutes, plus cooling time

Cooking time: 40 minutes

Serves 6

4 tbsp low-fat spread
5 tbsp all-purpose flour
2 eggs, beaten
²/₃ cup low-fat yogurt
²/₃ cup low-fat ready-made vanilla-flavored dessert topping
4 nectarines or peaches, peeled, pitted, and sliced
1 cup raspberries
1 tbsp powdered (confectioner's) sugar, to decorate
fresh mint sprigs, to decorate

1 Line a cookie sheet with nonstick baking paper.

2 Place the low-fat spread in a saucepan with ²/₃ cup water. Heat gently until the spread has melted, then bring to the boil.

3 Remove the pan from the heat, quickly add the flour, and beat well until the mixture is smooth and leaves the sides of the pan. Allow the mixture to cool slightly.

4 Gradually beat in the eggs, using a wooden spoon, until the mixture is smooth and shiny.

5 Drop spoonfuls of the dough onto the paper on the cookie sheet to form a ring, making sure they are just touching.

6 Bake in a preheated oven at 400° for about 40 minutes, until risen, golden brown, and crisp.

7 Immediately slice the ring horizontally in half to release the steam inside, and return to the oven for about 5 minutes to dry out. Carefully transfer to a wire rack to cool.

8 Place the bottom half of the choux ring on a serving platter. Combine the yogurt and dessert topping and spoon the mixture into the ring.

9 Top with the prepared fruits, then place the top of the choux ring over the fruit.

10 Sift the powdered (confectioner's) sugar over the choux ring, decorate with mint sprigs, and fill the centre of the ring with extra raspberries, if you like. Serve immediately in slices.

VARIATION
● Use other prepared fresh or canned fruits such as apricots and strawberries in place of the nectarines and raspberries.

NUTRITIONAL ANALYSIS
(figures are per serving)

Calories = 200
Fat = 7.9g
of which saturates = 2.7g
    monounsaturates = 2.9g
    polyunsaturates = 1.3g
Protein = 8.1g
Carbohydrate = 25.5g
Dietary fiber = 2.4g
Sodium = 0.1g

Percentage of total calories from fat = 35%
of which saturates = 10%
Good source of vitamin C

 # PROFITEROLES

A light version of this popular dessert, delicious served with fresh fruit such as strawberries, makes a perfect finale for a family feast or special-occasion meal.

Preparation time: 30 minutes, plus cooling time

Cooking time: 15-20 minutes

Serves 6

4 tbsp low-fat spread
5 tbsp all-purpose flour, sifted
2 eggs, beaten

FOR THE CHOCOLATE SAUCE
$2^1/2$ ounces ($2^1/2$ squares) baking chocolate, broken into pieces
6 tbsp dark corn syrup

1 cup low-fat vanilla ice cream or frozen dessert
1 pound strawberries
strawberry or mint leaves, to decorate

1 Line two cookie sheets with nonstick baking paper.

2 Place the low-fat spread in a saucepan with $^2/_3$ cup water. Heat gently until the spread has melted, then bring to the boil.

3 Remove the pan from the heat, quickly add the flour, and beat well until the mixture is smooth and leaves the sides of the pan. Allow the mixture to cool slightly.

4 Gradually beat in the eggs, using a wooden spoon, until the mixture is smooth and shiny. Spoon the mixture into a piping bag fitted with a medium-sized plain nozzle. Pipe walnut-sized balls of the mixture onto the prepared cookie sheets.

5 Bake in a preheated oven at 400° for 15-20 minutes, until crisp and golden.

6 With a sharp, pointed knife, carefully slice the top off each profiterole to allow steam to escape. Transfer to a wire rack to cool completely.

7 Meanwhile, make the chocolate sauce. Place the chocolate and syrup in a bowl over a pan of simmering water and stir until melted and well blended.

8 Spoon some ice cream into each profiterole and cover with the tops.

9 To serve, pile the profiteroles into small pyramids on individual serving plates. Arrange some strawberries on each plate. Pour some of the sauce over the profiteroles and strawberries, and serve with the remaining sauce handed separately. Decorate with strawberry or mint leaves.

VARIATIONS
● Use milk, white, orange, or mint-flavored chocolate in place of the baking chocolate, for variety.
● Use other flavored low-fat ice cream or frozen deserts such as strawberry or chocolate in place of the vanilla ice cream.
● A melon-baller is an ideal tool for scooping small portions of ice cream to fill the profiteroles.

NUTRITIONAL ANALYSIS

(figures are per serving)

Calories = 286
Fat = 9.4g
of which saturates = 3.6g
     monounsaturates = 3.6g
     polyunsaturates = 1.3g
Protein = 6g
Carbohydrate = 47.1g
Dietary fiber = 1.5g
Sodium = 0.2g

Percentage of total calories from fat = 30%
of which saturates = 10%
Good source of vitamin C

RASPBERRY MERINGUE NESTS

This is a simple but highly attractive dessert. Crispy meringue nests contrast with a creamy yogurt filling topped with fresh raspberries.

Preparation time: 25 minutes, plus cooling time
Cooking time: 2½-3 hours
Serves 6

3 egg whites
³/₄ cup sugar
³/₄ cup low-fat yogurt
1 cup black or red raspberries
fresh mint sprigs, to decorate

1 Line two cookie sheets with nonstick baking paper. Draw six 4-inch circles on the paper and turn over.

2 Place the egg whites in a bowl and whisk until stiff. Gradually whisk in half the sugar, whisking well after each addition.

3 Gradually whisk in the remaining sugar until well incorporated.

4 Spoon the meringue into a piping bag fitted with a large star nozzle. Pipe a continuous coil of meringue on each circle on the paper to make the bases, then pipe an extra ring of meringue on top of each circle around the edge to make a nest or basket shape.

5 Bake in a preheated oven at 225° for 2½-3 hours, until crisp and dry.

6 Leave to cool on a wire rack, then peel off the base paper. Place the meringue nests on serving plates.

7 Spoon some yogurt into each nest and top with some raspberries. Serve immediately, decorated with mint sprigs.

VARIATION
● Use different prepared fresh fruit.

70

SPICED APPLE
STRUDEL

*A popular choice for a dessert, this elegant strudel is perfect
for entertaining or for a special-occasion family meal.*

Preparation time: 25 minutes

Cooking time: 40 minutes

Serves 8

*1³/₄ pounds tart apples, such as Baldwin,
Cortland, or Newtown
finely grated rind and juice of 1 lemon
2 tbsp yellow raisins
2 tbsp dark raisins
2 tbsp ready-to-eat dried apricots, chopped
2 tbsp light soft brown sugar
2 tsp ground mixed spice
4 sheets phyllo dough (each about 18 x 10 inches)
2 tbsp sunflower oil
4 tbsp fresh white bread crumbs
1 tbsp powdered (confectioner's) sugar*

1 Peel, core, and slice the apples. Place them in a bowl with the lemon rind and juice, raisins, apricots, sugar, and spice and mix well.

2 Place 1 sheet of phyllo dough on a sheet of nonstick baking paper and brush the dough lightly with oil.

3 Place another sheet on top, brush lightly with oil, and layer the remaining 2 sheets of dough on top, brushing each one lightly with oil.

4 Sprinkle the bread crumbs over the dough, leaving a 1-inch border all around the edge.

5 Spread the apple mixture evenly over the bread crumbs, then fold the border edges over the fruit mixture.

6 With one long side toward you, using the nonstick baking paper, carefully roll up the strudel.

7 Place the strudel seam-side down on a cookie sheet lined with parchment paper. If the oven or cookie sheet is too small to take the strudel in a long roll, curve it into a horseshoe shape. Brush the strudel all over lightly with oil.

8 Bake in a preheated oven at 375° for about 40 minutes, until crisp and golden.

9 Dust with sifted powdered (confectioner's) sugar just before serving and serve hot or cold cut into slices with low-fat ice cream or reduced-fat cream.

VIRTUALLY FAT-FREE

Reducing the amount of fat in our diet is one of the most positive steps we can take towards a healthier lifestyle. And, in response to the endless recommendations from nutritionists and health experts, many people have taken up the challenge by cutting back on their intake of fat, and saturated fats in particular. However, making a drastic cut in the fat content of our meals is no mean feat and this section is intended for those with this goal in mind. All the recipes contain 5 grams or less of fat per serving and are suitable for those who need to lose weight or minimize their fat intake for medical reasons. Obviously these recipes are also suitable for anyone following a healthy eating plan, but in this case they do not need to be the main focus of the diet.

Fat is an important part of the flavor of many dishes and this is why it can be so hard to cut down its use. Using fat-free cooking methods and substituting other flavors are two techniques this section utilizes to bring you a delicious range of low-fat recipes that do not compromise on taste or flavor.

FAT-FREE STRATEGIES

Even if you have already reduced the fat in your diet to healthier levels, making a further reduction to under 5 grams of fat per serving does require that extra surge of willpower. Fortunately, there are strategies which will ensure that preparing, cooking, and eating food can still remain one of the greatest joys of life.

There are a surprising number of cooking techniques that don't require fat — simmering, dry-frying, broiling, microwaving, and pressure-cooking, to name a few. They also have the added benefit of not creating greasy dishes which need cleaning after the meal.

Flavor is an important element that people miss when they first give up fat. However, the richness of fat often masks more interesting and subtle flavors in the food. As your palate becomes clearer, you'll start to appreciate clean, natural tastes. If strong, satisfying flavors are what you enjoy, there is a wealth of aromatics and seasonings that offer exciting possibilities in place of fat — chilies, garlic, ginger, grated citrus rind and juice, soy sauce, pickles, wine, spirits, vegetable juices, sun-dried tomatoes, herbs, and spices will get your tastebuds tingling.

Fats also help to improve the appearance, palatability, and keeping qualities of food, particularly cakes and breads. But there are many "fat-free" or low-fat ingredients which can be used instead:
- Dried fruit purées can replace fat in some cake recipes, as well as contributing valuable nutrients.
- Fruit juice concentrates can be used as a glaze for cakes, sweet breads, cupcakes, and muffins which may look a little dry without any fat.
- Marinating foods in wine, soy sauce, or fruit juice instead of oil will help tenderize and moisten them, as well as improve their appearance and flavor.

TECHNIQUES FOR FAT-FREE COOKING

If you find you need to use a little fat, use oil from a spray, or combine oil with water, fruit juice, or broth and spray it from a plastic spray can or atomizer.

"FRYING"
- To wet-fry, bring a small amount of fat-free liquid (water, broth, wine, cooking liquid from steamed vegetables, meat, or fish) to the boil in a nonstick pan. Reduce the heat to medium-low, then add chopped vegetables, poultry, or meat. Cook, stirring, for 2-15 minutes depending on the ingredients, their size, and the degree of doneness required. Add a little more liquid if necessary.
- Meat containing "hidden" fats, and watery vegetables such as onions, celery, and mushrooms, can be dry-fried without fat in a nonstick skillet over low heat, until tender and even slightly browned.

STEAMING
- Steam vegetables, poultry, or fish in a steamer basket, set over boiling liquid. The liquid can be flavored with herbs and garlic. Save it to use for simmering and stewing.

BROILING AND BARBECUING
- Guaranteed to bring out the best in good quality meats, poultry, fish, and strong-tasting vegetables such as bell peppers, eggplant, and onions. The direct, dry heat quickly seals in juices beneath a crispy exterior.
- Broiling can be used as a flavorful alternative to stewing and simmering vegetables which need pre-cooking before being cooked in a soup, casserole, or oven-baked dish.
- Marinate the foods in blends of herbs, spices, fruit juices, soy sauce, or yogurt, and use the marinade to baste the food during cooking.

ROASTING
- For maximum flavor and moisture, bake fish, poultry, or corn in foil, parchment paper parcels, or sealed roasting bags with wine, citrus juice, or broth. Add herbs, spices, and slivers of vegetables for extra flavor.

COMBINED TECHNIQUES
- Lightly steam vegetables, fish, or poultry, then cook in a sauce.

NON-STICK COOKWARE

Many of these techniques depend on good-quality nonstick cookware to prevent food from sticking and to encourage it to brown without any oil — that way it looks more appetizing. Nonstick cookware has improved beyond belief in recent years. Generally speaking, the more you pay, the better the quality. Many of the newer ranges are dishwasher safe. Some are so durable that they can be used with metal utensils, but most manufacturers recommend using wooden or plastic tools. Use the virtually fat-free diet as an opportunity for treating yourself to some new equipment.

The following are indispensable items in fat-free cooking:

SKILLET — *6-inch*
SKILLET — *9-inch*
SKILLET WITH LID — *12-inch*
RIDGED BROILER PAN, *to use either under the broiler or on top of the stove if you don't have a griddle*
ROASTING PANS — *small and large*
COOKIE SHEETS

FAT-BUSTING TIPS

● Allow soups and stews to cool, then chill. The fat solidifies on the surface and can easily be removed.
● Choose extra-lean cuts of meat and trim off all visible fat. Remove skin from poultry.
● Limit red meats to 2 ounces per serving. Cut in small dice and bulk out with more vegetables and pulses.
● Drain off any fatty liquid from meat after browning.
● Use phyllo or strudel pastry, lightly sprayed with oil, instead of ordinary pastry.
● Use moist, fat-free fillings in sandwiches, then you won't need to use a spread.
● Use evaporated skimmed milk (4% fat) instead of skim milk in dishes such as creamed potatoes. It adds creaminess.
● Use arrowroot, potato starch, and cornstarch to thicken sauces. Unlike wheat flour, they don't need to be mixed with fat.

VIRTUALLY FAT-FREE SNACKS

Even when you're on a drastically fat-reduced diet, you still need tasty snacks. Here are some suggestions:

SUNFLOWER OR PUMPKIN SEEDS (PEPITAS) A tablespoon makes a tasty snack and contains about 2 grams of fat. Good to sprinkle on leafy salads with a low-fat dressing.
BRAZIL NUTS Two whole kernels contain 3.4 grams fat and plenty of carbohydrates, vitamins, and minerals.
FRESH OR DRIED DATES Sweet, energy-boosting, and virtually fat-free.
FRUITS of any description, fresh or dried, are virtually fat-free.
VEGETABLES Crisp sticks of carrot, celery, bell pepper, radishes, jicama, baby corn, and cherry tomatoes are great on their own or with yogurt.
LOW-FAT YOGURT Deliciously creamy and contains only 5% fat.
LOW-FAT CHEESES Virtually fat-free soft cheeses may contain as little as 0.2% fat. Mix them with puréed fruits or honey for extra richness.
FRUITCAKES OR SWEET BREADS These contain far less fat than ordinary cakes or cookies. A small slice contains 1-3 grams of fat.
OAT OR RICE CAKES These contain about 2 grams of fat per cake. Top with chopped banana and low-fat soft cheese.

HIDDEN FATS

Even if we cut down on the amount of fat used in preparation and cooking, there is still the fat already present in the food to consider. The combination of the two affects the overall fat content of the foods we eat. Here are some foods you may not think of as fatty:

Food	Average serving	Fat/g
lean steak	6 ounces	22
canned tomato soup	bowl	6.0
barbecue sauce	2 tbsp	7.0
whole milk	1¼ cups	11.7
peanut butter	2 tbsp	13.0
chocolate	1 ounce	7.4
popcorn	1 ounce	10.7
potato chips	1 ounce	8.5
sponge cake	small slice	26
ice cream	2 scoops	9.8
avocado pear	half	22

FAT-FREE BROTHS

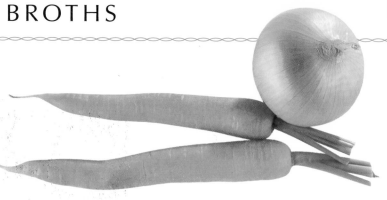

Broths are vital to fat-free cooking as they replace the flavor and moisture normally provided by fat. Broths will keep for 4-5 days in the refrigerator, but it's well worth making extra to freeze for later use.

Vegetable broths are not simmered for as long as meat broths because the flavor of some vegetables becomes unpleasant if overcooked. The vegetables should therefore be diced quite finely (about ³/₄ inch square) as this increases the surface area and encourages them to release their nourishing juices more quickly.

LIGHT VEGETABLE BROTH

1.8 g fat per cup
Makes about 3 quarts

This is a good base for light summer soups, stewed vegetables, or poached fish. Use it instead of chicken broth in vegetarian dishes.

1 onion, chopped
10 sprigs parsley, including stalks
2 bay leaves
6 large fresh basil leaves
3-4 fresh thyme sprigs
2 celery stalks, chopped
2 carrots, chopped
2 zucchini, chopped
¹/₂ cup chopped green beans
1 cup chopped large mushrooms
4 tomatoes, quartered
2 strips lemon zest
1 tsp salt
¹/₂ tsp freshly ground black pepper

1 Place the onion and herbs in a large saucepan with about ²/₃ cup water. Cook over a medium-high heat for 4-5 minutes, stirring, until the onion is soft.

2 Add the remaining ingredients, then cover and cook for 10 minutes, stirring occasionally. Pour in enough water to cover by about 2 inches. Bring to the boil, then simmer for 45 minutes.

3 Strain the broth through a fine-meshed sieve, pressing to extract all the liquid. Simmer for a little longer if you want a stronger flavor.

STRONG VEGETABLE BROTH

0.4 g fat per cup
Makes about 3 quarts

This makes a full-bodied broth which is good for hearty soups and casseroles. You can use it wherever you would normally use meat broth.

1 onion, chopped
10 sprigs parsley, including stalks
2 bay leaves
6 sprigs fresh thyme
4 celery stalks with leaves, chopped
3 carrots, chopped
3 tomatoes, quartered
2 leeks, green parts included, quartered lengthwise and chopped
³/₄ cup chopped mushrooms
1 tbsp dried wild mushrooms, soaked in boiling water for 15 minutes
1 eggplant, chopped
1 potato, diced
2 tbsp tamari or shoyu
1 tsp salt
¹/₂ tsp freshly ground black pepper

1 Place the onion and herbs in a large saucepan with about ²/₃ cup water. Cook, stirring, over medium-high heat for 4-5 minutes, until the onion is soft.

2 Add the remaining ingredients. Cover and cook for 10 minutes, stirring occasionally. Pour in enough water to cover by about 2 inches. Bring to the boil, then simmer for 45 minutes.

3 Strain the broth through a fine-meshed sieve or cheesecloth, pressing to extract all the liquid.

FAT-FREE CHICKEN BROTH

0.4 g fat per cup
Makes about 2 ¹/₂ quarts

1 x 5-pound chicken, cut in pieces
1 head of garlic, outer skin removed, clove tips sliced off
3 onions, quartered
2 leeks, split lengthwise
4 carrots, halved
4 celery stalks, halved
10 sprigs parsley
2 bay leaves
2 tsp salt
¹/₂ tsp freshly ground black pepper

1 Place all the ingredients in a large pot with enough water to cover by about 2 inches. Slowly bring to the boil, removing any scum. Simmer over very low heat for 3 hours.

2 Strain through a fine-meshed sieve or cheesecloth into a large bowl, then filter through paper towels. Leave to cool, then place in the refrigerator. When chilled, remove the solid layer of fat.

VERY LOW-FAT SALAD DRESSINGS

Forget about heavy oily dressings and bring your salad greens to life with nothing more than a squeeze of lemon or lime, a sprinkling of fresh herbs, coarse sea salt, and freshly ground black pepper — the clean, acidic flavors really wake up the palate. Or try one of these very low-fat dressings.

CITRUS DRESSING

1.5 g fat per tbsp

Makes 5 tbsp

1/2 tsp Dijon mustard
2 tsp olive oil
3 tbsp fresh orange juice
3 tbsp fresh lime juice
pinch of sugar
salt and pepper to taste

Liquidize all the ingredients in a blender until homogenized.

MUSTARD YOGURT DRESSING

0.1 g fat per tbsp

Makes 1 cup

6 tbsp nonfat yogurt
2 tsp Dijon-style mustard
1 tsp wine vinegar
1 tbsp chopped fresh herbs
finely grated zest of 1/2 lemon
freshly ground black pepper

Combine the yogurt, mustard, and vinegar. Stir in the herbs, grated lemon zest, and pepper.

ORIENTAL DRESSING

1.8 g fat per tbsp

Makes 6 tbsp

1 1/4 cups Fat-Free Chicken Broth
(page 76)
2 tbsp minced red onion
1/2 tsp minced fresh ginger root
1/2 tsp minced lemon grass
3 sprigs flat-leafed parsley
1 tbsp lime juice
1/2 tsp salt
2 tsp sesame seeds, toasted and crushed
1/2 tsp sugar
1 tsp tamari (Japanese soy sauce)
1 tsp dark sesame oil

1 Place the broth, onion, ginger, lemon grass, parsley, lime juice, and salt in a small saucepan. Bring to the boil. Cover and simmer for 5 minutes until reduced, then strain.

2 Place 6 tbsp of the liquid in a blender with the sesame seeds, sugar, tamari, and sesame oil. Liquidize until well homogenized.

VEGETABLES

*Containing the merest trace of fat, vegetables take on a justifiably high profile in
a virtually fat-free diet. They are a vital source of fiber, vitamins, and minerals.
Yellow and orange varieties, such as carrots, sweet potatoes, and butternut squash, are
bursting with beta-carotene, a powerful antioxidant known to help prevent cancer. Dark
green leafy vegetables also contain beta-carotene, as well as calcium, iron, and vitamin C.
Vegetables offer an infinite variety of tastes, textures, and flavors. Depending on type, the
buds, leaves, stems, flowers, and roots of vegetables are all at our disposal to be turned into
delicious and satisfying main meals, appetizers, and snacks.*

CARROT, TOMATO, &
PEPPER SOUP

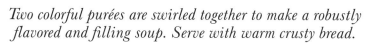

*Two colorful purées are swirled together to make a robustly
flavored and filling soup. Serve with warm crusty bread.*

Preparation time: 20 minutes

Cooking time: 30 minutes

Serves 4

2 large red bell peppers
2 large tomatoes
1 garlic clove, unpeeled
$^1/_2$-inch piece fresh ginger root, minced
2-3 fresh thyme sprigs
1 onion, chopped
1 small leek, split lengthwise and chopped
1 cup (8 ounces) thinly sliced carrots
$^1/_4$ cup (2 ounces) diced potato
3$^3/_4$ cups Fat-Free Chicken Broth (page 76)
or Strong Vegetable Broth (page 76)
salt and freshly ground black pepper
squeeze of lemon juice
toasted sesame seeds, to garnish

1 Preheat the oven to 425°. Place the bell
peppers, tomatoes, and garlic in a roasting
pan. Roast the garlic for about 10 minutes,
until soft. Roast the bell peppers and
tomatoes for a further 10 minutes, until
the skins are blackened and blistered.

2 Meanwhile, place the ginger, thyme,
and half the onion in a saucepan with

the leek, carrots, potato, and
$^2/_3$ cup of the broth. Wet-fry over
medium heat until the onion is soft.
Add a further 2 cups of broth and
seasoning. Cover and simmer over low
heat until the carrots are tender.

3 Remove the skin, core, and seeds from
the bell peppers, then roughly chop the
flesh. Peel the tomatoes and garlic,
reserving any juice. Transfer to a blender
or food processor with the remaining
onion and broth, and season with salt and
pepper. Purée until smooth, then transfer
to a small saucepan. Add a squeeze of
lemon juice, then simmer over low heat
for a few minutes.

4 Purée the carrot mixture, return to
the pan, and check the seasoning.
Reheat gently.

5 Pour the carrot soup into warm
bowls. Swirl the tomato and pepper
soup into the center. Garnish with
sesame seeds.

NUTRITIONAL ANALYSIS

(figures are per serving)

Calories = 74
Fat = 0.8g
of which saturates = 0.2g
      monounsaturates = 0.1g
      polyunsaturates = 0.5g
Protein = 2.3g
Carbohydrate = 15.4g
Dietary fiber = 4.5g
Sodium = 0.02g

Percentage of total calories from fat = 10%
of which saturates = 2%
Good source of vitamins A & C

MINTED ZUCCHINI & PEA
SOUP

A refreshing soup, ideal for a summer lunch.

Preparation time: 25 minutes
Cooking time: 30 minutes
Serves 6

2 shallots, chopped
1 garlic clove, minced
2 tbsp minced fresh mint
3³/₄ cups Fat-Free Chicken Broth (page 76)
1¹/₂ cups (9 ounces) mixed green and yellow
zucchini, finely diced
¹/₂ cup shelled peas (about 9 ounces unshelled)
¹/₂ cup corn kernels (from 1 large cob)
1 small potato, diced
squeeze of lemon juice
salt and freshly ground black pepper
small sprigs of mint, to garnish

1 Place the shallots, garlic, and mint in a nonstick saucepan with a ladleful of broth. Wet-fry over medium heat for 4-5 minutes, or until the shallots are softened.

2 Add the zucchini, the shelled peas, corn, potato, and another ladleful of broth to moisten. Cover and cook over medium heat for 10 minutes, until the vegetables are beginning to soften slightly.

3 Add the remaining broth and bring to the boil. Season to taste, then simmer for about 10 minutes, until the vegetables are just tender.

4 Leave about one-third of the mixture in the pan, then purée the rest until smooth. (If you prefer a completely smooth soup, purée all of it.)

5 Return the mixture to the pan and reheat gently. Add a squeeze of lemon juice to sharpen the flavor, and check the seasoning.

6 Pour into warm bowls. Garnish each serving with a sprig of mint. Serve with warm crusty bread or crackers.

VARIATIONS
● Use chopped asparagus in place of the zucchini.
● Use fresh coriander (cilantro) or flat-leafed parsley in place of the mint.

COOK'S TIP
● If you are short of time, use frozen corn and peas.

NUTRITIONAL ANALYSIS

(figures are per serving)

Calories = 60
Fat = 0.9g
of which saturates = 0.1g
      monounsaturates = 0.1g
      polyunsaturates = 0.4g

Protein = 3.4g
Carbohydrate = 10.1g
Dietary fiber = 2.0g
Sodium = 3 mg

Percentage of total calories from fat = 14% , of which saturates = 2%
Good source of vitamin C

GREEN PEPPER &
AVOCADO DIP

*Serve this colorful dip as an appetizer or snack,
or spooned over broiled fish or chicken.*

Preparation time: 20 minutes

Cooking time: 10 minutes

Serves 6

2 green bell peppers, halved, cored, and seeded
$^1/_2$ small fresh green chili, finely chopped
$^1/_2$ small avocado
2 garlic cloves, crushed
3 green onions (scallions), green parts
included, chopped
finely grated rind and juice of 1 lime
4 tbsp chopped fresh coriander (cilantro)
salt and freshly ground black pepper
4 small wheat tortillas, to serve
lime wedge and a sprig of fresh
coriander (cilantro), to garnish

1 Place the bell peppers cut side downward in a broiler pan. Broil under very high heat for 10 minutes, until blackened. Peel off the skin and roughly chop the flesh.

2 Place the bell peppers and the remaining ingredients in a food processor or blender. Purée until smooth. Check the seasoning and add more lime juice if necessary.

3 Spoon into a serving bowl, then cover and chill. Garnish with lime and coriander (cilantro) just before serving. Serve with the wheat tortillas and chunks of crisp, raw vegetables.

EGGPLANT & TOMATO
CROSTINI

Preparation time: 30 minutes
Cooking time: 2 hours 55 minutes
Serves 4

3 plum tomatoes, halved crosswise
pinch of dark brown sugar
pinch of fennel seeds (optional)
freshly ground black pepper
1 large eggplant
2 garlic cloves, unpeeled
1 small fresh red chili
¹/₄ cup minced red onion
2 tsp sun-dried tomato paste or tomato paste
1 tsp tamari (Japanese soy sauce)
1 tsp finely-grated lemon rind
¹/₂ tsp coriander (cilantro) seeds,
toasted and crushed
¹/₂-inch piece fresh ginger root, minced
salt
1 small French stick, thickly sliced
chopped fresh flat-leafed parsley, to garnish

1 Pack the tomatoes, cut side upward, in a single layer in a shallow ovenproof dish into which they fit snugly. Sprinkle with the sugar, fennel seeds (if using), and pepper. Roast in a preheated oven at 275° for 1¹/₂-2 hours, until beginning to shrivel. Remove from the dish with a slotted spoon, cut in half, and set aside.

2 Raise the oven temperature to 425°. Prick the eggplant in several places. Place in a roasting pan with the garlic and chilies. Roast until soft. The garlic and chilies will need 10-15 minutes, the eggplant 40-45 minutes.

3 Remove the skin and seeds from the chili, and the skin from the garlic. Peel the eggplant. Place in a food processor or blender with the onion,

tomato paste, tamari, lemon rind, coriander seeds, ginger, and salt and pepper. Process to a chunky purée.

4 Reduce the oven temperature to 300°. Spread the bread in a single layer on a cookie sheet and toast for 10 minutes until slightly crisp.

5 To serve, spread the toast with the eggplant purée, top with pieces of tomato, and sprinkle with parsley.

VARIATION
● Use slivers of raw tomato or red bell pepper instead of oven-dried tomatoes.

COOK'S TIP
● Serve at room temperature to allow the flavors to come through.

GREEN BEAN &
KOHLRABI SALAD

ORIENTAL
SALAD

A crisp and colorful salad of crunchy vegetables with a lemony yogurt dressing. Serve with rye bread as an appetizer or light entrée.

Preparation time: 30 minutes
Cooking time: 3 minutes
Serves 4

Serve as an appetizer or as an accompaniment to broiled or stir-fried fish, seafood, or poultry.

Preparation time: 15 minutes
Serves 4

6 ounces fine green beans, trimmed and cut into
1¹/₂-inch pieces
3 small kohlrabi, weighing about 4 ounces each
2 small carrots, thinly sliced
¹/₂ yellow bell pepper, seeded and finely diced
3 green onions (scallions),
green parts included, sliced
coarse sea salt and freshly ground black pepper
1 tbsp pumpkin seeds (pepitas)
1 tbsp chopped fresh dill
6 tbsp Mustard Yogurt Dressing (page 77)

1 Place the beans in a steamer over boiling water and steam for 2-3 minutes until just tender but still crunchy. Alternatively, cook them in a microwave oven. Allow to cool.

2 Peel and thinly slice the kohlrabi. Stack a few slices at a time and cut into matchstick strips.

3 Combine the beans, kohlrabi, carrots, bell pepper, and green onions (scallions) in a large bowl and season.

4 Divide the mixture between four serving plates. Sprinkle with pumpkin seeds (pepitas). Stir the dill into the dressing and spoon a little over each plate.

COOK'S TIPS
● Kohlrabi is a neglected vegetable which deserves to be used more often. It has a unique, slightly peppery flavor and the crunch and juiciness of an apple.
● Be sure to use small kohlrabi since the larger specimens tend to be tough and woody.

10 ounces mixed young oriental greens such as
mustard greens, bok choy, tatsoi, and mizuna
¹/₃ Chinese (Napa) cabbage, cut lengthwise
¹/₂ cup snow-peas, trimmed and thinly sliced
diagonally
¹/₃ cup brown mushrooms, very thinly sliced
2 green onions (scallions), cut crosswise into
1-inch strips
¹/₂ cup cold boiled rice
6 tbsp Oriental Dressing (page 77)
1 tsp toasted sesame seeds

1 Tear the greens and bok choy stalks into bite-sized pieces. Slice the Chinese cabbage crosswise.

2 Arrange all the greens and vegetables attractively on individual serving plates with a small mound of rice in the center.

3 Spoon the dressing over the top and sprinkle with the sesame seeds.

NUTRITIONAL ANALYSIS

(figures are per serving)

Calories = 78	Protein = 4.5g
Fat = 1.9g	Carbohydrate = 11.1g
of which saturates = 0.3g	Dietary fiber = 3.0g
monounsaturates = 0.4g	Sodium = 0.05g
polyunsaturates = 0.8g	

Percentage of total calories from fat = 22%
of which saturates = 3%
Good source of vitamin A & folic acid

NUTRITIONAL ANALYSIS

(figures are per serving)

Calories = 96	Protein = 4.6g
Kilojoules = 401	Carbohydrate = 12.8g
	Dietary fiber = 5.7g
Fat = 3.2g	Sodium = 0.09g
of which saturates = 0.5g	
monounsaturates = 0.9g	
polyunsaturates = 1.5g	

Percentage of total calories from fat = 30%
of which saturates = 4%
Good source of vitamins A & C, folic acid, & iron

PAPAYA & BEAN SPROUT
SALAD

Full of contrasting flavors and textures, this salad makes a delicious appetizer or low-calorie lunch.

Preparation time: 15 minutes

Serves 2

1 large, ripe papaya
squeeze of lime juice
7 ounces (about 4 handfuls) green and red salad leaves such as frisée, romaine, lamb's lettuce, and oakleaf lettuce, torn into bite-sized pieces
$^1/_2$ ounce (small handful) arugula
$^1/_2$ small cucumber, very thinly sliced
$^1/_2$ cup bean sprouts
$1^1/_2$ tbsp Citrus Dressing (page 77)

1 Halve the papaya lengthwise and scoop out the seeds, reserving a few for garnish. Using a small sharp knife, carefully remove the skin. Slice the flesh lengthwise into thin segments. Place in a shallow dish, and sprinkle with a squeeze of lime juice.

2 Arrange the leaves on individual plates. Scatter the cucumber, bean sprouts, and papaya over the top, and sprinkle with the reserved papaya seeds.

3 Spoon the dressing over the salad and serve at once with crackers or crusty bread.

VARIATIONS

● Add a tablespoon of cottage cheese for extra protein.
● Use muskmelon or mango instead of papaya.
● Replace the cucumber with thinly sliced mushrooms.

NUTRITIONAL ANALYSIS

(figures are per serving)

Calories = 109
Fat = 2.2g
of which saturates = 0.3g
      monounsaturates = 0.9g
      polyunsaturates = 0.6g
Protein = 3.2g
Carbohydrate = 20.4g
Dietary fiber = 6.4g
Sodium = 0.02g

Percentage of total calories from fat = 18%
of which saturates = 3%
Good source of beta-carotene, folic acid, vitamin C, & iron

STEAMED BROCCOLI
WITH LEMON & PARMESAN

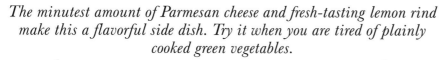

The minutest amount of Parmesan cheese and fresh-tasting lemon rind make this a flavorful side dish. Try it when you are tired of plainly cooked green vegetables.

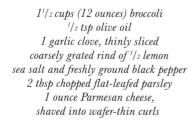

Preparation time: 15 minutes
Cooking time: 5 minutes
Serves 4

NUTRITIONAL ANALYSIS
(figures are per serving with half a baked potato)

Calories = 184
Fat = 3.4g
of which saturates = 1.5g
      monounsaturates = 1.0g
      polyunsaturates = 0.6g
Protein = 10.0g
Carbohydrate = 30.3g
Dietary fiber = 0.2g
Sodium = 0.09g

Percentage of total calories from fat = 17%
of which saturates = 7%
Good source of vitamin C & folic acid

1¹/₂ cups (12 ounces) broccoli
¹/₂ tsp olive oil
1 garlic clove, thinly sliced
coarsely grated rind of ¹/₂ lemon
sea salt and freshly ground black pepper
2 tbsp chopped flat-leafed parsley
1 ounce Parmesan cheese,
shaved into wafer-thin curls

1 Divide the broccoli into even-sized flowerets. Trim the woody end off the central stalk and cut the stalk into thin diagonal slices.

2 Transfer the flowerets and sliced stalk to a steamer basket. Steam over boiling water for 1 minute, until just tender.

3 Heat the oil in a nonstick skillet. Add the garlic and gently fry over medium-low heat for 30 seconds until just colored — do not allow it to burn. Add the broccoli, lemon rind, salt, pepper, and parsley. Toss for a few seconds, then add the Parmesan cheese. Toss again, then transfer to a heated dish, and serve immediately.

4 Serve the broccoli with baked potatoes to accompany fish, meat, or chicken.

VARIATIONS
● Use a mixture of broccoli and cauliflower flowerets.
● For a spicier flavor, sprinkle with dried red pepper flakes and omit the lemon rind.

ROASTED PAPRIKA
POTATOES

Serve these crispy cubes of oven-roasted potato as a side dish with red meats, chicken, fish, or with a vegetarian entrée.

Preparation time: 25 minutes

Cooking time: 45 minutes

Serves 4

1³/₄ pounds potatoes
1 tbsp chopped fresh rosemary
1 tbsp olive oil
1 tsp paprika
salt and freshly ground black pepper

1 Peel the potatoes and slightly trim the ends and sides to straighten. Cut into ³/₄-inch cubes.

2 Bring a saucepan of salted water to the boil. Boil the potatoes for 5 minutes, until just tender. Alternatively, cook them in a microwave oven. Tip into a colander and drain, shaking the colander to roughen the edges of the cubes, so that they become crisp when roasted.

3 Combine the rosemary, oil, paprika, and salt and pepper. Add to the potatoes and toss carefully to coat.

4 Arrange the potatoes in a single layer in a nonstick roasting pan. Roast in a preheated oven at 400°, tossing occasionally, for 35 minutes, until golden brown.

NUTRITIONAL ANALYSIS
(figures are per serving)

Calories = 178
Fat = 3.3 g
of which saturates = 0.4g
    monounsaturates = 2.0g
    polyunsaturates = 0.5g
Protein = 4.3g
Carbohydrate = 34.9g
Dietary fiber = 3.2g
Sodium = 0.01g

Percentage of total calories from fat = 16%
of which saturates = 2%
Good source of vitamin C

COOK'S TIP
● Make sure the roasting pan is large enough. If the potato cubes are crowded, they will steam in their own moisture rather than roast.

MIXED ROOT
VEGETABLES

Serve this as a side dish with broiled meats or chicken.

Preparation time: 35 minutes

Cooking time: 1¹/₂ hours

Serves 8

2 onions, thickly sliced
vegetable oil spray
14 ounces potatoes
1 pound 10 ounces mixed root vegetables such as turnip, parsnip, celery root (celeriac), carrot, jicama, yucca, and rutabaga
2 tbsp chopped fresh rosemary
1 tbsp chopped fresh thyme
salt and freshly ground black pepper
1¹/₂ cups Fat-Free Chicken Broth (page 76) or Strong Vegetable Broth (page 76)
2 tsp butter
chopped fresh parsley

1 Arrange the sliced onions in a single layer in the bottom of a nonstick roasting pan. Lightly spray with oil. Roast in a preheated oven at 475° for 10-12 minutes. Remove the pan from the oven and reduce the temperature to 375°.

2 Peel and thinly slice the potatoes and the other root vegetables. Lightly spray a 2-quart ovenproof dish with oil. Layer the onions and other vegetables in the dish, sprinkling each layer with the fresh herbs, salt, and pepper.

3 Pour in the broth. Cover tightly with foil and bake for 1 hour, or until tender. Remove the foil, dot the vegetables with the butter, and bake for another 20 minutes to brown the top.

NUTRITIONAL ANALYSIS
(figures are per serving)

Calories = 90
Fat = 1.8g
of which saturates = 0.8g
    monounsaturates = 0.4g
    polyunsaturates = 0.3g
Protein = 2.4g
Carbohydrate = 16.9g
Dietary fiber = 4.4g
Sodium = 0.04g

Percentage of total calories from fat = 18%
of which saturates = 8%
Good source of vitamins A & C, & folic acid

BROILING VEGETABLES

If you are following a virtually fat-free diet, broiling or oven-roasting vegetables is a wonderful way of preparing them. The best candidates for broiling are bell peppers, red onions, zucchini, eggplant, and tomatoes. If you use a nonstick roasting pan, you will not normally need to add any oil, but if the vegetables start to look dry, you may need to moisten them lightly with oil from a spray. To create that mouthwatering, charbroiled look, vegetables need to be subjected to intense heat. You can do this in a very hot oven or covered barbecue, or alternatively under a hot broiler or over hot coals.

Eaten hot, cold, or at room temperature, broiled vegetables make a delicious side dish, vegetarian main meal, or salad. They do not require any oily dressing since they produce their own juices, although a sprinkling of good quality vinegar or lemon juice adds a pleasantly sharp note. Pungent herbs such as rosemary, basil, and thyme are also good to use.

Broiling or oven-roasting are particularly useful techniques for vegetables that need softening before being added to a stew or soup. Wet-frying produces satisfactory results, but boiling provides the finished dish with the rich, mellow flavor usually supplied by fat.

NUTRITIONAL ANALYSIS
(figures are per serving)

Calories = 110
Fat = 1.7g
of which   saturates = 0.3g
    monounsaturates = 0.4g
    polyunsaturates = 0.7g

Protein = 5.1g
Carbohydrate = 20.0g
Dietary fiber = 6.3g
Sodium = 0.33g

Percentage of total calories from fat = 14%, of which saturates = 3%
Good source of vitamins A, C, E, & B vitamins

✳ RATATOUILLE ❧

Preparation time: 20 minutes
Cooking time: 40 minutes
Serves 6

olive oil spray
1 large eggplant, cut crosswise into 1 inch thick slices
2 cups large, flat-cap mushrooms, quartered
2 zucchini, halved lengthwise
2 large red bell peppers, halved, cored, and seeded
2-2¹/₂ cups Fat-Free Vegetable Broth (page 76)
2-3 sprigs of fresh thyme
1 tbsp chopped fresh rosemary
1 onion, minced
2 garlic cloves, minced
1 pound plum tomatoes, peeled and chopped
2 tbsp tamari (Japanese soy sauce)
2 slivers of lemon rind
¹/₂ tsp sugar
salt and freshly ground black pepper
pinch of dried red pepper flakes
2 tbsp flat-leafed parsley, trimmed and chopped

1 Lightly spray the eggplant, mushrooms, and zucchini all over with cooking oil from a spray can. Arrange in a nonstick broiler pan with the bell peppers, cut-side downward. Broil for 10-12 minutes, turning halfway through the cooking time, until they are beginning to blacken. Cut all the vegetables into even-sized chunks and set aside.

2 Pour ²/₃ cup of the broth into a heavy-based casserole or pan over medium heat. Add the thyme, rosemary, onion, and garlic. Wet-fry for 5 minutes, until the onion is soft.

3 Add the tomatoes and their juice, tamari, lemon rind, sugar, salt and pepper, and 1¼ cups of the broth. Bring to the boil, then simmer over low heat for 10 minutes, stirring occasionally, until slightly thickened.

4 Add the broiled vegetables, red pepper flakes, and all but 1 tbsp of the parsley. Bring to the boil, then cover and simmer for 10 minutes, adding a little more broth if necessary. Check the seasoning, and garnish with the remaining parsley before serving.

5 Serve at room temperature with some crusty bread, or hot with rice or cracked wheat as a light meal.

VARIATION
● Replace the eggplant or mushrooms with extra zucchini or peppers.

SPINACH & BELL PEPPER

FRITTATA

Preparation time: 20 minutes

Cooking time: 15 minutes

Serves 6

6 ounces (about 4 cups uncooked)
young spinach leaves
2 large eggs
4 egg whites (from large eggs)
³/₄ tsp ground turmeric
4 tbsp Fat-Free Chicken Broth (page 76) or
Strong Vegetable Broth (page 76)
3 green onions (scallions),
green parts included, minced
3 tbsp finely diced red bell pepper
2 cups cooked new potatoes, cut into small chunks
¹/₂-inch piece fresh ginger root, finely chopped
pinch of red pepper flakes
¹/₄ tsp olive oil
¹/₄ tsp salt
freshly ground black pepper

1 Wash the spinach thoroughly, remove any coarse stems, and roughly chop the leaves. Place in a saucepan without any extra water. Cook over medium heat for 2-3 minutes, or until just tender. Drain, squeeze dry, and place in a small bowl.

2 In a large bowl, lightly beat the whole eggs with the whites and ¹/₄ tsp of the turmeric.

3 Pour the broth into a nonstick 9 ¹/₂-10-inch skillet with the green onions (scallions), bell pepper, potatoes, ginger, red pepper flakes, and remaining turmeric. Wet-fry over medium heat for a minute or two, then mix with the spinach in the bowl.

4 Heat the oil in the pan, then pour in a thin layer of the egg mixture, and allow to set. Add the spinach mixture and remaining egg, stirring to distribute the spinach evenly. Cook over medium heat for about 5 minutes, until almost set.

5 Place under a preheated medium-hot broiler for a few minutes to brown the top.

6 Cut the frittata into wedges and serve warm with crusty bread, shredded lettuce, and sliced cherry tomatoes.

COOK'S TIP
● Normally made with whole eggs, the fat content of this frittata is reduced to a minimum by using a third of the usual amount of egg yolks.

NUTRITIONAL ANALYSIS
(figures are per serving)

Calories = 101
Fat = 4.0g
of which saturates = 1.1g
    monounsaturates = 1.6g
    polyunsaturates = 0.7g

Protein = 8.7g
Carbohydrate = 8.2g
Dietary fiber = 2.1g
Sodium = 0.17g

Percentage of total calories from fat = 35% , of which saturates = 10%
Good source of vitamin A

BRAISED
SPRING VEGETABLES

Serve these crunchy, tender young vegetables with
pasta as a vegetarian entrée.

Preparation time: 40 minutes

Cooking time: 10 minutes

Serves 6

2 tbsp sunflower margarine
6 large green onions (scallions), trimmed and
halved lengthwise
2-3 sprigs of thyme
sea salt
4 ounces ($^3/_4$ cup) baby carrots
$^2/_3$ cup baby corn cobs
$^3/_4$ cup fine green beans, trimmed
1 cup baby asparagus tips
$^3/_4$ cup broccoli flowerets, cut into small pieces
about $1^1/_2$ inches across
$^1/_2$ cup sugar snap peas
$^1/_2$ cup shelled young fava beans,
outer skins removed
3 tbsp chopped fresh mixed herbs such as
flat-leafed parsley, chives, and basil
1 tbsp lemon juice
freshly ground black pepper
1 pound 2 ounces (4 cups) pasta shapes, to serve

1 Have ready a large pan of boiling salted water over which you have fitted a steamer basket with a lid.

2 Melt half the margarine in a large nonstick skillet. Add the onions, thyme, sea salt, and $^3/_4$ cup water. Bring to the boil, cover, and simmer for 5 minutes.

3 Meanwhile, steam the carrots, corn, and beans together for 2 minutes. Add them to the onions in the pan and leave to simmer. Next, steam the asparagus and broccoli together for 1 minute, then add these to the pan containing the other vegetables, and continue to simmer. Finally, steam the sugar snap peas and shelled fava beans together for 1 minute, then add these to the pan as well.

4 When all the vegetables are in the pan, stir in the remaining margarine, the herbs, and lemon juice. Season with pepper and a little more salt if necessary. Cover and cook for a further minute.

5 Cook the pasta according to the instructions on the package and serve with the vegetables.

COOK'S TIP
● Make sure the pasta is ready to be served by the time you have finished cooking the vegetables.

NUTRITIONAL ANALYSIS

(figures are per serving including pasta)

Calories = 150

Fat = 4.5g

of which saturates = 0.9g

  monounsaturates = 0.9g

  polyunsaturates = 2.2g

Protein = 7.4g

Carbohydrate = 21.5g

Dietary fiber = 3.7g

Sodium = 0.06g

Percentage of total calories from fat = 27%

of which saturates = 6%

Good source of vitamins A & C, & folic acid

BEETS & GREENS
WITH CORIANDER SAUCE

*This makes a colorful and substantial
vegetarian entrée served with cooked soft grains
such as cracked wheat or buckwheat.*

Preparation time: 30 minutes

Cooking time: 1 hour 35 minutes

Serves 2-3

3 (about 9 ounces) uncooked small red beets
1/2 cup nonfat plain yogurt
2 tbsp chopped fresh coriander (cilantro)
1 garlic clove, crushed
salt and freshly ground black pepper
*6 ounces (about 3 cups) trimmed greens such as
collard greens, beet greens, turnip greens, or
cabbage, cut into ribbons*
1 tsp sunflower oil
4 tbsp Strong Vegetable Broth (page 76)
finely grated rind of 1/2 lemon

1 Wash the beets, taking care not to
tear the skins. Dry thoroughly and
wrap loosely in heavy-duty aluminum
foil. Roast in a preheated oven at
400° for 1-1½ hours, until tender.
Alternatively, they can be
cooked in a covered container
in a microwave oven.

2 Meanwhile, place the yogurt in a
small bowl and mix with the
coriander (cilantro), garlic, and
salt and pepper to taste.

3 Carefully peel the beets and cut into
quarters lengthwise. Keep them warm
while you cook the greens.

4 Heat a nonstick wok or
skillet over medium-
high heat. Add the
greens, sunflower oil,
broth, and lemon rind, and
wet-fry for 3-4 minutes,
until just tender and
still bright green.

5 Arrange the
greens and beets on
warmed serving
plates. Top with a
spoonful of the coriander sauce.

VARIATION

● Replace some or all of the greens with
stir-fried leeks or steamed green beans.

NUTRITIONAL ANALYSIS

(figures are per serving)

Calories = 111

Fat = 2.7 g

of which   saturates = 0.3g

monounsaturates = 0.4g

polyunsaturates = 1.6g

Protein = 7.2g

Carbohydrate = 15.5g

Dietary fiber = 8.8 g

Sodium = 0.1g

Percentage of total calories from fat = 22%, of which saturates = 2%

Good source of vitamins A & C, folic acid, & iron

STUFFED BELL
PEPPERS

With a vibrantly flavored stuffing of rice, lemon, and diced zucchini, these colorful peppers make a satisfying vegetarian entrée.

Preparation time: 50 minutes

Cooking time: 1 hour 15 minutes

Serves 4 (makes 4 peppers)

FOR THE STUFFING
2 tsp olive oil
2 tbsp Strong Vegetable Broth (page 76)
1 onion, minced
²/₃ cup long-grain rice
2 tbsp lemon juice
¹/₂ cup water
1 zucchini, very finely diced
3 tbsp chopped flat-leafed parsley
1 tbsp chopped fresh mint
¹/₄ tsp ground cinnamon
¹/₄ tsp ground allspice
salt and freshly ground black pepper

4 small red or yellow bell peppers
³/₄ cup tomato juice
salt and freshly ground black pepper
sprigs of flat-leafed parsley, to garnish

1 To make the stuffing, heat the oil and the broth in a small saucepan over medium heat. Add the onion, then cover and wet-fry for 4 minutes until soft.

2 Stir in the rice, lemon juice, and water. Cover and simmer for 10 minutes.

3 Mix the diced zucchini with the rice and cook for a further 2 minutes. Add a little more water or broth if the mixture becomes too dry. Stir in the parsley, mint, cinnamon, allspice, and salt and pepper.

4 With a small pointed knife, cut a circle around the top of the bell peppers, slightly wider than the base of the stem. Remove and discard the stem and core, reserving the tops to be used as "lids." Remove the seeds and ribs.

5 Fill the bell peppers with the rice mixture, leaving a little space for the rice to expand. Cover the tops with the lids.

6 Stand the bell peppers upright in a heavy-based saucepan into which they fit snugly. Add the tomato juice and enough water to come one-third of the way up their sides. Season with salt and pepper. Cover tightly and bring to the boil, then simmer for 30 minutes over very low heat.

7 Transfer the bell peppers to a serving dish and garnish with parsley sprigs. Spoon some of the cooking liquid over the peppers and serve the remainder in a jug. Serve the bell peppers with a bowl of nonfat plain yogurt and hunks of crusty bread for mopping up the juices.

VARIATION
● Use cracked wheat or buckwheat as a stuffing instead of the rice.

NUTRITIONAL ANALYSIS

(figures are per serving)

Calories = 206
Fat = 3.4g
of which saturates = 0.6g
    monounsaturates = 1.4g
    polyunsaturates = 0.9g
Protein = 5.2g
Carbohydrate = 41.4g
Dietary fiber = 4.1g
Sodium = 0.11g

Percentage of total calories from fat = 15%
of which saturates = 3%
Good source of vitamins A, C, E, & B vitamins

EASTERN
MEDITERRANEAN
✸ CASSEROLE

Bursting with color and flavor, this comforting casserole makes an excellent entrée for a fall dinner.

Preparation time: 25 minutes

Cooking time: 45 minutes

Serves 4-6

1 tsp cumin seeds
2 tsp coriander (cilantro) seeds
1 tbsp sesame seeds
2 tsp dried oregano
1 tsp vegetable oil
1 onion, chopped
3 garlic cloves, finely chopped
1 green chili, seeded and chopped
1¹/₂ cups Strong Vegetable Broth (page 76)
1 cup butternut squash or pumpkin flesh, cut into chunks
1 small eggplant, cut into chunks
1 red bell pepper, cut into squares
6 ounces green beans, chopped
6 ounces small new potatoes, unpeeled
14-ounce can peeled, chopped tomatoes
salt and freshly ground black pepper
6 ounces shredded green cabbage

1 Place the seeds in a small heavy-based pan without any oil. Heat until the aroma rises. Add the oregano and dry-fry for a few more seconds. Remove from the heat, crush with a pestle and mortar, and set aside.

2 Heat the oil in a heavy-based nonstick casserole. Gently fry the onion for a few minutes over medium-low heat until translucent. Add the garlic, chili, and 2 tbsp of the stock. Fry for 3 more minutes until soft. Stir in the seed mixture.

3 Add the squash, eggplant, bell pepper, beans, potatoes, and tomatoes. Bring to the boil, then cover and cook over medium-low heat for 10 minutes.

4 Pour in the remaining broth and season with salt and pepper. Bring to the boil then cover and simmer for 20 minutes. Add more broth if the mixture starts to look dry.

5 Stir in the cabbage and cook for 2-3 minutes until just wilted but still bright green. Serve immediately with plainly cooked rice or cracked wheat.

VARIATION
● Use 1 cup (8 ounces) mushrooms in place of the eggplant.

COOK'S TIP
● The toasted crushed seeds act as a thickener and also add a wonderfully earthy flavor to the dish.

NUTRITIONAL ANALYSIS
(figures are per serving)

Calories = 128
Fat = 2.7 g
of which saturates = 0.4g
    monounsaturates = 0.7g
    polyunsaturates = 1.2g
Protein = 5.5g
Carbohydrate = 22.4g
Dietary fiber = 5.8g
Sodium = 0.05g

Percentage of total calories from fat = 19%
of which saturates = 3%
Good source of vitamins A, C, & E,
folic acid & iron

POULTRY, MEAT, & GAME

Chicken, meat, and game contain valuable nutrients and add satisfying flavor to meals. The drawback is that these foods are a major source of cholesterol and saturated fats — the substances implicated in heart disease. Chosen with care, however, they can still have a place in a virtually fat-free diet. Part of the solution is to eat the meat and not the fat. But even if you choose lean cuts or trim visible fat from standard cuts, there is still the problem of the hidden fat, or marbling, so you'll need to cut down on serving sizes too. Think of meat as an accompaniment to vegetables, grains, or pasta, rather than the other way round. Choosing the variety is also important — poultry is lowest in fat, the white meat containing less fat than the dark meat. Game meats, such as venison, buffalo, and rabbit, are very lean.

BEEF & MUSHROOM
PHYLLO PARCELS

These spicy little phyllo parcels are ideal to serve with drinks or as a snack. Phyllo dough can be found in Greek stores; strudel dough can be substituted.

Preparation time: 40 minutes
Cooking time: 30 minutes
Makes 12

4 tbsp Fat-Free Meat Broth (page 76)
¹/₃ cup minced onion
1 garlic clove, finely chopped
¹/₂ tsp ground allspice
¹/₄ tsp ground cinnamon
freshly ground black pepper
²/₃ cup lean ground sirloin steak
1 cup finely chopped mushrooms
finely grated rind of 1 lemon
salt
4 sheets phyllo or studel dough,
measuring 10 ³/₄ x 10 inches
olive oil spray

1 Place the broth, onion, garlic, allspice, cinnamon, and pepper in a nonstick skillet. Wet-fry over medium-low heat for 2-3 minutes, until the onion is soft.

2 Add the beef and mushrooms. Raise the heat to medium and cook for a further 5-6 minutes, until the mushrooms are cooked. Stir in the lemon rind and season with salt. Allow to cool.

3 Cut the phyllo dough into 12 long strips measuring 3¹/₂ x 10 inches.

4 Lightly spray one strip with oil. Place about 2 level tablespoons of the filling in the bottom left-hand corner of a strip, and fold over diagonally to form a triangle. Continue to fold until you reach the end of the strip. Repeat with the remaining strips.

5 Place the triangles on a nonstick cookie sheet and lightly mist with oil. Bake in a preheated oven at 400° for 15-20 minutes, until golden.

6 Serve warm or at room temperature with crisp chunks of fresh vegetables and a bowl of nonfat plain yogurt mixed with some toasted cumin seeds and chopped fresh mint.

NUTRITIONAL ANALYSIS

(figures are per parcel)

Calories = 37
Fat = 0.9g
of which saturates = 0.3g
    monounsaturates = 0.3g
    polyunsaturates = 0.1g
Protein = 3.8g
Carbohydrate = 3.8g
Dietary fiber = 0.4g
Sodium = 0.01g

Percentage of total calories from fat = 21%
of which saturates = 7%
Good source of B vitamins

PORK
PITA POCKETS

Pita pockets stuffed with spicy morsels of ground broiled pork and crisp salad make a healthy, well-balanced snack or addition to a lunch box.

Preparation time: 25 minutes, plus chilling
Cooking time: 15 minutes
Serves 4

$^1/_4$ cup minced onion
6 tbsp minced flat-leafed parsley
1 cup extra-lean ground pork
2 tbsp fresh bread crumbs
$^1/_4$ tsp ground cumin
pinch of cayenne
salt and freshly ground black pepper
2 tbsp nonfat plain yogurt

TO SERVE
2 large pita breads
shredded lettuce
sliced tomatoes and cucumber
lemon wedges
nonfat plain yogurt

1 Place the onion and parsley in a blender and process until very finely minced.

2 Combine the pork, bread crumbs, cumin, cayenne, and salt and pepper in a mixing bowl. Add the onion-and-parsley mixture, mixing until evenly blended, then add the yogurt.

3 Form the mixture into 12 small cylindrical patties. Cover and chill for 1 hour. Thread onto 4 skewers.

4 Preheat the broiler until very hot. Broil for 15 minutes, turning, until brown and cooked through.

5 Cut the pita breads in half crosswise. Fill with salad, the grilled patties, and a lemon wedge. Top with a spoonful of yogurt.

VARIATION
● Replace the pork with ground turkey or chicken.

NUTRITIONAL ANALYSIS

(figures are per serving)

Calories = 88
Fat = 2.5g
of which saturates = 0.8g
    monounsaturates = 0.9g
    polyunsaturates = 0.4g
Protein = 13.0g
Carbohydrate = 3.6g
Dietary fiber = 0.9g
Sodium = 0.06g

Percentage of total calories from fat = 26%
of which saturates = 8%
Good source of B vitamins, iron, & zinc

TURKEY STIR-FRY
WITH BOK CHOY & NOODLES

Serve this as a light lunch or supper.

Preparation time: 20 minutes

Cooking time: 15 minutes

Serves 4

8 ounces thin rice noodles
1 tsp peanut oil
3 tbsp Fat-Free Chicken Broth (page 76)
2 garlic cloves, crushed
1-inch piece fresh root ginger, minced
2 fresh red chilies, seeded and very thinly sliced
1 pound turkey breast, cut into thin strips
3 green onions (scallions), sliced into 1-inch
diagonal pieces
1 cup thinly sliced brown mushrooms
1 pound 5 ounces bok choy, chopped
1 tbsp light soy sauce
2 tbsp chopped fresh coriander (cilantro)
salt and freshly ground black pepper

NUTRITIONAL ANALYSIS

(figures are per serving)

Calories = 372
Fat = 2.2g
of which saturates = 0.6g
    monounsaturates = 0.7g
    polyunsaturates = 0.6g
Protein = 34.7g
Carbohydrate = 52.1g
Dietary fiber = 1.0g
Sodium = 0.55g

Percentage of total calories from fat = 5%
of which saturates = 1%
Good source of vitamins A, C, & B vitamins,
iron, & zinc

1 Cook the noodles according to the instructions on the package. Rinse under a cold running faucet for a few seconds, then leave to drain and cool.

2 Heat a wok or large skillet over medium-high heat. When it is hot, add the oil and broth. Add the garlic, ginger, and chilies, and stir-fry for a few seconds.

3 Add the turkey and stir-fry for 2 minutes until no longer pink. Then add the onions, mushrooms, and soy sauce, and stir-fry for 2 minutes. Add the bok choy and stir-fry for another 2 minutes. Add the coriander (cilantro) and season to taste with salt and pepper.

4 Stir in the noodles until heated through. Serve the stir-fry immediately by itself or with steamed rice.

VARIATION
● If bok choy is unavailable, use Swiss chard or spinach instead.

RED ONION
MARMALADE

Preparation time: 10 minutes

Cooking time: 55 minutes

Makes ²/₃ cup

1 pound red onions, thinly sliced
4 tbsp Fat-Free Chicken Broth (page 76) or Strong
Vegetable Broth (page 76)
1 tbsp red wine vinegar
2 tsp olive oil
1 bay leaf, broken into pieces
freshly ground black pepper

1 Place the onion slices in a bowl and toss with the remaining ingredients.

2 Transfer the onion mixture to a large heavy-based nonstick skillet. Cover and cook over medium heat for 5 minutes, stirring occasionally, until the onions are translucent.

3 Reduce the heat to very low, then continue to cook, covered, for 45 minutes until very soft, stirring occasionally. Remove the lid and cook for a further 5 minutes, until very soft and thick.

4 Serve hot or cold with broiled meats, poultry, or fish.

LEMON & MINT
TURKEY BURGERS

These almost fat-free burgers are delicious cooked over hot coals. They are ideal for picnics or an informal light meal.

Preparation time: 25 minutes, plus 1 hour chilling

Cooking time: 6 minutes

Serves 4 (makes 8 patties)

1 pound ground turkey
¹/₂ small onion, grated
finely grated rind and juice of 1 small lemon
1 garlic clove, minced
3 tbsp minced fresh mint
pinch of dried red pepper flakes
salt and freshly ground black pepper
2 tbsp lightly beaten egg white
Red Onion Marmalade (see page 94), to serve

1 In a bowl, combine the turkey, onion, lemon rind and juice, garlic, mint, red pepper flakes, and salt and pepper, mixing thoroughly. Stir in the egg white to bind.

2 Shape the mixture into 8 patties about ¹/₂ inch thick. Cover and leave in the refrigerator for at least 1 hour to allow the flavors to develop.

3 Cook in a nonstick ridged skillet for 4-5 minutes each side. Alternatively, cook in a nonstick shallow roasting pan under a very hot broiler.

4 Serve the burgers with red onion marmalade, sesame buns, and a large salad.

VARIATION
● Serve with nonfat plain yogurt mixed with some toasted cumin seeds and chopped fresh mint instead of Red Onion Marmalade.

COOK'S TIP
● Drain off any excess liquid that appears after the burgers have been chilled.

NUTRITIONAL ANALYSIS
(figures are per serving including 2 tbsp Red Onion Marmalade)

Calories = 150
Fat = 1.7g
of which saturates = 0.4g
    monounsaturates = 0.8g
    polyunsaturates = 0.3g
Protein = 29.1g
Carbohydrate = 5.0g
Dietary fiber = 0.9g
Sodium = 0.08g

Percentage of total calories from fat = 35%
of which saturates = 6%
Good source of B vitamins & zinc

CHICKEN & VEGETABLE
STIR-FRY

Serve this as a light lunch or supper dish.

Preparation time: 20 minutes
Cooking time: 7 minutes
Serves 6

10 ¹/₂ *ounces skinless, boneless chicken breasts, cut*
into ³/₄*-inch cubes*
salt
4 tsp soy sauce
1 tbsp cornstarch
1 tbsp dry sherry or rice wine
6 tbsp Fat-Free Chicken Broth (page 76)
1 tbsp oyster sauce
4 green onions (scallions)
¹/₂ cup baby corn cobs
¹/₂ cup snow-peas, trimmed
1 cup canned water chestnuts, drained
1 red bell pepper
2 tsp ground nut oil
³/₄*-inch piece fresh ginger root, minced*
2 garlic cloves, minced
1 tsp dark sesame oil
1¹/₄ *tsp sesame seeds*

1 Place the chicken in a bowl with
¹/₄ tsp salt, 2 tsp of the soy sauce, the
cornstarch, and sherry, stirring to coat.
Leave to stand for 15 minutes.

2 Mix the remaining soy sauce with the
broth and oyster sauce, and set aside.

3 Diagonally slice the green onions
(scallions) into ³/₄-inch pieces. Cut the
corn into 3 pieces. Diagonally slice the
snow-peas into halves. Halve the water
chestnuts horizontally and cut the bell
pepper into similar sized pieces.

4 Place a nonstick wok or large skillet
over medium-high heat. When the pan is
hot, add the peanut oil. When it sizzles,
add the ginger, garlic, and green onions
(scallions). Stir quickly, then add the
onions, corn, water chestnuts, and bell
pepper. Stir-fry for 2 minutes. Sprinkle
with the sesame oil and a little salt.

5 Add the chicken and stir-fry for
3 minutes until it is no longer pink.

6 Add the snow-peas and the soy sauce
mixture. Stir-fry for 1 minute, until
thickened. Sprinkle with sesame seeds
and serve at once. Serve with plainly
cooked rice.

VARIATION
● Use broccoli flowerets in place
of the corn.

COOK'S TIP
● The secret of a successful stir-fry
is to cook over high heat for
the minimum amount of time.
You need to have all the
ingredients prepared
and to hand before
you begin.

CHICKEN TERIYAKI

In this dish, the chicken breasts are richly glazed with honey and soy sauce. Serve as a light lunch or supper.

Preparation time: 20 minutes, plus marinating
Cooking time: 10 minutes
Serves 6

6 skinless, boneless chicken breasts, weighing about 4 ounces each
vegetable oil spray

FOR THE MARINADE
3 tbsp clear honey
$^1/_2$ cup tamari (Japanese soy sauce)
$^1/_2$ cup dry sherry
1-inch piece fresh ginger root, minced
1 garlic clove, crushed
$^1/_2$ tsp freshly ground black pepper
lemon wedges and sprigs
of flat-leafed parsley, to garnish

1 Cut the chicken breasts in half diagonally and place in a bowl.

2 Place the marinade ingredients in a small saucepan and bring to the boil. Allow to cool, then pour the marinade over the chicken. Leave to marinate for at least 2 hours or overnight, turning occasionally.

3 Remove the chicken from the marinade and shake off the excess liquid. Reserve the marinade.

4 Lightly spray with oil a nonstick skillet large enough to take the chicken breasts in a single layer. Place over medium-high heat until hot, then add the chicken. Fry for 2-3 minutes until browned on both sides.

5 Add the reserved marinade. Bring to the boil, then reduce the heat slightly, and simmer briskly for 5 minutes.

6 Transfer the chicken breasts to a heated serving dish. Reduce the liquid remaining in the pan over a high heat and pour it over the chicken. Garnish with lemon wedges and sprigs of parsley.

7 Serve the chicken with boiled rice and a stir-fried leafy vegetable.

CHICKEN BREASTS
WITH VERMOUTH &
WATERCRESS SAUCE

*This quickly cooked entrée
would be ideal for a dinner party.*

Preparation time: 15 minutes

Cooking time: 25 minutes

Serves 4

*4 skinless, boneless chicken breasts, weighing
about 6 ounces each
freshly ground black pepper
²/₃ cup Fat-Free Chicken Broth (page 76)
2 shallots, minced
4 tbsp dry vermouth
1 bunch trimmed watercress, chopped
salt
2 tsp arrowroot, mixed with 1 tbsp orange juice or
cold water
orange segments, to garnish*

1 Cut the chicken breasts in half
diagonally. Season with plenty of coarsely
ground black pepper.

2 Fry the chicken in a heavy-based
nonstick skillet for 2-3 minutes each
side, to seal. Remove from the pan and
set aside.

3 Add 2 tbsp of the broth and the
shallots to the pan. Wet-fry for 2 minutes
until soft.

4 Add the vermouth and remaining
broth to the pan. Bring to the boil
and add the chicken. Reduce the heat,
cover, and simmer over low heat
for 15-20 minutes.

5 Stir in the watercress and season to
taste with salt and pepper.

6 Raise the heat, add the arrowroot, and
stir for 1 minute until thickened.

7 Transfer to a heated serving dish and
pour the sauce over the chicken. Garnish
with orange segments and serve with
steamed new potatoes and carrots cut
into matchstick strips.

VARIATIONS
● Use turkey
breast instead of
chicken.
● Replace the
watercress with
3 tbsp of chopped fresh
herbs such as tarragon or
basil.

COOK'S TIP
● Vermouth is a fortified wine,
enriched with herbs and spices,
which makes an aromatic basis for a
sauce. If you do not have any, use dry
white wine instead.

NUTRITIONAL ANALYSIS

(figures are per serving)

Calories = 214
Fat = 2.1g
of which saturates = 0.6g
monounsaturates = 0.9g
polyunsaturates = 0.4g
Protein = 42.5g
Carbohydrate = 3.5g
Dietary fiber = 0.5g
Sodium = 0.11g

Percentage of total calories from fat = 9%,
of which saturates = 2%
Good source of B vitamins, iron, & zinc

BROILED POUSSINS

With the skin removed, these spicy poussins make a delicious low-fat entrée.
Alternatively, use rock Cornish game hens instead of the poussins.

Preparation time: 30 minutes, plus marinating

Cooking time: 25 minutes

Serves 4

2 poussins or rock Cornish game
hens, weighing about 14 ounces each
1 tbsp lemon juice
1¼ tsp salt
¼ tsp freshly ground black pepper
¼ tsp cayenne pepper
6 tbsp nonfat plain yogurt
1-inch piece fresh root ginger, minced
½ small onion, grated
3 garlic cloves, crushed
1 tbsp coriander (cilantro) seeds,
toasted and crushed
vegetable oil spray

1 Place the poussins or rock Cornish game hens on a board, breast side downward. Using poultry shears or strong kitchen scissors, cut along the entire length of either side of the backbone. Discard the backbone, pope's nose, and leg and wing tips.

2 Halve the birds lengthwise by cutting through the breastbone. Remove the skin. Make parallel cuts through the thick part of the breast and thighs, almost to the bone.

3 Combine the lemon juice, salt, black pepper, and cayenne pepper. Rub the mixture over the poussins and into the flesh. Set aside for 30 minutes.

4 Combine the yogurt, ginger, onion, garlic, and coriander (cilantro) seeds. Add to the poussins, turning to coat and rubbing the mixture into the flesh. Cover and leave to marinate in the refrigerator for at least 4 hours or overnight.

5 Thread the poussin halves onto 4 skewers, pushing the skewer lengthwise through the leg and the wing.

6 Preheat the broiler until very hot. Place the poussins skin side upward on a rack in a broiler pan. Lightly spray with oil from a spray can. Position the pan 6 inches from the heat source. Broil for 15 minutes, then turn over and broil for a further 10 minutes, until the juices run clear when a skewer is inserted into the thigh.

7 Transfer to a warmed serving platter and serve with lime wedges, shredded lettuce, sliced tomatoes, onion rings, pita bread, and a bowl of nonfat yogurt.

NUTRITIONAL ANALYSIS

(figures are per serving)

Calories = 195
Fat = 2.5g
of which saturates = 0.5g
    monounsaturates = 1.1g
    polyunsaturates = 0.5g

Protein = 41.0g
Carbohydrate = 3.0g
Dietary fiber = 0.2g
Sodium = 0.1g

Percentage of total calories from fat = 11%, of which saturates = 3%
Good source of B vitamins

LAMB, EGGPLANT, & CHICK-PEA
CASSEROLE

Even lean lamb contains hidden fat, so this recipe contains a relatively small amount of meat but plenty of carbohydrate-rich chick-peas and pita bread. It is ideal for a comforting winter dinner.

Preparation time: 40 minutes, plus soaking and cooking the chick-peas

Cooking time: 1 hour 40 minutes

Serves 6

1 cup chick-peas (garbanzo beans), soaked overnight
1 eggplant, cut into ³/₄-inch slices
¹/₄ tsp ground cinnamon
large pinch of cayenne
large pinch of ground allspice
freshly ground black pepper
8 ounces extra-lean lamb, cut into ³/₄-inch cubes
1 large onion, chopped
1¹/₂ cups Fat-Free Meat Broth (page 76)
1 large red bell pepper, cut into ³/₄-inch squares
14-ounce can peeled, chopped tomatoes
finely grated rind of 1 lemon
salt
1 large pita bread, opened flat and toasted
¹/₃ cup nonfat plain yogurt
2 tbsp chopped fresh mint
1 garlic clove, crushed
toasted cumin seeds, to garnish

1 Drain the chick-peas (garbanzo beans), place in a saucepan with fresh water, and bring to the boil. Simmer briskly until just tender, then drain.

2 Arrange the eggplant slices in a single layer in a nonstick broiler pan. Broil for 10-12 minutes, turning once, until golden. Cut into bite-sized segments.

3 Rub the cinnamon, cayenne, allspice, and a little black pepper into the meat.

4 Place the onion and 2 tbsp of the broth in a nonstick skillet over medium heat. Wet-fry for 4-5 minutes, until translucent. Add the meat and sauté for 5 minutes, until browned.

5 Transfer the meat and onions to a heavy-based casserole. Add the bell pepper, eggplants, chick-peas (garbanzo beans), tomatoes, and remaining broth. Add the lemon rind and season with salt and pepper. Bring to the boil, then cover and simmer for 1-1¹/₄ hours until the lamb is tender.

6 Break the pita bread into pieces and spread it over the base of a shallow dish. Drain the meat and vegetables, reserving the liquid, and arrange over the bread. Spoon over a little of the liquid and pour the remainder into a sauceboat.

7 Mix the yogurt with the mint, garlic, and a little salt. Spoon this over the lamb, sprinkle with cumin seeds, and serve immediately with a salad.

VENISON CHILI

Being naturally very lean, venison makes a healthy alternative to beef.
Buffalo could be used instead.

Preparation time: 30 minutes, plus soaking beans

Cooking time: 1 hour 50 minutes

Serves 8

1 cup black turtle beans, soaked overnight
¹/₂ cup navy beans, soaked overnight
2 tsp cumin seeds
2 tsp coriander (cilantro) seeds
2 tsp dried oregano
1 tsp olive oil
2-3 cups Fat-Free Meat Broth (page 76)
3 pounds boneless venison, cubed
2 onions, chopped
3 garlic cloves, minced
2 red bell peppers, cored, seeded, and
cut into ³/₄-inch squares
2-3 tsp chili powder, or to taste
2 x 14-ounce cans peeled, chopped tomatoes
3 tbsp tomato paste
1 tsp sugar
1 tsp salt
6 tbsp chopped fresh coriander (cilantro)

1 Drain the beans, place in separate saucepans, and cover with fresh water. Boil rapidly for 15 minutes, then simmer until just tender. Drain and set aside.

2 Dry-fry the seeds over medium heat until fragrant. Add the oregano and fry for a few seconds more. Remove from the pan and lightly crush with a pestle in a mortar.

3 Fry the venison in a nonstick skillet, in batches if necessary, over medium-high heat for 15 minutes until browned and any moisture has evaporated. Sprinkle with half the toasted spices and fry for a few minutes more. Transfer to a casserole.

4 Add the oil and 4 tbsp of the broth to the skillet. Wet-fry the onion, garlic, bell pepper, chili, and remaining toasted spices over medium heat for 5 minutes, until the onion is soft.

5 Add the mixture to the meat, together with the tomatoes, tomato paste, sugar, salt, beans, and about 2 cups of the broth. Bring to the boil, then cover and simmer for 45 minutes, stirring occasionally.

6 Stir in the coriander (cilantro) and simmer for a further 5 minutes. Serve with boiled rice or warm tortillas and a green side salad.

FISH & SEAFOOD

Packed with protein, vitamins, and minerals and containing very little fat, fish and seafood are among the most nutritious foods available. The fat found in all fish is mainly of the unsaturated type and contains essential fatty acids which are important for health. However, the amount of fat present varies depending on the type of fish, and even the season of the year. White fish are lowest in fat — monkfish, cod, red snapper, and porgy (sea-bream) contain less than 1%. Seafood is also low in fat but it does contain cholesterol. Oily fish such as salmon, trout, and tuna contain 5-20 % fat, which makes these varieties difficult to include in a virtually fat-free diet, unless you eat them in very small quantities.

MUSSEL & POTATO
SOUP

Packed with robust flavors, this soup is a meal in itself. Serve it for lunch with plenty of salad and freshly baked bread.

Preparation time: 50 minutes

Cooking time: 50 minutes

Serves 4

3 ¹/₂ pounds mussels, cleaned and bearded
1 quart water
1 onion, minced
4 garlic cloves, minced
3 parsley sprigs
3 rosemary sprigs
1 bay leaf
¹/₄ tsp black peppercorns
1 cup sliced waxy new potatoes
2 plum tomatoes, seeded and finely diced
salt
chopped flat-leafed parsley, to garnish

1 Place the mussels in a large heavy-based saucepan with 1 cup of the water. Cook, tightly covered, over high heat for 5 minutes, until the shells open, shaking the pan occasionally.

2 Strain the cooking liquid through a sieve lined with cheesecloth and reserve it. Discard any mussels that have not opened. Set aside a few mussels for garnish. Remove the rest from their shells and reserve them.

3 Place the remaining water in a saucepan with the garlic, parsley, rosemary, bay leaf, and peppercorns. Bring to the boil, then simmer, partially covered, for 30 minutes.

4 Strain the garlic-and-herb infusion and mix with the mussel cooking liquid. Return the liquid to the pan and add the potatoes. Simmer for 15 minutes, until the potatoes are cooked.

5 Add the diced tomatoes and the mussels, including those in their shells. Simmer until the mussels are heated through.

6 Ladle the soup into warmed bowls, making sure each serving gets a few mussels in their shells. Garnish with parsley.

102

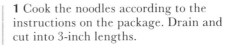

ORIENTAL
SEAFOOD SOUP

This light but satisfying soup relies on good quality homemade broth. Serve as an appetizer for a Chinese meal.

Preparation time: 15 minutes
Cooking time: 20 minutes
Serves 4

NUTRITIONAL ANALYSIS

(figures are per serving)

Calories = 246
Fat = 4.9g
of which saturates = 1.1g
      monounsaturates = 0.8g
      polyunsaturates = 1.7g
Protein = 32.0g
Carbohydrate = 19.7g
Dietary fiber = 1.9g
Sodium = 0.73g

Percentage of total calories from fat = 18%
of which saturates = 4%
Good source of potassium, iron, zinc, & B vitamins

2 ounces thin rice noodles
3 cups Fat-Free Chicken Broth (page 76)
2 stalks lemon grass, crushed
2 tsp ginger juice
6 green onions (scallions), thinly sliced
salt
12 ounces cod, skinned and cut into chunks
¹/₃ cup thinly sliced mushrooms
1 small green chili, seeded and thinly sliced
¹/₃ cup corn kernels
2 tsp fish sauce
pinch of sugar
2 tbsp lime juice
2 tbsp chopped fresh coriander (cilantro)

1 Cook the noodles according to the instructions on the package. Drain and cut into 3-inch lengths.

2 Place the broth, lemon grass, ginger juice, and green onions (scallions) into a saucepan. Bring to the boil and season with salt.

3 Add the fish, mushrooms, and chili. Simmer gently for 10 minutes until the fish is nearly cooked, then add the corn and cook for another 2 minutes.

4 Stir in the noodles, fish sauce, sugar, and lime juice. Simmer for another minute. Sprinkle with coriander (cilantro) and serve.

VARIATIONS
● Add a few bay shrimp to the fish.
● Use garden peas instead of corn.

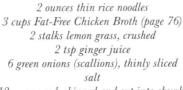

NUTRITIONAL ANALYSIS

(figures are per serving)

Calories = 198
Fat = 1.1g
of which saturates = 0.2g
      monounsaturates = 0.2g
      polyunsaturates = 0.4g
Protein = 18.7g
Carbohydrate = 27.6g
Dietary fiber = 0.9g
Sodium = 0.06g

Percentage of total calories from fat = 5%
of which saturates = 0.7%
Good source of potassium & B vitamins

SMOKED SALMON
SALAD

*This colorful salad is full of contrasting flavors and textures —
rich, velvety smoked salmon, juicy pink grapefruit, peppery watercress,
crunchy radishes, and crisp celery. Serve it as a tasty appetizer
or with a bowl of soup as a light lunch.*

Preparation time: 20 minutes
Serves 2

1 pink grapefruit
$^1/_2$ cup low-fat small curd cottage cheese
2 tbsp chopped fresh herbs, such as
dill, chives, or sorrel
salt and freshly ground black pepper
$^1/_2$ head radicchio, torn into bite-sized pieces
handful of small lettuce leaves
handful of watercress, trimmed
olive oil spray
2 slices (about 2 ounces) smoked salmon (lox),
cut into strips
4 radishes, sliced
2 small celery stalks, diagonally sliced
2 slices of whole-grain rye bread, to serve

1 Using a very sharp knife, cut a
horizontal slice from the top and bottom
of the grapefruit, exposing the flesh.
Remove the remaining peel and all the
white parts by cutting downward,
following the contours of the fruit.

2 Working over a bowl to catch the
juices, cut down between the flesh and
membrane of each segment and ease out
the flesh. Add the segments to the juice
in the bowl.

3 Mix the cottage cheese with the herbs,
salt, and pepper to taste.

4 Lightly spray the radicchio, lettuce,
and watercress with oil from a spray, and
sprinkle with a tablespoon of the
grapefruit juice. Season with freshly
ground pepper and a pinch of salt.

5 Arrange the leaves and watercress on
individual plates. Scatter with the
smoked salmon (lox), radishes, celery,
and half the grapefruit segments (use

the remainder in a fruit salad). Add a
small mound of the cottage cheese
mixture and serve with the rye bread.

VARIATIONS
● Use arugula instead of watercress.
● Replace the celery with asparagus.

NUTRITIONAL ANALYSIS
(figures are per serving)

Calories = 253
Fat = 4.1g
of which saturates = 0.9g
      monounsaturates = 1.1g
      polyunsaturates = 0.7g
Protein = 20.9g
Carbohydrate = 35.4g
Dietary fiber = 7.5g
Sodium = 1.06g

Percentage of total calories from fat = 15%, of
which saturates = 3%
Good source of calcium, potassium, iron, & B
vitamins

CEVICHE
OF SOLE

Raw fish is "cooked" in citrus juice in this colorful appetizer or entrée salad.

Preparation time: 35 minutes

Cooking time: 25 minutes

Serves 4

14 ounces sole, flounder,
or dab, skinned
juice of 2 oranges
juice of 2 limes
$^{1}/_{2}$ small red onion, minced
3 small green chilies,
seeded and finely diced
3 garlic cloves, peeled and minced
salt
freshly ground black pepper
1 medium sweet potato, unpeeled
6 tomatoes, puréed and sieved
2 tbsp sherry
4 handfuls crisp lettuce, such
as iceberg or romaine
$^{1}/_{2}$ green bell pepper, seeded
and finely diced
6 shelled cooked jumbo shrimp
3 tbsp chopped fresh coriander (cilantro)

1 Cut the fish into very thin strips and place in a non acid-reactive bowl.

2 Combine the orange and lime juice, onion, chilies, garlic, salt, and pepper. Pour the mixture over the fish and leave to marinate in the refrigerator for 3-4 hours. The fish will turn opaque and virtually cook.

3 Steam the sweet potato for 15-20 minutes, until just tender. Allow to cool, then remove the peel. Dice the flesh finely and set aside.

4 Remove the fish from the marinade, scraping back into the marinade as many of the diced vegetables as possible. Cover the fish and refrigerate. Pour the marinade into a small saucepan.

5 Add the puréed tomato and the sherry. Bring to the boil, then simmer briskly for about 5 minutes, until reduced. Leave to cool then check the seasoning, adding more salt and pepper if necessary.

6 Arrange the lettuce leaves on individual plates with the fish on top. Scatter the sweet potato and bell pepper over the top, then add the jumbo shrimp. Spoon over the sauce, and sprinkle with the coriander (cilantro). Serve with crusty bread.

NUTRITIONAL ANALYSIS

(figures are per serving)

Calories = 220
Fat = 2.7g
of which saturates = 0.5g
       monounsaturates = 0.5g
       polyunsaturates = 1.1g
Protein = 27.0g
Carbohydrate = 21.6g
Dietary fiber = 4.2g
Sodium = 0.21g

Percentage of total calories from fat = 11%
of which saturates = 2%
Good source of potassium, iron, zinc,
vitamins A, E, & B vitamins

SHRIMP & MONKFISH
KABOBS

Cooked over hot coals or under the broiler, these succulent kabobs make a light and tasty dinner.

Preparation time: 30 minutes, plus marinating

Cooking time: 10 minutes

Serves 4

FOR THE MARINADE
¹/₂ tsp dried oregano
¹/₂ tsp dried thyme
5 tbsp lemon juice
finely grated rind of ¹/₂ lemon
1 tbsp olive oil
1 garlic clove, crushed
salt and freshly ground black pepper

8 jumbo shrimp, unshelled
8 ounces monkfish fillets, cut into 1-inch cubes
¹/₂ yellow and ¹/₂ green bell pepper, cut into 1-inch squares
1 red onion, cut into 1-inch chunks
¹/₃ cup button mushrooms
lettuce, to serve

NUTRITIONAL ANALYSIS

(figures are per serving)

Calories = 107
Fat = 3.4g
of which saturates = 0.5g
      monounsaturates = 2.1g
      polyunsaturates = 0.5g
Protein = 14.8g
Carbohydrate = 4.6g
Dietary fiber = 1.4g
Sodium = 0.07g

Percentage of total calories from fat = 29%
of which saturates = 5%
Good source of potassium, iron, & B vitamins

1 First make the marinade. Dry-fry the oregano and thyme in a small heavy-based pan for a few seconds, until you smell the aroma. Mix with the remaining ingredients in a screw-top jar, and shake well.

2 Shell the shrimp, but leave the tail intact.

3 Place the shrimp and monkfish in a shallow dish, and the vegetables in another. Divide the marinade between each dish, turning the fish and vegetables until coated. Cover and leave in the refrigerator for at least 2 hours.

4 Thread the ingredients onto 4 skewers, alternating the monkfish and shrimp with the vegetables.

5 Cook over hot coals, or under a preheated hot broiler, for 10 minutes, turning occasionally.

6 Arrange the lettuce in a shallow serving dish and place the kabobs on top.

7 Serve with warm pita bread and a bowl of nonfat yogurt seasoned with chopped fresh mint, salt, and cayenne pepper.

BROILED CALAMARI
WITH TOMATO & LENTIL SALSA

Charbroiled calamari makes an excellent appetizer or light meal.

Preparation time: 35 minutes, plus marinating

Cooking time: 15 minutes

Serves 4

FOR THE SALSA
¹/₂ cup small brown lentils
juice of 2 limes
1 tsp grated orange rind
2 tsp olive oil
salt and freshly ground black pepper
¹/₂ cup finely diced fennel
3 firm tomatoes, seeded and finely diced
2 green onions (scallions),
green parts included, minced
3 tbsp chopped fresh fennel leaves
1 tbsp chopped or flat-leafed parsley

1 pound 5 ounces calamari (squid)
olive oil spray
salt
freshly ground black pepper
2 large handfuls of frisée or escarole
lime wedges, to garnish

1 To make the salsa, place the lentils in a saucepan, cover with water, and bring to the boil. Cover and simmer for 12-15 minutes, or until the lentils are just tender but with some bite.

2 Drain off any liquid from the lentils. While they are still warm, toss with the lime juice, orange rind, olive oil, and plenty of sea salt and coarsely ground black pepper. Allow to cool a little, then mix in the rest of the salsa ingredients. Leave to stand at room temperature for at least 1 hour.

3 Clean the squid, removing the beak and the inner quill, and discard the tentacles. Rinse in cold water, drain, and pat dry. Cut the fins from the pouch and reserve. Cut the pouch into 3-inch triangles. Lightly spray the triangles and fins with oil and season generously with salt and pepper.

4 Heat a ridged nonstick skillet or griddle until very hot. Place the squid pieces on it, and broil for about 30 seconds or until they start to curl. Turn over and broil the other side for another 30 seconds. Immediately remove from the broiler.

5 Arrange the frisée or escarole on individual plates. Add the squid, garnish with lime wedges, and serve with the salsa.

NUTRITIONAL ANALYSIS

(figures are per serving)

Calories = 191
Fat = 4.4g
of which saturates = 0.8g
monounsaturates = 1.6g
polyunsaturates = 1.1g

Protein = 23.7g
Carbohydrate = 15.3g
Dietary fiber = 1.1g
Sodium = 0.14g

Percentage of total calories from fat = 21%, of which saturates = 4%
Good source of potassium, iron, zinc, B vitamins, & vitamin E

HALIBUT STEAKS
PROVENÇAL

Meaty halibut and a broiled tomato sauce topped with diced peppers, zucchini, and eggplant make a richly flavored but low-fat main meal.

Preparation time: 35 minutes

Cooking time: 35 minutes

Serves 4

FOR THE SAUCE
1¼ pounds plum tomatoes
4 large garlic cloves, unpeeled
1 red bell pepper, halved and seeded
2 tsp dried oregano
2 tbsp Fat-Free Chicken Broth (page 76)
½ onion, minced
2 tsp wine vinegar
½ tsp sugar
½ tsp salt
freshly ground black pepper

4 halibut steaks, weighing about 6 ounces each
salt and freshly ground black pepper
flour, for dusting
olive oil spray
5 tbsp Fat-free Chicken Broth (page 76)
¼ cup each of finely diced zucchini, eggplant, and red and yellow bell peppers

1 First make the sauce. Place the tomatoes, garlic, and bell peppers in a roasting pan, allowing plenty of space between them. Roast in a preheated oven at 450°, until the skins blacken and blister. The garlic will need about 10 minutes, and the tomatoes and bell pepper 20 minutes.

2 Peel the garlic and bell pepper, but leave the tomatoes unpeeled.

3 Dry-fry the oregano in a small heavy-based pan until you can smell the aroma.

4 Heat the broth in another small pan. Wet-fry the onion until translucent. Add the vinegar and oregano and cook for another minute.

5 Purée the tomatoes, garlic, and bell peppers with the onion mixture until smooth. Press through a sieve, then pour into a small saucepan. Add the sugar, and salt and pepper to taste. Reheat gently and keep warm.

6 Season the fish well and dust with flour. Lightly spray a nonstick skillet with oil, and place over medium heat. Add the fish, then cover and cook for about 10 minutes, turning frequently, until golden and just cooked through. Remove from the pan and keep warm.

7 Add the broth to the pan over high heat. Add the diced vegetables and cook for 4-5 minutes, or until just tender. Season with salt and pepper.

8 Spoon some of the sauce over 4 warmed plates. Place the fish in the center and add the diced vegetables. Serve with boiled new potatoes.

NUTRITIONAL ANALYSIS

(figures are per serving)

Calories = 217
Fat = 3.9g
of which saturates = 0.7g
     monounsaturates = 1.22g
     polyunsaturates = 1.11g
Protein = 34.7g
Carbohydrate = 11.3g
Dietary fiber = 3.5g
Sodium = 0.35g

Percentage of total calories from fat = 16%
of which saturates = 3%
Good source of potassium, iron, vitamins A, E, & B vitamins

FLOUNDER FILLETS
WITH MUSHROOM, DILL, & LEMON

These lettuce-wrapped flounder fillets with a light lemony stuffing make an elegant entrée when you have company.

Preparation time: 25 minutes

Cooking time: 15 minutes

Serves 4

NUTRITIONAL ANALYSIS

(figures are per serving)

Calories = 95
Fat = 1.8g
of which saturates = 0.3g
      monounsaturates = 0.5g
      polyunsaturates = 0.5g
Protein = 19.3g
Carbohydrate = 0.6g
Dietary fiber = 0.6g
Sodium = 0.14g

Percentage of total calories from fat = 17%
of which saturates = 3%
Good source of potassium
& B vitamins

8 large crisp lettuce leaves, such as iceberg or romaine
1/3 cup finely diced mushrooms
finely grated rind of 1 large lemon
2 tbsp chopped fresh dill
coarse sea salt
freshly ground black pepper
1 pound flounder fillets, skinned
2 tbsp lemon juice
fresh dill fronds, to garnish

1 Plunge the lettuce leaves into a large pan of boiling salted water for a few seconds. Drain under cold running water. Shave away any thick pieces of stalk and spread out to dry on paper towels.

2 Combine the mushroom, grated lemon rind, and dill with a pinch of sea salt and plenty of freshly ground black pepper.

3 Cut the fillets into 8 pieces and sprinkle with the lemon juice. Place a little of the mushroom mixture on top of each piece and roll up. Wrap each roll in a lettuce leaf, folding over the sides as for a burrito.

4 Place the parcels in a single layer in a steamer basket (cook in batches if necessary).

5 Place the basket over boiling water. Cover and steam for 10 minutes. Remove from the pan and keep warm.

6 Serve, garnished with the dill, with new potatoes and lightly steamed carrot or zucchini strips.

VARIATION
● Use chard or silverbeet leaves instead of lettuce leaves. Remove the ribs and tough stalks.

RED SNAPPER
PARCELS

*Baked in a foil parcel with orange rind and herbs,
red snapper makes an impressive entrée.*

Preparation time: 25 minutes

Cooking time: 30 minutes

Serves 4

*1 red snapper, weighing about 2 pounds, cleaned
2 tsp olive oil
salt and freshly ground black pepper
juice and thinly pared rind of $^1/_2$ orange
2 tbsp chopped fresh marjoram
2 tbsp chopped fresh thyme
$1^1/_2$ pounds new potatoes, to serve
orange segments, to garnish*

1 Slash the fish on each side with a
sharp knife. Place on a large double
thickness rectangle of aluminum foil.
Brush the oil over the fish, season with
salt and pepper, and sprinkle with the
orange juice.

2 Reserve a tablespoon each of the
marjoram and thyme. Sprinkle the
remainder over both sides of the fish,
stuffing it into the slashed flesh. Cut the
orange rind into thin shreds and scatter
over the fish.

3 Wrap the foil loosely round the fish,
sealing the edges securely to prevent the
juices from escaping.

4 Place on a baking sheet under a preheated hot broiler. Cook for 15 minutes
each side, until cooked through.

5 Transfer to a warmed serving dish.
Sprinkle with the reserved herbs, pour the
cooking juices over the top, and garnish
with orange segments. Serve with the
potatoes and some steamed snow-peas.

NUTRITIONAL ANALYSIS

(figures are per serving, including potatoes)

Calories = 324
Fat = 5.0g
of which saturates = 1.1g
       monounsaturates = 1.6g
       polyunsaturates = 1.2g
Protein = 46.9g
Carbohydrate = 24.5g
Dietary fiber = 2.6g
Sodium = 0.19g

Percentage of total calories
from fat = 14%, of which saturates = 3%
Good source of iron, zinc, selenium,
iodine, & B vitamins

SEAFOOD
RAGOUT

*This hearty Mediterranean-style
fish stew makes an excellent
low-fat entrée.*

Preparation time: 25 minutes

Cooking time: 35 minutes

Serves 6

*2 tsp olive oil
1 small onion, chopped
1 small red bell pepper,
seeded and diced
1 small green bell pepper,
seeded and diced
3 garlic cloves, minced
14-ounce can peeled, chopped tomatoes
3 tbsp chopped flat-leafed parsley
1 tbsp tomato paste
$^2/_3$ cup dry red wine
2 thin slices of lemon rind
salt and freshly ground black pepper
12 ounces thick cod steaks, skinned and cubed
6 peeled jumbo shrimp
1 pound fresh mussels, scrubbed and bearded
8 ounces large scallops, sliced*

NUTRITIONAL ANALYSIS

(figures are per serving)

Calories = 225
Fat = 3.8g
of which saturates = 0.7g
    monounsaturates = 1.1g
    polyunsaturates = 1.0g
Protein = 35.2g
Carbohydrate = 8.9g
Dietary fiber = 1.8g
Sodium = 0.41g

Percentage of total calories from fat = 15%
of which saturates = 3%
Good source of iron, zinc, iodine,
vitamin A, & B vitamins

1 Heat the oil in a heavy-based flameproof casserole. Gently sauté the onion and bell peppers until soft. Add the garlic and sauté for another minute. Stir in the tomatoes, 2 tbsp of the parsley, the tomato paste, wine, salt, and pepper. Bring to the boil, then gently simmer for 10-15 minutes, until slightly thickened.

2 Stir in the cod. Cover and simmer for 5 minutes. Add the shrimp and mussels. Cover and simmer for a further 5 minutes, stirring occasionally. Finally add the scallops. Cook for 2-3 minutes more.

3 Discard any mussels that have not opened. Check the seasoning and sprinkle with the remaining parsley.

4 Serve immediately, accompanied by saffron-flavored rice or boiled new potatoes.

VARIATIONS
● Use fat-free fish broth instead of the wine.
● Replace the cod with monkfish, anglerfish, or redfish.

SEARED COD
WITH GREEN CHILI SAUCE

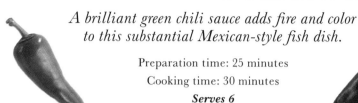

A brilliant green chili sauce adds fire and color to this substantial Mexican-style fish dish.

Preparation time: 25 minutes
Cooking time: 30 minutes
Serves 6

FOR THE SAUCE
3-4 tomatillos (green tomatoes)
2 green bell peppers, halved and seeded
3 fleshy green chilies
2 garlic cloves, unpeeled
1/4 cup chopped onion
1/4 cup trimmed and chopped fresh coriander (cilantro)
1/2 cup Fat-Free Chicken Broth (page 76)
1/4 tsp salt
1 small tortilla, cut into strips
2 tsp peanut oil
squeeze of lime juice

6 cod steaks, weighing about 6 ounces
salt and freshly ground black pepper
olive oil spray
1 1/2 cups boiled rice, to serve
lime wedges, to garnish

1 To make the sauce, place the tomatillos, bell peppers, chilies, and garlic in a roasting pan, leaving plenty of space between them. Roast in a preheated oven at 450°, turning occasionally until the skins blacken and blister. The chilies and garlic will need about 10 minutes, the tomatillos 10-15 minutes, and the bell peppers 20 minutes.

2 Remove the skin from the garlic and bell peppers, and the skin and seeds from the chilies. Leave the tomatillos unpeeled.

3 Place all the sauce ingredients, except the oil and lime juice, in a food processor or blender. Purée until smooth.

4 Heat the peanut oil in a small saucepan until almost smoking. Add the sauce and cook for 1-2 minutes, stirring constantly. Add a squeeze of lime juice and check the seasoning. Keep warm.

5 Season the cod with salt and pepper. Spray lightly with olive oil. Place the fish in a nonstick roasting pan under a very hot preheated broiler for 7-9 minutes, without turning, until the flesh is uniformly opaque.

6 Serve with the chili sauce and rice, and garnish with lime wedges.

The green chili sauce is suitable for freezing.

NUTRITIONAL ANALYSIS

(figures are per serving including rice)

Calories = 174
Fat = 2.9g
of which saturates = 0.5g
    monounsaturates = 0.8g
    polyunsaturates = 1.0g
Protein = 29.2g
Carbohydrate = 6.3g
Dietary fiber = 2.1g
Sodium = 0.10g

Percentage of total calories from fat = 15%
of which saturates = 3%
Good source of selenium, iodine, &
B vitamins

GRAINS & BEANS

*T*here is hardly a country in the world that does not have a whole-grain or bean-based dish as part of its traditional cuisine, and with good reason. Grains and beans (also known as legumes or pulses) are a rich source of fiber, vitamins (particularly B vitamins), minerals, and carbohydrates. Also, being low in fat, they satisfy the appetite without piling on the pounds. Grains and beans can be used in a variety of sweet and savory dishes and make satisfying vegetarian entrées. Being naturally bland, they combine well with robustly flavored ingredients such as garlic, onions, tomatoes, chilies, soy sauce, ginger, and lime. These complement the subtle earthiness of grains and beans, which in turn adds a mellow balance to the stronger flavors.

BREAKFAST BULGUR
WHEAT WITH DRIED FRUIT

Cooked with grated orange zest and sweet spices, bulgur wheat makes an energizing and virtually fat-free breakfast.

Preparation time: 10 minutes, plus overnight soaking

Cooking time: 20 minutes

Serves 4

¹/₃ cup pitted dried apricots
¹/₃ cup pitted prunes
¹/₄ cup dried apple rings
²/₃ cup bulgur wheat
¹/₄ cup yellow or dark raisins
3 thin slivers of orange zest
crushed seeds from 3 cardamom pods
¹/₄ tsp freshly grated nutmeg

1 Place the dried apricots, prunes, and apple rings in a bowl, cover with boiling water, and leave to soak overnight.

2 Rinse the bulgur wheat in several changes of water. Drain and put in a saucepan with the raisins, orange rind, cardamom, and nutmeg. Add enough water to cover by the depth of your thumbnail. Bring to the boil, then cover and simmer over very low heat for 15 minutes until the liquid has been absorbed.

3 Divide the bulgur between individual serving bowls, discarding the orange slivers, and fluff with a fork. Allow to cool slightly.

4 Drain the fruit and arrange on top of the bulgur wheat.

5 Serve with a spoonful of nonfat yogurt and a drizzle of clear honey.

VARIATION
● Use cracked wheat or wheat berries, soaked overnight, instead of bulgur wheat.

COOK'S TIP
● If the cooked bulgur wheat seems too dry, serve with skim milk or apple juice.

BUTTERMILK
PANCAKES

Buttermilk gives these delicious light pancakes a pleasantly tangy flavor. Serve them at a lazy Sunday breakfast or brunch.

Preparation time: 10 minutes, plus 30 minutes resting

Cooking time: 25 minutes

Makes 15

1 cup self-rising flour
pinch of salt
¹/₄ tsp baking soda
1 tbsp sugar
1 extra-large egg
1¹/₄ cups buttermilk
1 tbsp sunflower or grapeseed oil
sunflower oil spray

1 Sift the flour, salt, and baking soda into a bowl. Stir in the sugar.

2 Beat the egg lightly and combine with the buttermilk.

3 Make a well in the center of the flour. Pour in half the egg-and-buttermilk mixture, and the oil. Beat with a wooden spoon, gradually drawing in the flour from around the edge. Add the remaining liquid, and whisk gently to form a smooth mixture. Pour into a measuring-jug and leave to rest for 30 minutes.

4 Lightly spray a nonstick skillet or omelet pan with oil. Heat over a medium flame. Pour in about 2 tbsp of the mixture, tilting the pan so that the batter spreads to a 5-inch circle. Cook until bubbles appear on the surface and the edges look dry. Flip over and brown the other side. Keep warm in a low oven while you cook the remaining pancakes.

5 Serve with wedges of orange and a sprinkling of sweetener or fruit purée, or a mixture of yogurt and honey.

QUINOA SALAD
WITH GRAPES & SNOW-PEAS

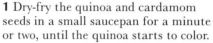

This makes a light but satisfying appetizer, or you could also serve it as an accompaniment to broiled chicken or fish.

Preparation time: 20 minutes
Cooking time: 15 minutes, plus standing
Serves 4

³/₄ cup quinoa
seeds from 4 cardamom pods, crushed
2 cups water
salt
2 tsp lemon juice
1 tsp tamari (Japanese soy sauce)
2 tsp olive oil
freshly ground black pepper
²/₃ cup trimmed snow-peas
³/₄ cup halved seedless black grapes
3 tbsp snipped chives
radicchio and Bibb lettuce

NUTRITIONAL ANALYSIS
(figures are per serving)

Calories = 181
Fat = 3.9g
of which saturates = 0.5g
    monounsaturates = 1.7g
    polyunsaturates = 1.1g
Protein = 7.3g
Carbohydrate = 31.4g
Dietary fiber = 1.3g
Sodium = 0.1g

Percentage of total calories from fat = 19%
of which saturates = 2%
Good source of iron, zinc, & B vitamins

1 Dry-fry the quinoa and cardamom seeds in a small saucepan for a minute or two, until the quinoa starts to color.

2 Add the water and ¹/₂ tsp salt. Bring to the boil, then cover and simmer over very low heat for 15 minutes, until the liquid is absorbed.

3 Remove from the heat, fluff with a fork, and stir in the lemon juice, tamari, and olive oil. Transfer to a bowl and leave to cool.

4 Plunge the snow-peas into boiling water for 30 seconds, then drain. Slice diagonally into three, and stir into the quinoa.

5 Set aside a few grapes as a garnish, and add the remainder to the quinoa.

6 Stir in the chives, and salt and pepper to taste.

7 When ready to serve, arrange the lettuce leaves around the edge of a shallow serving dish or on individual plates, and pile the quinoa salad on top. Garnish with the reserved grapes and serve with crackers.

VARIATIONS
● To serve this salad as an entrée, add a tablespoon of very low-fat cottage cheese.
● Use bulgur wheat instead of quinoa.
● Use thinly sliced celery or cucumber instead of the snow-peas.

ORIENTAL
NOODLE SALAD
WITH CHICKEN

Flavored with ginger, chili, and lime,
this substantial salad can be served as an entrée
for a light lunch or an appetizer.

Preparation time: 30 minutes

Cooking time: 5 minutes

Serves 6

FOR THE MARINADE
2 fresh green or red chilies, seeded and sliced into
shreds
³/₄-inch piece fresh root ginger, minced
2 garlic cloves, crushed
3 tbsp lime juice
3 tbsp chopped fresh coriander (cilantro)
3 tbsp tamari or shoyu (Japanese soy sauce)
2 tbsp Fat-Free Chicken Broth (page 76)
¹/₂ tsp sugar
¹/₄ tsp salt
2 tsp grapeseed oil
1 tsp sesame oil

6 ounces thin cellophane noodles
or rice noodles
6 ounces cooked chicken breast
3 green onions (scallions),
cut into 3-inch lengths and shredded
¹/₄ cup thinly-sliced brown mushrooms
¹/₃ cup cucumber, cut into
matchstick strips
¹/₃ cup carrot, cut into matchstick strips
1 cup tender spinach, stalks removed

1 Combine all the marinade ingredients in a bowl and leave to stand for 15 minutes.

2 Prepare the noodles as directed on the package. Drain and rinse in cold water. Drain again, then cut into 6-inch lengths. Toss with half the marinade and set aside.

3 Tear the chicken into shreds and toss with the remaining marinade. Add the

green onions (scallions), mushrooms, cucumber, and carrot.

4 Stack the spinach leaves and cut them crosswise into thin ribbons. Toss with the noodles.

5 Arrange a mound of noodles and spinach on individual serving dishes. Top with the chicken mixture and serve.

NUTRITIONAL ANALYSIS

(figures are per serving)

Calories = 177
Fat = 1.5g
of which saturates = 0.3g
      monounsaturates = 0.5g
      polyunsaturates = 0.5g
Protein = 12.6g
Carbohydrate = 27.5g
Dietary fiber = 1.2g
Sodium = 0.47g

Percentage of total calories from fat = 8%,
of which saturates = 2%
Good source of iron, vitamin A, & B vitamins

VERMICELLI
WITH TOMATO & BASIL

*With a refreshing uncooked tomato sauce, this quickly made
Italian classic makes the perfect light lunch for a hot summer's day.*

Preparation time: 30 minutes, plus standing

Cooking time: 10 minutes

Serves 4

1¹/₄ pounds ripe plum tomatoes, peeled
1 tbsp extra virgin olive oil
1 garlic clove, crushed
salt and freshly ground black pepper
4 tbsp fresh basil
*4 ounces thin pasta, such as vermicelli, taglierini,
or spaghettini*
fresh basil sprigs, to garnish

1 Slice the tomatoes, discarding the
seeds and juice. Chop the flesh
into ¹/₄-inch dice and place in a bowl
with the olive oil, garlic, and salt and
pepper to taste.

2 Remove the basil stalks and tear
the leaves into thin shreds. Mix with
the tomatoes in the bowl and leave to
stand for 30 minutes to allow the
flavors to develop.

3 Cook the pasta in a large pan of
boiling salted water until *al dente* —
tender but still with some bite. Drain
and transfer to a warm serving dish.

4 Check the sauce and add more
seasoning if necessary, then pour over the
pasta. Toss gently and serve immediately,
garnished with small basil sprigs.

5 Serve the pasta with crusty bread
and a simple mixed leaf salad dressed
with a squeeze of lemon and plenty of
chopped herbs.

COOK'S TIPS

● As with all simple dishes, success
depends on top-quality ingredients.
You will need perfectly ripe tomatoes
with a good fruity flavor and firm flesh
— they should not be at all watery.
Failing this, it is better to use good
quality canned tomatoes.
● The sauce needs to be well seasoned,
otherwise the finished dish will be bland
and tasteless.

NUTRITIONAL ANALYSIS
(figures are per serving)

Calories = 150
Fat = 3.7g
of which saturates = 0.6g
       monounsaturates = 2.2g
       polyunsaturates = 0.7g
Protein = 4.7g
Carbohydrate = 26.0g
Dietary fiber = 3.3g
Sodium = 0.01g

Percentage of total calories from fat = 22%
of which saturates = 4%
Good source of iron & B vitamins

FUSILLI
WITH ZUCCHINI & LEMON

*Deliciously flavored with plenty of grated lemon zest and fresh herbs,
this pasta dish is perfect for a light lunch or dinner.*

Preparation time: 25 minutes, plus draining

Cooking time: 20 minutes

Serves 4

*1 pound mixed yellow and green zucchini
salt
6 tbsp Light Vegetable Broth (page 76) or Fat-Free
Chicken Broth (page 76) for non-vegetarians
4 green onions (scallions), green parts included,
thinly sliced
1 tbsp chopped fresh rosemary
1 tbsp chopped fresh flat-leafed parsley
1 tbsp chopped fresh thyme
finely grated rind of 1 lemon
freshly ground black pepper
10 1/2 ounces pasta shapes, such as fusilli,
penne, or conchiglie (shells)
1 tbsp lemon juice
2 tbsp freshly grated Parmesan cheese*

1 Cut the zucchini into 3-inch
long matchstick strips. Put
them in a colander,
sprinkle with salt, and
leave to drain for 30
minutes. Pat dry
with paper towels.

2 Heat the broth in a large nonstick
skillet over medium heat. Add the onions,
herbs, lemon zest, and zucchini. Wet-fry
for 4-5 minutes until just tender, stirring
frequently. Season with pepper to taste.

3 Meanwhile, cook the pasta in a large
pan of boiling salted water until *al dente*
— tender but still with some bite.

4 Drain the pasta and add it
immediately to the zucchini mixture.
Stir in the lemon juice. Sprinkle with the
cheese, toss lightly, and serve.

VARIATION
● Replace the zucchini with
strips of summer squash or thin
asparagus spears.

COOK'S TIP
● Reserve some of the pasta cooking
water and add a little to the finished
dish if it seems dry.

NUTRITIONAL ANALYSIS
(figures are per serving)

Calories = 321

Fat = 4.4g

of which saturates = 1.9g

      monounsaturates = 0.8g

      polyunsaturates = 0.9g

Protein = 14.3g

Carbohydrate = 59.6g

Dietary fiber = 3.9g

Sodium = 0.09g

Percentage of total calories from fat = 12%, of which saturates = 5%

Good source of iron, zinc, selenium, vitamin A, & B vitamins

CORIANDER & CHILI
POLENTA
WITH SPICY SAUCE

*Colorful and bursting with vibrant flavors, this dish
can be served as a meat-free entrée, or in smaller quantities as an
accompaniment to broiled poultry or fish.*

Preparation time: 30 minutes

Cooking time: 45 minutes

Serves 8

NUTRITIONAL ANALYSIS
(figures are per serving)

Calories = 148
Fat = 2.6g
of which saturates = 0.3g
     monounsaturates = 0.6g
     polyunsaturates = 0.8g
Protein = 3.9g
Carbohydrate = 27.0g
Dietary fiber = 2.5g
Sodium = 0.04g

Percentage of total calories from fat = 16%
of which saturates = 2%
Good source of vitamins A, C, & E

1¼ pounds plum tomatoes
4 fleshy green or red chilies
4 red bell peppers, halved lengthwise and seeded
2 garlic cloves, unpeeled
2 tbsp sun-dried tomato paste
1 tsp coriander (cilantro) seeds, toasted and crushed
¾-inch piece fresh ginger root, minced
finely grated rind of 1 lemon
½ tsp sugar
salt and freshly ground black pepper
2 cups yellow cornmeal
1 quart water
5 tbsp chopped fresh coriander (cilantro)
fresh coriander (cilantro) sprigs, to garnish

1 Place the tomatoes, chilies, bell peppers, and garlic on a cookie sheet, leaving plenty of space between them. Roast in a preheated oven at 450°, turning occasionally, until the skins blacken and blister. The chilies and garlic will need about 10 minutes, and the tomatoes and bell peppers about 20 minutes.

2 Remove the skin from the garlic and bell peppers, and the skin and seeds from the chilies. Leave the tomatoes unpeeled.

3 Mince 3 of the chilies and set aside.

4 Place the remaining chili in a food processor or liquidizer with the bell peppers, tomatoes, and garlic. Add the tomato paste, coriander (cilantro) seeds, ginger, grated lemon rind, sugar, and salt and pepper. Blend to a purée, then press through a sieve. Pour into a small saucepan and keep warm.

5 Place the cornmeal, 1 tsp of salt, and the water into a large saucepan. Bring slowly to the boil, stirring constantly with a wooden spoon or wooden stick.

6 Stir in the reserved chopped chilies and 3 tbsp of the coriander (cilantro). Cook over low heat for 15-20 minutes, stirring vigorously and frequently, until the mixture starts to pull away from the sides of the pan.

7 Pour the polenta into a 12 x 9-inch roasting pan. Spread it out evenly, smoothing the surface with dampened hands. Cut into 16 squares or diamonds. Place under the broiler to reheat if necessary.

8 Arrange 2 pieces of polenta on individual serving plates and spoon some of the sauce over it. Garnish with the remaining coriander (cilantro).

9 Serve with lightly cooked green cabbage or spinach.

VARIATION
● Instead of cutting the polenta into shapes, serve it straight from the saucepan, in the same way as creamed potato.

COOK'S TIP
● Polenta is what they call cornmeal mush in northern Italy, where it is eaten as a staple. It can be used instead of pasta, rice, or potatoes.

CHICK-PEA & MIXED-BEAN
CASSEROLE

*This hearty casserole makes a meat-free entrée,
ideal for a midweek winter dinner.*

Preparation time: 25 minutes, plus soaking

Cooking time: 1 hour

Serves 6

*¹/₂ cup chick-peas (garbanzo beans),
soaked overnight*
¹/₂ cup red kidney beans, soaked overnight
¹/₂ cup navy beans, soaked overnight
salt
2 cups Strong Vegetable Broth (page 76)
1 onion, minced
2 carrots, sliced
3 garlic cloves, finely chopped
¹/₄ cup green or brown lentils
14-ounce can peeled, chopped tomatoes
2 tbsp tomato paste
1 tsp dried oregano
1 tsp toasted cumin seeds
freshly ground black pepper
1¹/₂ cups green beans, sliced
*4 tbsp chopped
flat-leafed parsley*

1 Drain the chick-peas
(garbanzo beans)
and dried beans.

Place them in a
large saucepan
with fresh water to
cover. Bring to the
boil and boil rapidly for 15 minutes.
Reduce the heat to a lively simmer, and
continue to cook until tender. Add salt
during the last 10 minutes of cooking.
Drain and set aside.

2 Place 5 tbsp of the broth in a heavy-
based casserole with the onion, carrot,
and garlic. Wet-fry over a medium heat
for 4 minutes, until softened.

3 Add the lentils, tomatoes, tomato
paste, oregano, cumin, and salt and
pepper. Fry for a minute or two.

4 Add the cooked chick-peas (garbanzo
beans) and beans, and the remaining
broth. Bring to the boil, then cover and
simmer for 25 minutes.

5 Stir in the green beans and simmer for
another 10-12 minutes until tender.
Check the seasoning and stir in the
parsley before serving.

6 Serve with baked potatoes and nonfat
plain yogurt.

WILD & BASMATI RICE
PILAF
WITH DRIED CRANBERRIES

*With its fruity flavors, this brightly colored pilaf makes a beautiful
vegetarian main course to serve during the holidays. Served in smaller
portions it makes a very low-fat accompaniment to roast turkey or chicken.*

Preparation time: 25 minutes, plus cooking rice

Cooking time: 10 minutes

Serves 6

NUTRITIONAL ANALYSIS
(figures are per serving)

Calories = 222
Fat = 3.7g
of which saturates = 0.7g
      monounsaturates = 1.7g
      polyunsaturates = 0.9g
Protein = 4.3g
Carbohydrate = 45.9g
Dietary fiber = 5.1g
Sodium = 0.02g

Percentage of total calories from fat = 15%
of which saturates = 3%
Good source of vitamin A

1 red onion, minced
1¼ cups Light Vegetable Broth (page 76) or Fat-Free Chicken Broth (page 76) (for non-vegetarians)
3 tender celery stalks, leaves included, finely sliced
3 carrots, coarsely grated
1 fresh green chili, seeded and finely chopped
4 green onions (scallions), green parts included, thinly sliced
⅓ cup dried cranberries
1 tbsp olive oil
2¼ cups cooked wild rice
1 cup cooked brown basmati rice
finely grated rind of 1 small orange
juice of 3 small oranges (about ½ cup)
1 tsp salt
¼ tsp freshly ground black pepper

1 Place the onion and 6 tablespoons of
the broth in a large nonstick skillet.
Cook for 3-4 minutes, until translucent.

2 Add the celery, carrots, chilies, green
onions (scallions), and cranberries. Wet-
fry over medium heat for 2 minutes,
until the vegetables are just tender but
still crisp and brightly colored. Remove
from the pan and set aside.

3 Add the oil to the pan over high heat.
Stir in the rice and toss for 2 minutes to
heat through. Lower the heat and stir in
the grated orange rind, juice, remaining
broth, and salt and pepper. Simmer for
1 minute.

4 Return the vegetables to the pan
and toss with the rice to heat through
before serving.

5 Serve the pilaf with Indian bread,
Armenian bread, or pita pockets and a
bowl of nonfat plain yogurt.

VARIATION
● Stir some puréed mango, chopped
fresh coriander (cilantro), and toasted
cumin seeds into the yogurt.

TUNISIAN COUSCOUS

Serve this as a vegetarian entrée, or add 12 ounces diced extra-lean lamb.

Preparation time: 30 minutes
Cooking time: 50 minutes
Serves 6

*3 cups Strong Vegetable Broth (page 76) or
Fat-Free Chicken Broth (page 76)
(for non-vegetarians)
1 onion, coarsely chopped
2 garlic cloves, crushed
1 tsp cumin seeds, toasted and crushed
1 cup canned peeled, chopped tomatoes
4 carrots, quartered
1 small celery root, cut into 1-inch pieces
4 potatoes, quartered
$^1/_2$ tsp hot sauce or chili powder
$^1/_2$ tsp salt
$^1/_4$ tsp freshly ground black pepper
$2^1/_2$ cups couscous
3 zucchini, cut
into 1-inch slices
chopped fresh coriander
(cilantro), to garnish*

1 Heat 6 tbsp of the broth in a large saucepan over which a steamer will fit. Add the onion and cook over medium heat until soft.

2 Add the garlic, cumin, and tomatoes and cook for 2-3 minutes, stirring.

3 Add the carrots, celery root, potatoes, remaining broth, hot sauce or chili, and salt and pepper. Bring to the boil, cover, and simmer for 20 minutes.

4 Soak the couscous in warm water for 10 minutes. Drain thoroughly and put in a metal sieve or cheesecloth-lined steamer.

5 Add the zucchini to the vegetables, then fit the steamer over the saucepan, making sure the bottom does not touch the stew. Steam the couscous, covered, for 30 minutes, until heated through.

6 To serve, turn the couscous into a shallow serving dish and fluff with a fork. Moisten with a little broth from the vegetables. Using a slotted spoon, arrange the vegetables in the middle and garnish with coriander (cilantro). Serve the remaining vegetable broth in a pitcher.

7 Serve the couscous with pita bread and a bowl of nonfat yogurt sprinkled with ground coriander (cilantro) and a pinch of cayenne pepper.

NUTRITIONAL ANALYSIS

(figures are per vegetarian serving)

Calories = 235
Fat = 1.3g
of which saturates = 0.1g
       monounsaturates = 0.0g
       polyunsaturates = 0.4g
Protein = 7.0g
Carbohydrate = 51.8g
Dietary fiber = 3.5g
Sodium = 0.06g

Percentage of total calories from fat = 5%
of which saturates = 0.5%
Good source of iron, vitamin A, & B vitamins

FRUITS & DESSERTS

*P*acked with vitamins, minerals, and fiber, and containing only minuscule
amounts of fat, fruit is a key component in a virtually fat-free diet. It supplies
the digestive system with essential bulk and fiber and, being rich in carbohydrates, helps
replace the energy normally provided by fat.
Fruit is the obvious choice for dessert, including luscious but low-fat tarts and flans and
refreshing fruit salads, yet it has a variety of other uses too. Fruit purées can
be used instead of fat to make wonderfully moist and virtually fat-free fruit bars,
and fruit soups are ideal for lazy brunches or a summer's afternoon snack.

BUTTERMILK &
RED FRUIT SOUP

*Serve this delicious fruit soup for breakfast or
as a refreshing energy-boosting snack on a hot day.*

Preparation time: 10 minutes

Cooking time: 5 minutes

Serves 4

1 tsp sunflower margarine
6 tbsp rolled (old-fashioned) oats
2 tbsp sugar
1 pound strawberries, hulled and sliced
1 cup raspberries
2¹/₂ cups buttermilk

1 Melt the margarine in a saucepan. Add
the oats and 2 tsp of the sugar. Fry over
gentle heat for a few minutes until golden.

2 Reserve one cup of the strawberries and
half a cup of the raspberries. Place the
remainder of the fruit in a blender with
the remaining sugar. Liquidize until
smooth.

3 Divide the buttermilk between 4 shallow
soup plates. Pour the berry purée into the
center and swirl slightly to mix.

4 Add the reserved whole fruit and
sprinkle with the oatmeal.

NUTRITIONAL ANALYSIS

(figures are per serving)

Calories = 218
Fat = 4.9g
of which saturates = 0.9g
       monounsaturates = 0.8g
       polyunsaturates = 0.9g
Protein = 8.9g
Carbohydrate = 36.8g
Dietary fiber = 5.3g
Sodium = 0.11g

Percentage of total calories from fat
= 20%, of which saturates = 4%
Good source of potassium, calcium,
B vitamins, & vitamin C

PEACH & MINT
SOUP

*This cooling soup would be ideal to serve as an appetizer
for a summer lunch or for a lazy weekend breakfast.
It is essential to use perfectly ripe peaches with a good flavor.*

Preparation time: 25 minutes
Serves 4

2³/₄ pounds peaches
4 tbsp lime juice
2 tbsp orange juice
2 tbsp sugar, or to taste
4 tbsp chopped fresh mint
¹/₃ cup small-curd cottage cheese
¹/₃ cup very low-fat yogurt
4 mint sprigs, to decorate

1 Using a small sharp knife, cut the peaches all the way round the indentation to the pit. Twist the two halves in opposite directions and ease out the pit. Remove the peel.

2 Roughly chop the flesh of all but one peach. Put the chopped flesh in a food processor or blender with 3 tbsp of the lime juice, the orange juice, sugar, and chopped mint. Liquidize until smooth. Pour into a bowl, cover, and chill.

3 Slice the remaining peach lengthwise into thin segments. Sprinkle with the remaining lime juice and set aside.

4 When ready to serve, divide the peach purée between individual serving bowls. Combine the cottage cheese and yogurt and swirl this mixture into the purée. Arrange the reserved peach slices on top and decorate with a sprig of mint.

VARIATION
● Use nectarines instead of peaches.

NUTRITIONAL ANALYSIS
(figures are per serving)

Calories = 148
Fat = 0.4g
of which saturates = 0.04g
monounsaturates = 0.04g
polyunsaturates = 0.02g
Protein = 5.9g
Carbohydrate = 32.0g
Dietary fiber = 6.3g
Sodium = 0.02g

Percentage of total calories from fat = 3%
of which saturates = 0.2%
Good source of potassium, B vitamins, & vitamin C

FRESH FIGS
WITH BERRIES & ORANGE CREAM

*A beautiful and quickly made light summer dessert served with
a low-fat, orange-flavored creamy topping.*

Preparation time: 10 minutes, plus chilling
Serves 4

*³/₄ cup very low-fat curd cheese or
sour cream substitute
2 tbsp buttermilk
1 tsp finely grated orange zest
1¹/₂ tsp sugar
4 fresh figs
1 pound fresh berries, such as raspberries,
loganberries, blueberries, mulberries, or a mixture
mint sprigs, to decorate*

1 Place the curd cheese or sour cream substitute, buttermilk, and sugar in a blender and liquidize for 1 minute, until very smooth. Scrape into a bowl and stir in the orange zest. Cover and chill.

2 Remove the stalks from the figs. Using a small sharp knife, make a cut like a cross in the top of each fruit, cutting three-quarters of the way down to the base. Hold the base with your thumb and fingertips, and press gently so that the fig opens out like a flower.

3 Place the figs on individual plates with a handful of berries, and decorate with a mint sprig. Serve with a spoonful of the orange cream.

VARIATIONS
● Replace the figs with ripe peaches, peeled and cut into segments.
● Mix the very low-fat curd cheese, or low-fat sour cream substitute, and buttermilk with sieved passion fruit pulp instead of orange zest, or try a few drops of rose water.

COOK'S TIP
● Use perfectly ripe, plump figs and serve them at room temperature to bring out their flavor.

NUTRITIONAL ANALYSIS
(figures are per serving)

Calories = 89
Fat = 0.4g
of which saturates = 0.1g
      monounsaturates = 0.1g
polyunsaturates = 0.1g
Protein = 7.1g
Carbohydrate = 14.4g
Dietary fiber = 7.5g
Sodium = 0.02g

Percentage of total calories from fat = 4%
of which saturates = 1%
Good source of potassium, calcium,
B vitamins, & vitamin C

ORANGE & DATE
SALAD

A light and simple Middle Eastern-style dessert, full of interesting flavors.
It would be perfect after a filling grain-based entrée, such as couscous.

Preparation time: 25 minutes, plus standing time

Cooking time: 8 minutes

Serves 4

3 tbsp sugar
²/₃ cup water
7 oranges
1 tbsp shelled pistachio nuts
¹/₃ cup fresh dates, sliced lengthwise into slivers
pinch of ground cinnamon

1 Melt the sugar in a small saucepan over a gentle heat. When it turns golden, immediately remove from the heat and add the water. Return to the heat and stir until any lumps have dissolved. Allow to cool, then stir in the strained juice of one of the oranges.

2 Cover the pistachio nuts with boiling water. Leave for 5 minutes, then slip off their skins. Chop the nuts finely and set aside.

3 Using a very sharp knife, cut a horizontal slice from the top and bottom of the remaining oranges to expose the flesh. Remove the remaining peel and all the white parts by cutting downward, following the contours of the fruit.

4 Cut the flesh horizontally into thin slices, removing any seeds. Arrange attractively on individual serving dishes with the date slivers on top.

5 Spoon over some of the caramel sauce. Sprinkle with the chopped pistachio nuts and a pinch of cinnamon.

VARIATION
● Replace the dates with the seeds from 2 pomegranates.

NUTRITIONAL ANALYSIS

(figures are per serving)

Calories = 230

Fat = 2.7g
of which saturates = 0.3g
          monounsaturates = 1.1g
          polyunsaturates = 0.7g
Protein = 3.4g
Carbohydrate = 50.8g
Dietary fiber = 5.5g
Sodium = 0.04g

Percentage of total calories from fat = 11%
of which saturates = 1%
Good source of calcium, potassium,
& vitamin C

STRAWBERRY
CHOCOLATE FLAN

An elegant dessert of luscious strawberries and sweetened yogurt in an almost fat-free chocolate sponge base.

Preparation time: 30 minutes
Cooking time: 25 minutes
Serves 10

sunflower oil spray
2 tsp each sugar and all-purpose flour, for sprinkling
2 eggs
2 tbsp light brown sugar
3 tbsp all-purpose flour
1 tbsp cocoa powder
1 cup nonfat plain yogurt
1 tsp sugar
1 cup strawberries, halved
mint sprig, to decorate

1 Lightly spray with oil a 9-inch raised-base pie pan. Sprinkle with sugar, tilting to coat evenly. Sprinkle with flour, tapping the pan to remove any excess.

2 Using a hand-held electric beater, whisk the eggs and sugar in a deep bowl until creamy and thick. The mixture should double in volume and leave a trail which you can still see for 5 seconds after the whisk has been removed.

3 Sift the flour and cocoa over the surface. Lightly fold in with a metal spoon.

4 Pour the mixture into the prepared pan and level the surface. Place on a cookie sheet and bake in a preheated oven at 350° for 20-25 minutes, until springy to touch. Turn out on to a wire rack and leave to cool.

5 Mix the yogurt and sugar together, then spread over the base. Arrange the strawberries on top and decorate with a sprig of mint.

The flan base is suitable for freezing.

NUTRITIONAL ANALYSIS

(figures are per serving)

Calories = 93
Fat = 1.9g
of which saturates = 0.6g
      monounsaturates = 0.7g
      polyunsaturates = 0.2g
Protein = 4.4g
Carbohydrate = 15.9g
Dietary fiber = 0.7g
Sodium = 0.04g

Percentage of total calories from fat = 18%
of which saturates = 6%
Good source of vitamin C

RHUBARB, STRAWBERRY, & ANISE
PHYLLO PIE

Rhubarb and strawberries flavored with anise are a surprisingly good combination. The pastry case made of phyllo dough keeps the fat content down.

Preparation time: 35 minutes
Cooking time: 25 minutes
Serves 8

1 pound trimmed young rhubarb
1¹/₄ pounds strawberries
²/₃ cup sugar
1¹/₂ tbsp cornstarch
finely grated rind of 2 oranges
seeds from 6 star anise pods, crushed
6 sheets phyllo dough, measuring
10 inches square, defrosted
2 tsp grapeseed oil
1 tbsp powdered (confectioner's) sugar
1 tsp orange flower water

1 Slice the rhubarb diagonally into 1¹/₂-inch lengths. Cut the strawberries in half lengthwise.

2 Combine the sugar and cornstarch in a shallow ovenproof dish. Add the rhubarb and strawberries, and sprinkle with the grated orange rind and half the star anise seeds, turning to coat. Leave to stand, turning occasionally while you prepare the pastry case.

3 Cover the phyllo sheets with a clean, damp kitchen towel. Taking one sheet at a time, lightly dab with oil on one side only. Place in a lightly greased 9-inch diameter 1¹/₂-inch deep loose-bottomed pie pan. Gently press the dough into the edge of the pan. Cover with the remaining dough, rotating each sheet so the corners are offset to resemble the petals of a flower.

4 Mix the powdered (confectioner's) sugar and orange flower water to a paste and use to paint the dough "petals."

5 Bake the rhubarb-and-strawberry mixture and the pastry case separately in a preheated oven at 375°. Bake the pastry for 10-15 minutes until golden and crisp, taking care that the edges do not burn. Bake the filling for 15-20 minutes, until the rhubarb is only just tender and still holds its shape.

6 Carefully ease the pastry out of the pan and place on a serving platter. Using a perforated cooking spoon, fill the case with the strawberries and rhubarb.

7 Pour the juice into a small saucepan. Bring to the boil and cook until it has a syrupy consistency. Spoon the syrup over the fruits. Sprinkle with the reserved star anise seeds. Serve warm.

COOK'S TIP
● Remove the filling from the oven while the rhubarb is still firm. It quickly loses its shape if overcooked.

NUTRITIONAL ANALYSIS

(figures are per serving)

Calories = 142
Fat = 1.11g
of which saturates = 0.1g
      monounsaturates = 0.1g
      polyunsaturates = 0.5g
Protein = 1.9g
Carbohydrate = 33.4g
Dietary fiber = 2.7g
Sodium = 0.01g

Percentage of total calories from fat = 7%,
of which saturates = 0.5%
Good source of potassiun & vitamin C

TROPICAL
TAPIOCA

Preparation time: 15 minutes

Cooking time: 15 minutes

Serves 6

³/₄-inch piece fresh ginger root, minced
4 tbsp pearl tapioca
2¹/₂ cups skim milk
8 passion fruits (granadillas)
2 tbsp sugar
3 tbsp lime juice
lime twists, to decorate

1 Place the ginger, pearl tapioca, and milk in a saucepan. Bring to the boil, stirring, then simmer, continuing to stir, for 15 minutes, until thickened. Leave to cool.

2 Scoop out the pulp from the passion fruits (granadillas), including the seeds. Mix with the sugar and lime juice.

3 Stir the passion fruit (granadilla) mixture into the tapioca. Pour into a serving bowl or sundae glasses. Add extra sugar or lime juice to taste. Cover and chill.

4 Decorate with twists of lime and serve.

NUTRITIONAL ANALYSIS

(figures are per serving)

Calories = 122
Fat = 0.4g
of which saturates = 0.2g
monounsaturates = 0.1g
polyunsaturates = 0.1g
Protein = 4.2g
Carbohydrate = 27.4g
Dietary fiber = 0.0g
Sodium = 0.06g

Percentage of total calories from fat = 3%
of which saturates = 1%
Good source of iron & B vitamins

BAKED BANANAS WITH
LIME CREAM

Hot, fragrant bananas with a lime-flavored creamy topping are a heavenly combination in this easy dessert.

Preparation time: 20 minutes

Cooking time: 20 minutes

Serves 4

3 tbsp clear honey
juice of 2 limes
4 bananas
4 tbsp very low-fat curd cheese or
very low-fat small-curd cottage cheese
1 tbsp buttermilk
1 tbsp plain nonfat yogurt
¹/₂ tbsp sugar, or to taste

1 Melt the honey in a small saucepan, then mix with all but 1 tbsp of the lime juice.

2 Peel the bananas and halve lengthwise. Place in a shallow ovenproof dish into which they fit snugly. Spoon the honey mixture over them. Bake in a preheated oven at 425° for 10-15 minutes, until soft and slightly bubbling.

3 Meanwhile, beat the curd cheese or small-curd cottage cheese, buttermilk, yogurt, and sugar until smooth. Stir in the remaining lime juice.

4 Arrange the bananas on individual plates and pour the juices over them. Serve at once with a spoonful of lime cream.

VARIATION

● Flavor the honey with minced stem ginger, or the seeds from 8 cardamom pods.

NUTRITIONAL ANALYSIS

(figures are per serving)

Calories = 148
Fat = 0.4g
of which saturates = 0.1g
monounsaturates = 0.0g
polyunsaturates = 0.1g

Protein = 3.6g
Carbohydrate = 34.8g
Dietary fiber = 3.1g
Sodium = 0.01g

Percentage of total calories from fat = 2%, of which saturates = 0.7%
Good source of potassium

BROILED PEPPERED
PINEAPPLE

This impressive dessert requires a very ripe, sweet pineapple for success.

Preparation time: 30 minutes

Cooking time: 15 minutes

Serves 4

1 tbsp shelled pistachio nuts
6 tbsp clear honey
12 black or green peppercorns, crushed
juice of 1 orange
2 tbsp lime juice
2 small pieces preserved ginger, minced
1 small ripe pineapple
4 tsp sugar

1 Cover the pistachio nuts with boiling water and leave to stand for 5 minutes. Slip off the skins, chop the nuts finely, and set aside.

2 Place the honey, peppercorns, grated orange rind and juice, lime juice, and ginger in a small saucepan. Bring to the boil, then simmer for 5 minutes until reduced by half.

3 Peel and core the pineapple, and cut into about 8 ½-inch thick slices. Cut in half and arrange in a single layer in a nonstick ovenproof dish. Sprinkle with the sugar. Place under a preheated very hot broiler for 5-8 minutes, turning once, until browned and bubbling. Pour the sauce over the slices and broil for 1 minute more.

4 Arrange on individual plates and spoon the juices over the fruits. Sprinkle with the pistachio nuts and serve hot.

VARIATION
● Peppercorns add a subtle warm flavor which contrasts well with the pineapple, but you can omit them if you wish.

NUTRITIONAL ANALYSIS
(figures are per serving)

Calories = 183
Fat = 2.7g
of which saturates = 0.3g
     monounsaturates = 1.3g
     polyunsaturates = 0.9g
Protein = 1.7g
Carbohydrate = 40.7g
Dietary fiber = 2.1g
Sodium = 0.03g

Percentage of total calories from fat = 13%,
of which saturates = 2%
Good source of potassium & vitamin C

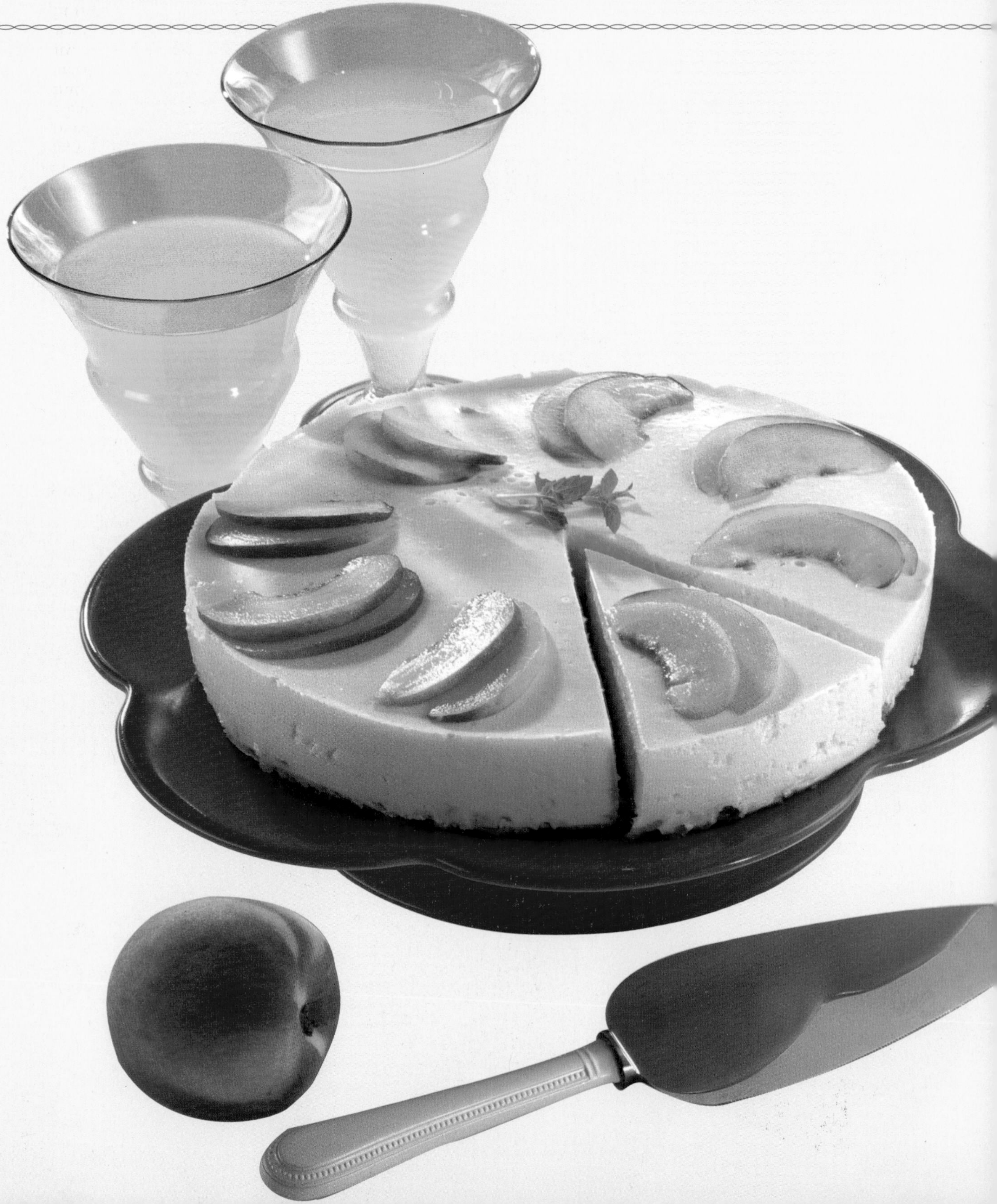

HIGH ENERGY

Choosing the right balance of foods helps us stay healthy, gives us more energy and promotes a sense of well-being. If you enjoy your food, lead a busy lifestyle, and want to get the most out of life, then the recipes in this section are tailor-made for you.

High-energy cooking is perfect for anyone who is trying to make healthy lifestyle changes, particularly in relation to diet and exercise, as well as for people looking to maximize their energy levels. Those who have physically demanding occupations or who have to work long hours, or anyone engaged in sport and fitness activities, will also benefit from these healthy, energy-giving recipes.

These energy-enhancing dishes are bursting with flavor and are full of carbohydrates for effective body refueling. And, as a bonus to all those who are constantly on the move, they are quick and easy to prepare. Featuring high-energy foods such as breads, cereals and pasta alongside beans, lentils, fruit and vegetables, this section offers choice and variety, as well as tips on how to get the most out of your cooking.

FOODS FOR ENERGY

Whether you are physically active through work or exercise, or just lead a busy life, you will need energy. Energy is supplied in different amounts by the food we eat.

Carbohydrates and fats supply most of the energy needed for exercise and physical activity. Although fat provides more than twice the amount of energy per unit weight than carbohydrate, it is carbohydrate that is the most important fuel for exercise, because this is the most accessible form of energy for your working muscles. The recipes in this book are all high in carbohydrate to keep your energy levels high, whether for exercise or sport, or if you lead a busy lifestyle or have a demanding job.

It may be helpful to eat small, frequent meals rather than three main meals, especially if you are on the move all the time. If you exercise regularly, make sure that you eat (or drink) a carbohydrate-rich snack or meal within one to two hours after exercising, to maximize your refueling.

Here we present two illustrated examples of everyday meals, showing quick and easy ways of boosting their carbohydrate content.

1 fresh banana, peeled and sliced

HIGH-ENERGY BRAN FLAKES
4 tbsp bran flakes, skim milk, low-fat, or 2% milk, or low-fat plain yogurt, plus any one or more of the following:

4 tbsp ready-to-eat dried apricots

2 tbsp dried apple rings, chopped

4 tbsp raisins/4 tbsp yellow raisins

HIGH-ENERGY SNACKS

- Banana Sandwich (2 slices bread)
- 3 small Bananas
- Homemade Bran Muffin, such as Pineapple Bran Muffins *(page 143)*
- Fruit Bars *(page 143)*
- ⅓ cup Dried Fruits, such as raisins
- 6 Crispbreads with 1 tbsp Honey

- 1 x 8-ounce baked jacket potato with low-fat topping *(page 168)*
- Bowl of Cereal (such as ½ cup granola or whole-wheat, sugarless cereal) with skim milk
- Salad Sandwich and one piece of Fruit

- Bowl of Fruit Salad with a small carton of Low-Fat, Fruit-flavored Yogurt
- Bowl of Potato & Carrot Soup with Whole-wheat Bread Roll *(page 164)*
- Raisin & Lemon Cookies *(page 142)*
- Fruit & Spice Coffeecake *(page 139)*

CARBOHYDRATE BOOSTERS

● Plan all your meals and snacks around a carbohydrate-rich food, so that more than half your plate is filled with it. It could be a low-fat sauce on a bed of pasta; a baked potato with low-fat filling; thick sandwiches, or a pita pocket with a small amount of filling. Serve extra bread with other dishes, such as pizzas and pasta dishes.

● Experiment with different pastas and noodles, adding a variety of sauces, especially vegetable-based ones which are low in fat. Try adding kidney beans or lentils in place of meat, such as Lamb & Lentil Casserole (page 179) or the Chicken Medley (page 180).

● Enjoy plenty of fresh fruits, or try canned fruits in natural juice for a change. Add dried fruits to breakfast cereals to boost carbohydrates and fiber.

● Breakfast cereals can be a nutritious snack at any time of the day. Choose high-fiber, low-sugar varieties whenever possible, and serve with skim milk or 2% milk.

● Cakes, cookies, and candies are high in fat. Choose bread-based snacks, speciality breads, and rolls (but not croissants), and spread them with jelly, jam, honey, or preserves and a scraping of low-fat spread.

HIGH-ENERGY SMOKED CHICKEN & MUSHROOM RISOTTO
(recipe on page 162)
This risotto using cooked, skinless and boneless smoked chicken, mushrooms, and peas, has been boosted to "high-energy" status by:
– *increasing the quantity of rice and slightly reducing the quantity of chicken*
– *adding some frozen fava beans along with the peas*
– *adding some canned, drained chick-peas (garbanzo beans)*
– *adding some yellow raisins*

Choose from a wide variety of delicious breads to serve with your meal, for an extra energy booster.

HIGH-ENERGY SIDE DISHES

a baked potato with delicious crispy skin, garnished with sprigs of fresh herbs and served with mixed salad leaves

a mixture of standard and sweet potatoes, sliced, tossed in a little olive oil, and open-roasted on a cookie sheet

boiled baby new potatoes tossed in chopped mixed fresh herbs

cooked couscous mixed with chopped fresh herbs and chopped green onions (scallions)

cooked long-grain and wild rice, mixed together and garnished with fresh herbs

cooked brown long-grain rice mixed with diced red, yellow, and green bell peppers, chopped red onion, and cooked corn kernels

BREADS

*B*read has been part of the staple diet of many countries for thousands of years, and is a most nutritious and versatile food that can be eaten and enjoyed at any time of the day. It is healthy, wholesome, and filling, and is available in many delicious varieties. As a good source of carbohydrate, bread is also low in fat and contains some B vitamins, calcium, and iron. The whole-wheat varieties are also high in fiber.
When making or choosing sandwiches, watch out for high-fat fillings and choose reduced-fat alternatives for foods such as cheese, mayonnaise, and coleslaw. Use fat spread sparingly and choose low- or reduced-fat spreads in preference to butter or margarine. Fill sandwiches with plenty of fresh vegetables or salad ingredients for extra flavor and nutrients.

BRAIDED CHEESE &
POPPYSEED BREAD

Try serving this bread with a bowl of hot homemade soup.

Preparation time: 20 minutes, plus kneading and rising time
Cooking time: 35-45 minutes
Makes one 1¹/₂-pound loaf (10 slices)

4 cups all-purpose flour
2 tbsp soft margarine
¹/₃ cup finely shredded sharp Cheddar cheese
2 tsp mustard powder
1¹/₂ tsp salt
freshly ground black pepper
1 tbsp fresh yeast or 1 envelope active dry yeast
1¹/₄ cups lukewarm low-fat or 2% milk,
for glazing
poppyseeds, for sprinkling

1 Place the flour in a large bowl and rub in the margarine. Add the cheese, mustard, salt, and pepper, mix well and make a well in the center.

2 Blend the yeast and milk together. Add the yeast liquid to the dry ingredients and mix well to form a soft but not sticky dough.

3 Turn onto a floured surface and knead for about 10 minutes, until the dough feels smooth and elastic. Shape into a round, place in a bowl, and cover with a clean kitchen towel. Leave to rise in a warm place for about 45 minutes, until doubled in size.

4 Turn onto a floured surface and knead again for about 5 minutes, until smooth and elastic. Divide, and roll the dough into two strands. Place side by side and pinch together at one end. Loosely braid the strands, then pinch them together at the other end. Place on a lightly floured baking sheet.

5 Cover with a clean kitchen towel and leave to rise in a warm place for about 30 minutes. Brush with milk to glaze and sprinkle with some poppyseeds.

6 Bake in a preheated oven at 375º for 35-45 minutes, until well-risen and golden brown. Cover the bread with foil if it is browning too much. Transfer to a wire rack to cool.

CHEESE, HERB, & ONION
BREAD

NUTRITIONAL ANALYSIS

(figures are per slice)

Calories = 225
Fat = 6.7g
of which saturates = 2.7g
monounsaturates = 1.7g
polyunsaturates = 1.8g
Protein = 9.0g
Carbohydrate = 35.6g
Dietary fiber = 1.4g
Sodium = 0.4g

Percentage of total calories from fat = 27%
of which saturates = 10%
Percentage of total calories from carbohydrate
= 59%, of which sugars = 4%

*This bread is quick and easy to make, with delicious results.
Serve it warm or cold as a snack, for a sandwich, or to accompany
a meal such as a pasta dish or salad.*

Preparation time: 25 minutes
Cooking time: 1-1¼ hours
Makes one 2-pound loaf (12 slices)

*1 large onion, minced
2 cups all-purpose flour
2 cups whole-wheat flour
1 tsp double-acting baking powder
2 tsp salt
freshly ground black pepper
2 tsp mustard powder
¼ cup soft margarine
⅔ cup finely shredded reduced-fat sharp Cheddar
cheese
4 tbsp minced fresh mixed herbs or 1 tbsp dried
mixed herbs
2 eggs, beaten
1¼ cups low-fat or 2% milk*

1 Dry-fry the onion in a heavy-based
nonstick skillet for 5 minutes.

2 Mix the flours, baking powder, salt,
pepper, and mustard powder in
a bowl. Rub in the margarine until
the mixture resembles fine bread crumbs.

Add the cheese, herbs, and onion and
mix well.

3 Add the eggs and milk and mix
together thoroughly. Turn the dough
mixture into a lightly greased 2-pound
loaf pan and level the surface.

4 Bake in a preheated oven at 375º for
1-1¼ hours, until risen and golden brown.

5 Turn out and cool on a wire rack. Serve
warm or cold in slices.

VARIATIONS
● Halve the quantities if you would like
to make a 1-pound loaf, or divide the
mixture between two 1-pound loaf pans
and bake for slightly less time.
● Use other reduced-fat hard cheeses,
such as Monterey jack or Swiss, in place
of the Cheddar cheese.
● Use all white all-purpose or whole-
wheat flour in place of the mixture.

NUTRITIONAL ANALYSIS

(figures are per slice)

Calories = 219
Fat = 7.5g
of which saturates = 2.3g
monounsaturates = 2.1g
polyunsaturates = 2.4g

Protein = 10.4g
Carbohydrate = 29.2g
Dietary fiber = 2.6g
Sodium = 0.5g

Percentage of total calories from fat = 31%
of which saturates = 9%
Percentage of total calories from carbohydrate = 50%, of which sugars = 5%

SUN-DRIED TOMATO & OLIVE
SODA BREAD

This bread is both attractive and full of flavor, and can be eaten as an everyday bread or served as part of a special meal. Serve freshly baked.

Preparation time: 20 minutes

Cooking time: 30-40 minutes

Serves 8 (8 wedges)

4 cups all-purpose flour
3 tsp double-acting baking soda
1 tsp salt
freshly ground black pepper
2 tsp dried mixed herbs
¹/₄ cup soft margarine
¹/₃ cup sun-dried tomatoes in olive oil, drained thoroughly and finely chopped
¹/₃ cup pitted black olives, drained thoroughly and finely chopped
1¹/₄ cups buttermilk

1 Sift the flour and double-acting baking powder into a bowl, add the salt, pepper, and herbs and mix well. Rub in the margarine until the mixture resembles fine bread crumbs.

2 Add the chopped tomatoes and olives and mix well. Add the buttermilk and mix to a soft dough. Knead lightly, shape into an 8-inch round, and place on a lightly greased baking sheet. Mark the round into 8 even wedges.

3 Bake in a preheated oven at 400º for 30-40 minutes, until risen and golden brown. Serve warm or cold, cut into wedges.

VARIATIONS
● Replace all or half of the all-purpose flour with whole-wheat flour.
● Use whole, low-fat, or 2% milk in place of the buttermilk.

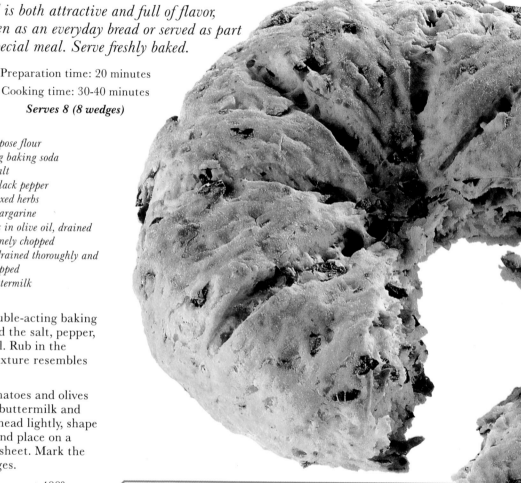

NUTRITIONAL ANALYSIS
(figures are per wedge)

Calories = 300
Fat = 11.1g
of which saturates = 1.9g
    monounsaturates = 3.2g
    polyunsaturates = 5.0g

Protein = 6.8g
Carbohydrate = 45.9g
Dietary fiber = 2.1g
Sodium = 0.7g

Percentage of total calories from fat = 33%, of which saturates = 6%
Percentage of total calories from carbohydrate = 57%, of which sugars = 4%

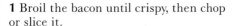

CLUB SANDWICH

Preparation time: 15 minutes

Cooking time: 5 minutes

Serves 2

2 slices lean smoked bacon, trimmed
5 tsp reduced-calorie mayonnaise
5 tsp low-fat plain yogurt
6 thick slices whole-wheat bread
2 slices (2 ounces) cooked, skinless,
boneless chicken breast
¹/₃ cup drained canned corn kernels
2 tbsp yellow raisins
shredded crisp lettuce
salt and freshly ground black pepper
1 tomato, sliced
2 tbsp chopped watercress

1 Broil the bacon until crispy, then chop or slice it.

2 Meanwhile, combine the mayonnaise and yogurt. Place two slices of bread on individual plates and spread each with some of the mayonnaise mixture.

3 Place the chicken, corn, yellow raisins, and lettuce over the mayonnaise, season, and top each with another slice of bread.

4 Spread these slices of bread with the mayonnaise mixture and place the bacon, tomato, and watercress on top.

5 Top each with a third slice of bread to make two club sandwiches.

6 Press lightly together and cut in half diagonally, then in half again to make quarters. Serve immediately.

VARIATIONS
● Use other breads such as white, mixed-grain, or rye bread.
● Sprinkle some minced fresh herbs over the fillings.
● Use unsmoked bacon in place of the smoked bacon.

NUTRITIONAL ANALYSIS

(figures are per sandwich)

Calories = 547
Fat = 13.9g
of which saturates = 3.7g
monounsaturates = 4.4g
polyunsaturates = 4.2g

Protein = 31.9g
Carbohydrate = 78.4g
Dietary fiber = 9.2g
Sodium = 1.6g

Percentage of total calories from fat = 23%, of which saturates = 6%
Percentage of total calories from carbohydrate = 54%, of which sugars = 12%

CHEESE & DATE BREAD

Preparation time: 20 minutes

Cooking time: 35-45 minutes

Makes one 1-pound loaf (10 slices)

2 cups self-rising flour
pinch of salt
¹/₄ cup soft margarine
¹/₃ cup finely shredded reduced-fat sharp Cheddar
cheese
¹/₂ cup dried pitted dates, finely chopped
2 eggs
²/₃ cup low-fat or 2% milk

1 Sift the flour and salt into a bowl. Rub in the margarine until the mixture resembles fine bread crumbs. Add ¹/₃ cup of the cheese and the dates and mix well.

2 Beat the eggs and milk together, add to the date mixture, and mix well. Turn the mixture into a lightly greased 1-pound loaf pan and level the surface. Sprinkle with the remaining cheese.

3 Bake in a preheated oven at 375º for 35-45 minutes, until risen and golden brown. Turn out and cool on a wire rack. Serve warm or cold in slices.

NUTRITIONAL ANALYSIS

(figures are per slice)

Calories = 192
Fat = 7.5g
of which saturates = 2.2g
monounsaturates = 2.1g
polyunsaturates = 2.5g
Protein = 7.0g
Carbohydrate = 25.7g
Dietary fiber = 1.2g
Sodium = 0.3g

Percentage of total calories from fat = 35%
of which saturates = 10%
Percentage of total calories from carbohydrate = 50%, of which sugars = 17%

1 Reserve 2 tbsp whole-wheat flour and set aside. Sift the remaining flours into a bowl with the baking powder and salt.

2 Melt the margarine and mix together with the sugar, egg, milk, and grated orange rind.

3 Pour the mixture over the dry ingredients and fold the ingredients gently together — just enough to combine the mixture. The mixture should look quite lumpy, which is correct since over-mixing will result in heavy muffins.

4 Toss the raisins in the remaining flour and fold gently into the muffin mixture.

5 Spoon the mixture into an 8- or 12-cup lightly greased muffin pan.

6 Bake in a preheated oven at 400º for 15-20 minutes, until well risen and golden brown.

7 Allow to cool in the pan for a few minutes, then unmold onto a wire rack to cool completely.

8 Store in an airtight container at room temperature for up to 2 days. The muffins may be reheated before serving.

VARIATIONS
● Use peeled, cored, and chopped tart apples, fresh or frozen raspberries, loganberries, or blueberries in place of the raisins and orange rind.
● Add 1-2 tsp ground mixed spice, pumpkin pie spice, or cinnamon to the mixture before baking.

WHOLE-WHEAT RAISIN & ORANGE
MUFFINS

These light muffins are best served warm on their own, or spread with a small amount of low-fat spread or jelly. Try one of the variations to sample some different flavors for breakfast, brunch, or a snack. Serve the muffins with a piece of fresh fruit for a change.

Preparation time: 25 minutes
Cooking time: 15-20 minutes
Makes 8 large or 12 medium-sized muffins

*1 cup whole-wheat flour
$^1/_3$ cup all-purpose flour
1 tbsp baking powder
pinch of salt
$^1/_4$ cup soft margarine
2 tbsp sugar
1 egg, beaten
$^7/_8$ cup low-fat or 2% milk
finely grated rind of 1 orange
$^1/_2$ cup raisins*

NUTRITIONAL ANALYSIS
(figures are per muffin) = serving 8 (making 8 large muffins)

Calories = 222	Protein = 4.9g
Fat = 7.3g	Carbohydrate = 36.4g
of which saturates = 1.7g	Dietary fiber = 1.9g
monounsaturates = 1.9g	Sodium = 0.3g
polyunsaturates = 3.1g	

Percentage of total calories from fat = 29%, of which saturates = 7%
Percentage of total calories from carbohydrate = 61%
of which sugars = 32%

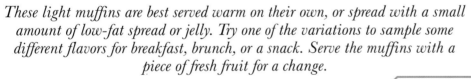

FRUIT & SPICE
COFFEECAKE

This tasty coffeecake is ideal for a filling breakfast or a quick snack at any time of the day. Try toasting slices of the coffeecake for a bedtime snack.

Preparation time: 20 minutes

Cooking time: 1 hour

Makes one 2-pound loaf (12 slices)

2 cups self-rising flour
$1/2$ tsp baking soda
1 tbsp ground mixed spice
$2/3$ cup light soft brown sugar
$1/2$ cup yellow raisins
$1/2$ cup raisins
$1/2$ cup currants
$1/2$ cup finely chopped ready-to-eat dried apricots
2 eggs
$1^1/4$ cups low-fat or 2% milk

1 Sift the flour, baking soda, and mixed spice into a bowl. Add the sugar and dried fruits, and mix well.

2 Beat the eggs and milk together and add to the fruit mixture. Beat until thoroughly mixed.

3 Turn the mixture into a lightly greased 2-pound loaf pan and level the surface.

4 Bake in a preheated oven at 350º for about 1 hour, until risen, golden brown, and firm to the touch.

5 Leave in the pan to cool for a few minutes, then transfer to a wire rack to cool completely.

6 Serve the coffeecake, warm or cold, in slices on its own. Alternatively, spread the coffeecake with a small amount of reduced-sugar jelly or jam, or honey.

VARIATIONS
● Use chopped candied cherries or candied peel in place of the currants.
● Add the finely grated rind of 1 lemon or 1 orange to the mixture before baking.

NUTRITIONAL ANALYSIS
(figures are per slice)

Calories = 209
Fat = 1.6g
of which saturates = 0.5g
    monounsaturates = 0.5g
    polyunsaturates = 0.2g

Protein = 4.4g
Carbohydrate = 47.8g
Dietary fiber = 1.8g
Sodium = 0.1g

Percentage of total calories from fat = 7%
of which saturates = 2%
Percentage of total calories from carbohydrate = 85%
of which sugars = 60%

CEREALS

*C*ereals *such as wheat and oats form a valuable and nutritious part of our diet.
Wheat (often eaten as flour) and oats (most commonly eaten as oatmeal) are a good
source of carbohydrates. They are low in fat, some contain fiber, and they have
many uses in cooking — in breads, cookies, biscuits, and scones.
In addition, oats contain soluble fiber, which can be helpful in lowering blood cholesterol levels
if eaten as part of a low-fat diet. Some cereals, including oats and wheat, provide the basis for
the wide variety of breakfast cereals available. Many breakfast cereals, including granola, are
fortified with vitamins and minerals, and the whole-grain varieties are also high in fiber.*

COD, CORN, & BROCCOLI CRÊPES

*These filled crêpes are ideal for serving as a light lunch or brunch.
Serve with some fresh crusty bread or hot toast.*

Preparation time: 25 minutes

Cooking time: 20 minutes

Serves 4 (two pancakes per serving)

¹/₂ cup all-purpose flour
¹/₂ cup whole-wheat flour
pinch of salt
1 egg
1¹/₄ cups low-fat or 2% milk
1 cup small broccoli flowerets
*1 tsp sunflower oil, plus extra for cooking the
pancakes*
1 small onion, minced
1 clove garlic, crushed
1 cup canned, peeled tomatoes, chopped
1 tbsp tomato ketchup
salt and freshly ground black pepper
1 cup cubed skinless cod fillets
³/₄ cup drained canned corn kernels
2 tbsp minced fresh coriander (cilantro)

1 Make the crêpe mixture following Steps
1 and 2 for the Orange and Cinnamon
Crêpes on page 147.

2 Cook the broccoli in a saucepan of
boiling water for about 5 minutes, until
just cooked. Drain and keep warm.

3 Meanwhile, heat 1 tsp oil in a
saucepan, add the onion and garlic,
and cook gently for 5 minutes,
stirring occasionally.

4 Add the tomatoes, tomato
ketchup, and seasoning, mix well
and bring to the boil. Add the
cod and corn and stir gently to
mix.

5 Cover and cook gently for about
10 minutes, stirring occasionally,
until the fish is just cooked. Add
the broccoli and coriander
(cilantro) and stir gently to mix.
Keep hot while cooking the
pancakes.

6 Cook the crêpes following Steps
4 and 5 for the Orange and Cinnamon
Crêpes on page 147.

7 Place some filling onto one half of a
crêpe. Fold the other half over the filling,
then fold in half again to form a triangle.

NUTRITIONAL ANALYSIS

(figures are per serving)

Calories = 299
Fat = 6.9g
of which saturates = 1.8g
      monounsaturates = 1.8g
      polyunsaturates = 2.4g
Protein = 21.7g
Carbohydrate = 40.0g
Dietary fiber = 4.1g
Sodium = 0.5g

Percentage of total calories from fat = 21%
of which saturates = 5%
Percentage of total calories from carbohydrate =
50%, of which sugars = 16%

CHEESE & PEAR
SCONES

Dried fruits — pears in this case — combine well with cheese and make these scones full of flavor. Serve them freshly baked, warm or cold, with your favorite spread or preserve.

Preparation time: 20 minutes
Cooking time: 10 minutes
Makes about 16 scones

$1^{1}/_{2}$ cups all-purpose whole-wheat flour
$^{1}/_{2}$ cup graham flour
pinch of salt
2 tsp baking powder
3 tbsp soft margarine
$^{1}/_{2}$ cup finely shredded, reduced-fat sharp
Cheddar cheese
$^{2}/_{3}$ cup finely chopped ready-to-eat dried pears
$^{2}/_{3}$ cup low-fat or 2% milk, plus extra for glazing

1 Mix the flour, graham flour, salt, and baking powder in a bowl, then rub in the margarine until the mixture resembles bread crumbs.

2 Stir in all but 1 tbsp of the cheese and the pears and mix well. Add enough milk to form a soft but not sticky dough.

3 Turn onto a lightly floured surface and knead very lightly.

Roll or pat the dough out lightly until about $^{3}/_{4}$ inch thick. Using a 2-inch plain cookie cutter, cut the dough into approximately 16 rounds.

4 Place on lightly floured baking sheets. Brush the tops with milk and sprinkle with the remaining cheese.

5 Bake in a preheated oven at 425º for about 10 minutes, until risen and golden brown. Transfer to a wire rack to cool. Serve warm or cold.

VARIATIONS

● Use other dried fruits, such as apples or apricots, in place of the pears.
● Use other reduced-fat hard cheese such as Monterey jack in place of the Cheddar.
● Use white all-purpose flour or a mixture of white and whole-wheat in place of the whole-wheat flour.

NUTRITIONAL ANALYSIS

(figures are per scone)

Calories = 107
Fat = 3.9g
of which saturates = 1.3g
      monounsaturates = 1.0g
      polyunsaturates = 1.3g

Protein = 4.5g
Carbohydrate = 14.5g
Dietary fiber = 1.9g
Sodium = 0.2g

Percentage of total calories from fat = 32%, of which saturates = 10%
Percentage of total calories from carbohydrate = 51%, of which sugars = 19%

RAISIN
& LEMON
COOKIES

These crumbly, melt-in-the-mouth cookies are an ideal treat to enjoy as a snack with coffee or tea. Once you have tasted one of these delicious cookies, you'll find it hard to resist eating more!

Preparation time: 15 minutes

Cooking time: 15-20 minutes

Makes about 18 cookies

¹/₂ cup soft margarine
¹/₂ cup sugar
finely grated rind of 1 lemon
1 egg, beaten
1¹/₂ cups all-purpose flour
2 tsp baking powder
pinch of salt
4 tbsp raw medium oatmeal
1 cup raisins

1 Cream the margarine, sugar, and lemon rind together until pale and fluffy. Gradually add the egg, beating well after each addition.

2 Sift the flour, baking powder, and salt together and add to the creamed mixture with the raw oatmeal, mixing well. Add the raisins and mix well.

3 Place heaping teaspoons of the mixture onto two lightly greased baking sheets and flatten them slightly with the back of a fork.

4 Bake in a preheated oven at 375º for 15-20 minutes, until golden brown. Allow to cool for a couple of minutes, then transfer to a wire rack.

VARIATIONS
● Add 1 tsp ground mixed spice to the mixture before baking.
● Use other dried fruits such as chopped apricots in place of the raisins.

NUTRITIONAL ANALYSIS

(figures are per cookie)

Calories = 156
Fat = 6.0g
of which saturates = 1.2g
      monounsaturates = 1.6g
      polyunsaturates = 2.8g

Protein = 1.9g
Carbohydrate = 25.1g
Dietary fiber = 0.8g
Sodium = 0.1g

Percentage of total calories from fat = 35%, of which saturates = 7%
Percentage of total calories from carbohydrate = 60%
of which sugars = 37%

PINEAPPLE BRAN
MUFFINS

These light muffins make a tempting snack at any time of the day, freshly baked on their own, or spread with a little low-fat spread or preserve.

Preparation time: 25 minutes
Cooking time: 15-20 minutes
Makes 8 large or 12 medium-sized muffins

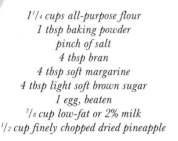

*1¹/₄ cups all-purpose flour
1 tbsp baking powder
pinch of salt
4 tbsp bran
4 tbsp soft margarine
4 tbsp light soft brown sugar
1 egg, beaten
⁷/₈ cup low-fat or 2% milk
¹/₂ cup finely chopped dried pineapple*

1 Reserve 2 tbsp flour and set aside. Sift the remaining flour into a bowl with the baking powder and salt. Stir in the bran.

2 Melt the margarine and mix with the sugar, egg, and milk.

3 Pour the mixture over the dry ingredients and fold in, just enough to combine the mixture. The mixture should look quite lumpy, which is correct since over-mixing will result in heavy muffins.

4 Add the pineapple to the remaining flour and fold gently into the muffin mixture.

5 Spoon the mixture into a 8- or 12-cup lightly greased muffin pan.

6 Bake in a preheated oven at 400º for 15-20 minutes, until well risen and golden brown.

7 Allow to cool in the pan for a few minutes, then unmold onto a wire rack to cool completely.

8 Store the muffins in an airtight container at room temperature for up to 2 days.

VARIATIONS
● Use other dried fruits such as peaches, apricots, pears, raisins, or yellow raisins in place of the pineapple.
● Use granulated sugar in place of the soft brown sugar.

NUTRITIONAL ANALYSIS
(figures are per muffin) = serving 8 (making 8 large muffins)

Calories = 213
Fat = 7.6g
of which saturates = 1.7g
    monounsaturates = 1.9g
    polyunsaturates = 3.2g

Protein = 4.8g
Carbohydrate = 33.9g
Dietary fiber = 4.2g
Sodium = 0.3g

Percentage of total calories form fat = 32%
of which saturates = 7%
Percentage of total calories from carbohydrate = 60%
of which sugars = 33%

FRUIT
BARS

Preparation time: 20 minutes
Cooking time: 20-30 minutes
Makes 10 bars

*¹/₂ cup low-fat spread
¹/₃ cup light soft brown sugar
2 tbsp dark corn syrup
2 tbsp molasses
1¹/₄ cups fine raw oatmeal
³/₄ cup medium oatmeal
1 tsp ground cinnamon
2 tbsp ready-to-eat dried apricots, finely chopped
2 tbsp ready-to-eat dried pitted dates, finely chopped*

1 Place the low-fat spread, sugar, syrup, and molasses in a saucepan and heat gently, stirring, until melted.

2 Remove from the heat, add the remaining ingredients, and mix well.

3 Turn the mixture into a lightly greased, shallow 7-inch square cake pan.

4 Bake in a preheated oven at 350º for 20-30 minutes, until lightly browned.

5 Allow to cool slightly, then mark into bars. When firm, remove from the pan, break into bars, and cool on a wire rack.

NUTRITIONAL ANALYSIS
(figures are per bar)

Calories = 207

Fat = 6.5g
of which saturates = 1.5g
    monounsaturates = 0.3g
    polyunsaturates = 1.6g

Protein = 3.8g
Carbohydrate = 35.3g
Dietary fiber = 1.2g
Sodium = 0.03g

Percentage of total calories from fat = 28%
of which saturates = 7%
Percentage of total calories from carbohydrate = 64%, of which sugars = 38%

CORN, LEEK, & MUSHROOM
PIZZA

This pizza has a crispy bread base, topped with lots of tasty,
nutritious vegetables — ideal for serving as a filling lunch, or as
a main course meal with a large green salad.

Preparation time: 45 minutes, plus kneading and
rising time for the pizza dough

Cooking time: 30-40 minutes

Makes one 10-inch pizza

FOR THE PIZZA BASE
1 tbsp fresh yeast or 1 envelope active dry yeast
$^{1}/_{2}$ tsp sugar
$1^{1}/_{4}$ cups lukewarm water
1 cup all-purpose flour
1 cup whole-wheat flour
$^{1}/_{2}$ tsp salt
1 tbsp olive oil

FOR THE TOMATO SAUCE
14-ounce can peeled, chopped tomatoes
1 small onion, minced
1 clove garlic, crushed
1 tbsp tomato paste
1 tbsp minced fresh mixed herbs or 1 tsp dried herbs
pinch of sugar
salt and freshly ground black pepper

FOR THE TOPPING
2 tbsp minced fresh tarragon or 2 tsp dried tarragon
1 tsp olive oil
1 cup trimmed, washed, and sliced leeks
$1^{1}/_{4}$ cups sliced mushrooms
$1^{1}/_{4}$ cups canned corn kernels
$^{1}/_{2}$ cup finely shredded Monterey jack cheese, finely grated

1 To make the pizza base, blend fresh yeast with the sugar and water and set aside in a warm place until frothy. If using dry yeast, mix the sugar with the water, sprinkle the yeast over the water, then set aside until frothy.

2 In a bowl, stir together the flours and salt. Make a well in the center and add the yeast liquid and oil. Mix the flour into the liquid to make a firm dough.

3 Turn the dough out onto a lightly floured surface and knead for about 10 minutes, until the dough feels smooth and elastic, and is no longer sticky.

4 Place the dough in a clean bowl, cover with plastic wrap or a clean kitchen towel, and leave in a warm place until doubled in size — about 45 minutes.

5 Meanwhile, make the tomato sauce. Place the tomatoes, onion, garlic, tomato paste, herbs, sugar, and seasonings in a saucepan and mix well. Bring to the boil, then simmer, uncovered, for 15-20 minutes, until the sauce becomes fairly thick, stirring occasionally. Adjust the seasoning and set aside.

6 Turn the pizza dough out onto a lightly floured surface and knead again for 2-3 minutes.

7 Roll the dough out to a circle roughly 10 inches in diameter. Place on a baking sheet, making the edges of the dough slightly thicker than the center.

8 For the topping, spread the tomato sauce evenly over the pizza base and sprinkle the tarragon over the top. Heat the oil in a saucepan, add the leeks and mushrooms, cover, and cook gently for 10 minutes, stirring occasionally.

9 Add the corn, mix well, then spoon the mixture over the tomato sauce. Sprinkle the cheese over the pizza.

10 Bake in a preheated oven at 425º for 30-40 minutes, until the dough is risen and golden brown.

11 Serve the pizza hot or cold in slices, with a tossed green salad or homemade low-calorie coleslaw and fresh crusty bread or a baked potato.

VARIATIONS
- Use chopped cooked chicken or turkey in place of the mushrooms.
- Use other herbs such as mixed herbs or coriander (cilantro) in place of the tarragon.
- Use one large onion in place of the leeks.

NUTRITIONAL ANALYSIS
(figures are per serving of a 6-slice pizza)

Calories = 278
Fat = 6.7g
of which saturates = 2.4g
 monounsaturates = 2.6g
 polyunsaturates = 1.0g
Protein = 13.9g
Carbohydrate = 43.4g
Dietary fiber = 3.6g
Sodium = 0.4g

Percentage of total calories from fat = 21%
of which saturates = 7%
Percentage of total calories from carbohydrate = 58%
of which sugars = 11%

PEACH & LEMON
CHEESECAKE

*This irresistible cheesecake combines a crunchy granola base with a creamy,
fruity topping — bound to satisfy those sweet tastebuds every time.*

Preparation time: 30 minutes, plus chilling time

Serves 8

²/₃ cup dark corn syrup
1 cup unsweetened granola
14-ounce can peaches in fruit juice
1 tbsp powdered gelatin
1¹/₄ cups cottage cheese, sieved
finely grated rind and juice of 1 lemon
1¹/₄ cups reduced-fat light cream
²/₃ cup reduced-fat sour cream
2 tbsp sugar
peach slices and mint sprigs,
to decorate

1 Pour the corn syrup in a
saucepan and heat gently
until hot but not
boiling, stirring.

2 Remove from the
heat and stir in the
granola. Spread the
mixture evenly over
the base of an 8-inch
loose-bottomed cake pan
or springform pan. Chill in
the refrigerator while making the
filling. When the base is chilled and
firm, press it down to level the surface.

3 Drain the peaches, reserving the juice
and fruit. Pour the peach juice into a
small bowl and sprinkle it with the
gelatin. Leave to soak for a few minutes,
then place the bowl
over a pan of
simmering water.
Stir until the
gelatin has dissolved.
Set aside to cool.

4 Place the peaches, cottage
cheese, lemon rind and juice, cream,
sour cream, and sugar in a blender or
food processor and blend until smooth

146

and thoroughly mixed. Add the cooled gelatin and blend until well mixed.

5 Pour the peach mixture over the granola base and chill in the refrigerator for several hours until set.

6 To serve, carefully remove the cheesecake from the pan and place it on a serving platter. Decorate with fresh peach slices and mint sprigs before serving.

The syrup can be heated and the gelatin can be dissolved in a microwave oven.

VARIATIONS

● Use other canned fruits such as apricots, pears, cherries, or raspberries in place of the peaches.
● Use crushed reduced-fat graham crackers, mixed grain cereal, or cornflakes in place of the granola.

NUTRITIONAL ANALYSIS

(figures are per serving)

Calories = 261
Fat = 5.7g
of which saturates = 3.2g
    monounsaturates = 1.4g
    polyunsaturates = 0.6g
Protein = 10.3g
Carbohydrate = 44.6g
Dietary fiber = 2.2g
Sodium = 0.2g

Percentage of total calories from fat = 20%
of which saturates = 10%
Percentage of total calories from carbohydrate = 64%, of which sugars = 46%

ORANGE & CINNAMON
CRÊPES

The addition of cinnamon brings extra flavor to these light and crispy crêpes. Served with the yellow raisin and orange sauce, they will provide a satisfying conclusion to any meal.

Preparation time: 25 minutes
Cooking time: 20 minutes
Serves 4 (2 crêpes per serving)

1 cup all-purpose flour
pinch of salt
1 tbsp ground cinnamon
1 egg
1 1/4 cups low-fat or 2% milk
2 tsp sunflower oil
1 1/4 cups unsweetened orange juice
1 cup yellow raisins

1 To make the crêpes, sift the flour, salt, and cinnamon into a bowl and make a well in the center. Break in the egg and add a little milk, beating well with a wooden spoon.

2 Gradually beat in the remaining milk, drawing the flour in from the sides to make a smooth mixture. Cover and set aside while making the sauce.

3 To make the sauce, place the orange juice and yellow raisins in a saucepan and stir to mix. Bring to the boil and cook gently for about 15 minutes, stirring occasionally, until most of the liquid has evaporated and the yellow raisins have plumped up.

4 Meanwhile, cook the crêpes. Brush a heavy-based 7-inch nonstick skillet with a little oil and heat until hot. Beat the mixture to ensure it is well mixed, then pour in enough to thinly coat the pan base.

5 Cook until golden brown, then turn and cook on the other side. Transfer the crêpe to a warmed plate and keep hot. Repeat with the remaining mixture to make 8 crêpes. Arrange the cooked crêpes on top of one another with a sheet of parchment paper in between each crêpe.

6 Spoon some raisin and orange sauce over each crêpe, roll the crêpes up, and serve immediately.

NUTRITIONAL ANALYSIS

(figures are per serving)

Calories = 350
Fat = 5.0g
of which saturates = 1.5g
    monounsaturates = 1.4g
    polyunsaturates = 1.3g
Protein = 8.9g
Carbohydrate = 71.9g
Dietary fiber = 2.1g
Sodium = 0.3g

Percentage of total calories from fat = 13%
of which saturates = 4%
Percentage of total calories from carbohydrate = 77%, of which sugars = 54%

PASTA

*P*asta is an essential item in every kitchen, and is an excellent basis for many quick and tasty meals. There are two main types of pasta: egg pasta and eggless pasta. Both are available fresh or dried, and homemade pasta is also a popular choice. Filled pasta shapes such as tortellini and ravioli are also available in fresh and dried forms.
There are many shapes of pasta to choose from, as well as a range of different flavors, including spinach, tomato, chili, herb, or black squid ink. Pasta is naturally high in carbohydrates and low in fat. Whole-wheat varieties also contain fiber and some B vitamins. Avoid high-fat pasta sauces, especially the cream-based varieties. Tomato-based sauces tend to be much lower in fat and are just as flavorsome.

PASTA TWISTS WITH SMOKED HAM & TOMATO SAUCE

Fresh tomatoes always provide a good basis for a pasta sauce. They combine particularly well with mushrooms and smoked ham in this recipe to create a nutritious and filling meal.

Preparation time: 15 minutes

Cooking time: 20 minutes

Serves 4

4¹/₂ cups tomatoes, skinned and chopped
1 large onion, chopped
2 cloves garlic, crushed
1³/₄ cups button mushrooms, halved
1 tbsp tomato ketchup
1 tbsp tomato paste
salt and freshly ground black pepper
6 ounces cooked lean smoked ham, diced
1 pound pasta twists
2 tbsp chopped fresh mixed herbs
fresh Parmesan cheese shavings, to serve

1 Place the tomatoes, onion, garlic, mushrooms, tomato ketchup, tomato paste, and seasoning in a saucepan and mix well.

2 Cover, bring to the boil, then simmer gently for 15-20 minutes, stirring occasionally, until the vegetables are tender. Stir in the ham and cook gently for 5 minutes.

3 Meanwhile, cook the pasta in a large saucepan of lightly salted, boiling water for 10-12 minutes, until just cooked or *al dente*.

4 Drain the pasta thoroughly and toss it with the tomato sauce and fresh herbs, or spoon the sauce over the pasta. Serve immediately, sprinkled with some shavings of fresh Parmesan cheese. Serve with fresh crusty bread rolls and a mixed green salad.

The pasta sauce is suitable for freezing, and can also be cooked in a microwave oven.

VARIATIONS
● Use unsmoked ham or cooked chicken in place of the smoked ham.
● Use two 14-ounce cans peeled, chopped tomatoes in place of the fresh tomatoes.

148

NUTRITIONAL ANALYSIS

(figures are per serving)

Calories = 430
Fat = 5.4g
of which saturates = 1.9g
     monounsaturates = 0.9g
     polyunsaturates = 1.6g
Protein = 23.9g
Carbohydrate = 75.4g
Dietary fiber = 6.9g
Sodium = 0.1g

Percentage of total calories from fat = 11%
of which saturates = 4%
Percentage of total calories from
carbohydrate = 66% , of which sugars = 10%

WHOLE-WHEAT SPAGHETTI WITH COUNTRY-STYLE CHICKEN SAUCE

Preparation time: 20 minutes

Cooking time: 1 hour

Serves 4

2 tsp olive oil
1 onion, sliced
1 clove garlic, crushed
1¹/₂ cups skinless, boneless chicken breast, diced
3 slices smoked lean back bacon, diced
1 green bell pepper, seeded and sliced
1¹/₂ cups sliced carrots
1¹/₄ cups sliced mushrooms
2¹/₂ cups chicken broth
2 tbsp dry sherry
2 tbsp tomato paste
2 tsp dried mixed herbs
salt and freshly ground black pepper
2 tbsp cornstarch
1 pound whole-wheat spaghetti
chopped fresh parsley to garnish

1 Heat the oil in a large saucepan and cook the onion, garlic, and chicken for 5 minutes, stirring occasionally. Add the bacon, green bell pepper, carrots, and mushrooms and mix well.

2 Combine the broth, sherry, tomato paste, herbs, and seasoning and add to the pan, mixing well. Cover, bring to the boil, then simmer for 45-60 minutes, stirring occasionally, until the chicken is cooked and the vegetables are tender.

3 Blend the cornstarch with 3 tbsp water and stir into the chicken sauce. Bring back to the boil, stirring continuously, then simmer for 3 minutes, stirring.

4 Meanwhile, cook the pasta in a large saucepan of lightly salted, boiling water for 10-12 minutes, until the pasta is just cooked or *al dente*.

5 Drain the pasta thoroughly and serve it with the chicken sauce spooned over the top. Garnish with chopped fresh parsley. Serve with fresh crusty bread.

VARIATION
● Use tomato sauce in place of the tomato paste.

NUTRITIONAL ANALYSIS

(figures are per serving)

Calories = 516
Fat = 8.8g
of which saturates = 1.5g
     monounsaturates = 2.4g
     polyunsaturates = 1.8g

Protein = 38.2g
Carbohydrate = 78.0g
Dietary fiber = 7.0g
Sodium = 0.7g

Percentage of total calories from fat = 12%, of which saturates = 3%
Percentage of total calories from carbohydrate = 57%, of which sugars = 8%
Good source of vitamin A

PASTA SHELLS WITH

SMOKED FISH,
SHRIMP, & GARDEN PEAS

Serve this sumptuous pasta dish, rich in flavor, texture, and color, with some warm, crusty whole-wheat bread. Choose other types of pasta, such as fettuccine or pasta twists, for variety.

Preparation time: 15 minutes

Cooking time: 25 minutes

Serves 4

NUTRITIONAL ANALYSIS
(figures are per serving)

Calories = 639
Fat = 15.3g
of which saturates = 4.2g
monounsaturates = 3.5g
polyunsaturates = 6.0g
Protein = 42.7g
Carbohydrate = 88.1g
Dietary fiber = 9.3g
Sodium = 1.2g

Percentage of total calories from fat = 22%
of which saturates = 6%
Percentage of total calories from
carbohydrate = 52%, of which sugars = 10%
Good source of calcium

6 ounces skinless smoked cod
or white fish fillet
1 bay leaf
6 black peppercorns
1 stick celery, chopped
3 cups low-fat or 2% milk
1¹/₄ cups broccoli flowerets
³/₄ cup cauliflower flowerets
1¹/₄ cups frozen garden peas
3 tbsp soft margarine
1 red onion, chopped
3 tbsp all-purpose flour
8 cooked jumbo shrimp, deveined and shelled
2 tbsp minced fresh coriander (cilantro) (optional)
salt and freshly ground black pepper
1 pound pasta shells

1 Place the smoked fish in a saucepan with the bay leaf, peppercorns, and celery. Add the milk, cover, and heat gently until almost boiling. Simmer for 7-10 minutes, until the fish is just cooked. Remove the fish from the pan using a slotted spoon and keep warm.

2 Strain and reserve the milk, and discard the flavorings. Cook the broccoli, cauliflower, and garden peas in boiling water for 5 minutes, until just tender. Drain and keep warm.

3 Meanwhile, melt the margarine in a large saucepan and cook the onion for 5 minutes, stirring. Add the flour and cook gently for 1 minute, stirring. Remove the pan from the heat and gradually stir in the milk.

4 Heat gently, stirring continuously, until the sauce comes to the boil and thickens. Simmer gently for 3 minutes, stirring.

5 Flake the cooked fish and add to the sauce with the cooked vegetables, shrimp, coriander (cilantro), if using, and seasoning, and mix well. Reheat gently until the sauce is piping hot.

6 Meanwhile, cook the pasta in a large saucepan of lightly salted, boiling water for 10-12 minutes, until just cooked or *al dente*.

7 Drain the pasta thoroughly and serve immediately with the sauce spooned over the top, or tossed with the pasta.

VARIATION
● Use 1 cup cooked, shelled, and deveined bay shrimp or cooked, shelled mussels in place of the jumbo shrimp.

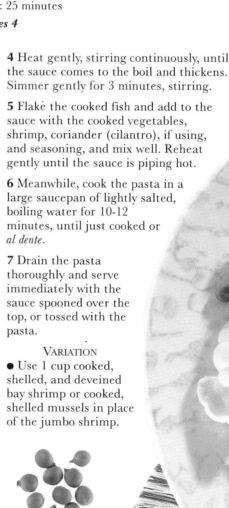

MEDITERRANEAN
PASTA MEDLEY
WITH TUNA & CORN

Some of the typical flavors of the Mediterranean are brought together in this pasta sauce to create a delectable entrée — perfect to enjoy in the evening or at midday alfresco.

Preparation time: 15 minutes

Cooking time: 25 minutes

Serves 4

14-ounce can peeled chopped tomatoes
1 onion, minced
1 clove garlic, crushed
1 red bell pepper, seeded and cut into large dice
2 cups sliced zucchini
1 cup minced celery
2/3 cup dry white wine
1 tbsp tomato paste
14-ounce can tuna in water, drained and flaked
2 cups corn kernels, drained
2 tbsp chopped fresh basil
1 tbsp chopped fresh parsley
salt and freshly ground black pepper
1 pound penne noodles

1 Place the tomatoes, onion, garlic, pepper, zucchini, celery, wine, and tomato paste in a saucepan and mix well. Cover, bring to the boil, and simmer for about 10 minutes, stirring occasionally. Uncover the pan and cook for a further 5 minutes, stirring occasionally.

2 Add the tuna, corn, herbs, and seasoning and stir to mix. Reheat gently for about 5 minutes, until the sauce is piping hot.

3 Meanwhile, cook the pasta in a large saucepan of lightly salted, boiling water for 10-12 minutes, until just cooked or *al dente*.

4 Drain the pasta thoroughly, toss with the tuna sauce, and serve immediately with some fresh, crusty French bread or warm multi-grain rolls and a mixed leaf salad.

VARIATIONS
● Use other canned fish such as salmon in place of the tuna.
● Use 2 cups sliced mushrooms in place of the corn.
● Use red wine in place of the white wine, or grape juice.
● Use chopped fresh mixed herbs in place of the basil and parsley.

NUTRITIONAL ANALYSIS
(figures are per serving)

Calories = 565
Fat = 4.2g
of which saturates = 0.7g
      monounsaturates = 0.6g
      polyunsaturates = 1.7g
Protein = 34.3g
Carbohydrate = 97.7g
Dietary fiber = 7.6g
Sodium = 0.6g

Percentage of total calories from fat = 7%
of which saturates = 1%
Percentage of total calories from carbohydrate = 65%
of which sugars = 13%

FETTUCCINE
WITH SPINACH & BLUE CHEESE SAUCE

Preparation time: 15 minutes

Cooking time: 15 minutes

Serves 4

1 pound fettuccine
2 tbsp soft margarine
1 clove garlic, crushed
4 shallots, finely chopped
2 tbsp all-purpose flour
2 cups low-fat or 2% milk
3 cups cooked, drained spinach
$1/3$ cup blue cheese, crumbled
salt and freshly ground black pepper
minced fresh parsley, to garnish

1 Cook the pasta in a large saucepan of lightly salted, boiling water for 10-12 minutes, until just cooked or *al dente*.

2 Meanwhile, make the spinach and blue cheese sauce. Melt the margarine in a saucepan, add the garlic and shallots, and cook gently for 5 minutes, stirring.

3 Add the flour and cook for 1 minute, stirring. Remove the pan from the heat and gradually stir in the milk.

4 Heat gently, stirring continuously, until the sauce comes to the boil and thickens. Reduce the heat and simmer gently for 3 minutes, stirring.

5 Press any excess water out of the spinach using the back of a wooden spoon, then chop the spinach.

6 Add the spinach, cheese, and seasoning to the sauce and mix well. Reheat gently, stirring continuously, until the cheese has melted and the sauce is piping hot.

7 Drain the cooked pasta thoroughly, then toss it with the sauce and serve immediately, garnished with some minced parsley. Alternatively, serve the pasta with the sauce spooned over it. Serve this dish with crusty bread rolls and a mixed leaf salad.

VARIATIONS
● Use other types of pasta such as whole-wheat spaghetti or pasta shapes in place of the fettuccine.
● Use 1 small standard or red onion or 1 bunch of green onions (scallions) in place of the shallots.
● Use a sharp yellow cheese instead of blue cheese.
● Add $1/3$ cup diced lean ham or cooked bacon to the sauce before serving.

NUTRITIONAL ANALYSIS
(figures are per serving)

Calories = 527
Fat = 15.7g
of which saturates = 6.2g
      monounsaturates = 3.9g
      polyunsaturates = 4.2g
Protein = 22.7g
Carbohydrate = 78.6g
Dietary fiber = 5.9g
Sodium = 0.4g

Percentage of total calories from fat = 27%
of which saturates = 10%
Percentage of total calories from carbohydrate = 56%
of which sugars = 7%s
Good source of calcium & vitamin A

SPAGHETTI
WITH MIXED
VEGETABLES

Preparation time: 15 minutes

Cooking time: 25 minutes

Serves 4

2 tsp olive oil
1 red onion, sliced
2 cloves garlic, crushed
14-ounce can peeled, chopped tomatoes
1-pound can chick-peas (garbanzo beans), rinsed and drained
1 cup sliced zucchini
1 cup baby corn, halved
³/₄ cup okra, trimmed
²/₃ cup tomato sauce
2 tbsp red wine
1 tbsp tomato paste
1 tsp sugar
2 tsp dried mixed herbs
salt and freshly ground black pepper
1 pound tricolor spaghetti
1 cup cherry tomatoes, halved
chopped fresh parsley, to garnish

1 Heat the oil in a saucepan, add the onion and garlic, and cook for 5 minutes, stirring occasionally. Add the tomatoes, chick-peas (garbanzo beans), zucchini, corn, okra, tomato sauce, wine, tomato paste, sugar, herbs, and seasoning and mix well.

2 Cover, bring to the boil, and simmer for 15-20 minutes, stirring occasionally.

3 Meanwhile, cook the pasta in a large saucepan of lightly salted, boiling water for 10-12 minutes, until just cooked or *al dente*.

4 Drain the pasta thoroughly. Stir the cherry tomatoes into the vegetable sauce. Toss the pasta with the vegetable sauce and serve immediately, sprinkled with fresh parsley. Serve with crusty bread rolls and a green side salad.

The mixed vegetable pasta sauce can be cooked in a microwave oven.

NUTRITIONAL ANALYSIS
(figures are per serving)

Calories = 482
Fat = 6.7g
of which saturates = 0.9g
   monounsaturates = 1.9g
   polyunsaturates = 2.3g
Protein = 20.8g
Carbohydrate = 88.8g
Dietary fiber = 10.7g
Sodium = 0.7g

Percentage of total calories
from fat = 12%
of which saturates = 2%
Percentage of total calories
from carbohydrate = 69%
of which sugars = 11%

QUICK & EASY
VEGETARIAN PASTA SAUCES

CHEDDAR & LEEK
Follow the recipe for Fettucine with Spinach & Blue Cheese Sauce on page 152 but replace the blue cheese with ¹/₂ cup grated sharp Cheddar cheese and the spinach with 2 cups sliced steamed leeks. Add 1 tbsp chopped fresh tarragon to the sauce for extra flavor.

MUSHROOM & ZUCCHINI
Alternatively, follow the recipe on page 152, replacing the shallots with 1 onion. Use 1 cup sliced, sautéed mushrooms and 1 cup sliced, sautéed zucchini in place of the spinach and use grated Monterey jack cheese in place of the blue cheese.

CHILI &
MACARONI BAKE

This macaroni bake makes a tasty entrée for serving at lunchtime or in the evening. Serve with a crisp green salad and fresh crusty French bread.

Preparation time: 1¹/₂ hours
Cooking time: 25-30 minutes
Serves 6

NUTRITIONAL ANALYSIS

(figures are per serving)

Calories = 415
Fat = 9.9g
of which saturates = 4.2g
  monounsaturates = 2.5g
  polyunsaturates = 1.3g
Protein = 25.3g
Carbohydrate = 55.4g
Dietary fiber = 6.7g
Sodium = 0.4g

Percentage of total calories from fat = 21%
of which saturates = 9%
Percentage of total calories from
carbohydrate = 50%
of which sugars = 13%
Good source of vitamin
A & B vitamins

8 ounces extra-lean ground beef
1 onion, minced
1 clove garlic, crushed
³/₄ cup finely diced carrots
³/₄ cup finely chopped mushrooms
1 small red bell pepper, seeded and finely diced
2 small fresh red chilies, seeded and finely chopped
1 cup canned peeled, chopped tomatoes
²/₃ cup red wine
²/₃ cup tomato sauce
1 tsp dried mixed herbs
salt and freshly ground black pepper
1 pound canned red kidney beans, rinsed and drained
12 ounces short-cut macaroni
2 tbsp low-fat spread
2 tbsp all-purpose flour
2¹/₂ cups low-fat or 2% milk
4 tbsp finely grated reduced-fat sharp Cheddar cheese
2 tbsp fresh whole-wheat bread crumbs

1 To make the chili, place the ground beef, onion, and garlic in a saucepan and cook gently until the meat is browned all over.

2 Add the carrots, mushrooms, red bell pepper, chilies, tomatoes, red wine, tomato sauce, herbs, and seasoning, and mix well. Cover, bring to the boil, and simmer for 30 minutes, stirring occasionally.

3 Add the kidney beans and mix well. Cover and cook for a further 15 minutes, stirring occasionally.

4 Meanwhile, cook the macaroni in a large saucepan of lightly salted, boiling water for about 10 minutes, until just cooked, then drain thoroughly and keep warm.

5 Place the low-fat spread, flour, and milk in a saucepan and heat gently, whisking continuously, until the sauce comes to the boil and thickens. Simmer gently for 3 minutes, whisking, then season with salt and pepper.

6 Mix together the chili and cooked macaroni and transfer to an ovenproof dish. Pour the white sauce over the top. Mix the cheese and bread crumbs together and sprinkle them over the chili.

7 Bake in a preheated oven at 350° for 25-30 minutes, until golden and bubbling. Serve immediately.

VARIATIONS
● Use ground soya protein or other lean ground meats such as pork or turkey in place of the beef.
● Use dry white wine in place of the red wine.
● Use other reduced-fat hard cheese such as Monterey jack in place of the Cheddar cheese.
● Use one tsp dried chili flakes in place of the fresh red chilies.

TORTELLINI PRIMAVERA

Filled pasta is often served on its own or tossed in melted butter or oil. Try this hearty and flavorful alternative, consisting of tortellini tossed with a mixture of colorful vegetables combined to make an exciting sauce.

Preparation time: 15 minutes

Cooking time: 25 minutes

Serves 4

14-ounce can peeled, chopped tomatoes
²/₃ cup tomato sauce
6 shallots, sliced
1 clove garlic, crushed
1¹/₄ cups sliced mushrooms
1¹/₄ cups sliced zucchini
1 red bell pepper, seeded and sliced into strips
8 canned asparagus spears, chopped
2 tbsp sun-dried tomatoes, finely chopped
1 bay leaf
salt and freshly ground black pepper
¹/₂ cup frozen peas
1 pound meat-filled tortellini
2-3 tbsp chopped fresh mixed herbs
4 tbsp finely grated fresh Parmesan cheese, to serve
fresh basil sprigs, to garnish

1 Place the canned tomatoes, tomato sauce, shallots, garlic, mushrooms, zucchini, bell pepper, asparagus, sun-dried tomatoes, bay leaf, and seasoning in a saucepan and mix well.

2 Cover, bring to the boil, and simmer gently for 15 minutes, stirring occasionally. Remove the bay leaf, stir in the peas, and cook for a further 5 minutes, stirring occasionally.

3 Meanwhile, cook the tortellini in a large saucepan of lightly salted, boiling water for 16-18 minutes (or according to the manufacturer's instructions), until cooked and tender.

4 Drain the pasta thoroughly. Toss the tortellini with the sauce and herbs, and sprinkle with Parmesan cheese. Garnish with fresh basil sprigs and serve with fresh crusty bread.

VARIATIONS
● Use cheese-filled tortellini in place of the meat-filled tortellini.
● Use frozen lima beans in place of the peas.
● Use 4 large skinned and chopped fresh tomatoes in place of the canned tomatoes.
● Use baby corn in place of the asparagus.
● Use reduced-fat Cheddar cheese in place of the Parmesan.

NUTRITIONAL ANALYSIS

(figures are per serving)

Calories = 502
Fat = 12.9g
of which saturates = 5.6g
monounsaturates = 4.3g
polyunsaturates = 2.0g
Protein = 28.4g
Carbohydrate = 68.5g
Dietary fiber = 7.8g
Sodium = 0.6g

Percentage of total calories from fat = 23%
of which saturates = 10%
Percentage of total calories from carbohydrate = 51%
of which sugars = 8%
Good source of vitamins A & C

FUSILLI SALAD

The dressing in this recipe, with a refreshing hint of horseradish, combines well with the pasta and vegetables to make an attractive and nutritious salad, ideal as a entrée or a filling evening snack.

Preparation time: 15 minutes

Cooking time: 10-12 minutes

Serves 4

14 ounces tricolor fusilli or spiral pasta
5 tsp olive oil
4 shallots, sliced
2 cloves garlic, crushed
2 cups zucchini, cut into matchstick strips
2 cups fresh wild mushrooms such as oyster or shiitake
1 tbsp pitted black olives, finely chopped (optional)
²/₃ cup reduced-fat sour cream
²/₃ cup low-fat plain yogurt
2 tbsp horseradish sauce
salt and freshly ground black pepper
2 tbsp chopped fresh mixed herbs

1 Cook the pasta in a large saucepan of lightly salted, boiling water for 10-12 minutes, until just cooked or *al dente*.

2 Meanwhile, heat the oil in a saucepan, add the shallots, and garlic, and cook for 3 minutes, stirring occasionally. Add the zucchini and mushrooms, mix well, cover, and cook for 5 minutes, stirring occasionally. Add the olives, if using, and mix well.

3 In a bowl, mix together the sour cream, yogurt, horseradish sauce, seasoning, and herbs.

4 Drain the pasta thoroughly, then toss together with the mushroom mixture.

5 Toss the pasta and sour cream mixtures together and serve warm or cold with thick slices of fresh whole-wheat bread.

NUTRITIONAL ANALYSIS
(figures are per serving)

Calories = 426

Fat = 13.6g

of which saturates = 5.1g

   monounsaturates = 5.1g

   polyunsaturates = 2.0g

Percentage of total calories from fat = 29%

of which saturates = 10%

Percentage of total calories from carbohydrate = 56%

of which sugars = 8%

Protein = 15.7g

Carbohydrate = 63.9g

Dietary fiber = 5.4

Sodium = 0.2g

VARIATIONS
● Use 1 small onion in place of the shallots.
● Use button or closed cup mushrooms in place of the wild mushrooms.
● Use a flavored oil such as chili or herb oil in place of the olive oil.

BELL PEPPER, TOMATO, & SPINACH
PASTA SALAD

This colorful salad is tossed with a delicious mustard and herb-flavored dressing. Serve warm for a brunch or a light evening meal, or make it in advance and pack it up for a tasty brown bag lunch.

Preparation time: 15 minutes

Cooking time: 10-12 minutes

Serves 4

12 ounces pasta shapes
5 tbsp olive oil
2 tbsp red wine vinegar
2 tsp whole-grain mustard
1 clove garlic, crushed
1 tbsp chopped fresh basil
1 tbsp chopped fresh oregano
salt and freshly ground black pepper
1 red bell pepper, seeded and diced
1 yellow bell pepper, seeded and diced
1¹/₂ cups cherry tomatoes, halved
1 cup fresh baby spinach leaves, washed and dried
³/₄ cup snow peas, chopped
1 bunch green onions (scallions), chopped
2 tbsp arugula

1 Cook the pasta in a large saucepan of lightly salted, boiling water for 10-12 minutes, until just cooked or *al dente*.

2 Meanwhile, place the oil, vinegar, mustard, garlic, herbs, and seasoning in a bowl and whisk together until thoroughly combined. Set aside.

3 Place the bell peppers and tomatoes in a bowl. Tear the spinach leaves into smaller pieces, add to the bowl with the snow peas, green onions (scallions), and arugula, and toss the ingredients together.

4 Drain the pasta thoroughly, whisk the dressing once again, and toss the pasta and dressing together. Toss the pasta and vegetables together and serve warm or cold with fresh crusty bread.

NUTRITIONAL ANALYSIS

(figures are per serving)

Calories = 422
Fat = 16.5g
of which saturates = 2.4g
     monounsaturates = 10.1g
     polyunsaturates = 2.8g

Protein = 12.6g
Carbohydrate = 59.5g
Dietary fiber = 6.7g
Sodium = 0.1g

Percentage of total calories from fat = 35%, of which saturates = 5%
Percentage of total calories from carbohydrate = 53%
of which sugars = 10%
Good source of vitamins A & C

RICE & GRAINS

*T*here are many types of rice and grains to choose from, which come in an assortment of shapes and sizes, and all varieties are nutritious. They are high in carbohydrates, provide a good source of energy, and are low in fat. Whole-grain varieties are higher in dietary fiber and contain some B vitamins. Rice also contains some protein.
Rice has excellent absorbent properties, and this makes it and other grains ideal for absorbing the flavors from other foods, so creating a wide range of delicious dishes. Often requiring little or no preparation, rice and grains can be used in many dishes including salads, risottos, stir-fries, dressings, soups, and desserts.

BULGUR WHEAT, MUSHROOM, & GARLIC SALAD

Serve this tasty salad as a side salad with chicken or fish, or as a light meal with fresh crusty bread. Bulgur wheat, also known as burghul or bulghur wheat, is obtainable from Middle Eastern stores. If it is hard to find, use cracked wheat.

Preparation time: 10 minutes, plus soaking time for the bulgur wheat
Cooking time: 10 minutes, plus cooking time for the bulgur wheat (if applicable)

1¹/₂ cups bulgur wheat or cracked wheat
2 tsp olive oil
1 red onion, chopped
2 cloves garlic, crushed
2 cups mushrooms, sliced
4 tomatoes, skinned and chopped
salt and freshly ground black pepper
3 tbsp chopped fresh mixed herbs
fat-free French or Italian dressing

1 Soak and cook (if applicable) the bulgur wheat according to the package instructions.

2 Heat the oil in a saucepan, add the onion and garlic, and cook for 5 minutes, stirring occasionally.

3 Add the mushrooms, cover, and cook for 5 minutes, stirring occasionally.

4 Add the drained, cooked bulgur wheat, tomatoes, seasoning, and herbs, and stir to mix. Sprinkle with some French or

Italian dressing and toss together to mix. Serve warm or cold with crusty French bread.

VARIATIONS
● Use zucchini in place of the mushrooms.
● Use 6 shallots in place of the onion.
● Sprinkle the salad with some finely grated fresh Parmesan cheese just before serving.

FRUIT & NUT
PILAF

A combination of mild spices adds subtle flavor to this delicious pilaf, which is ideal for serving on its own as a light meal, or with some crusty bread and broiled fish or meat for a more substantial meal.

Preparation time: 15 minutes

Cooking time: 30 minutes

Serves 4

2 tsp olive oil
2 cloves garlic, crushed
1 onion, chopped
1 small red chili, seeded and finely chopped
1 tsp ground cumin
1 tsp ground coriander (cilantro)
1 cup brown long-grain rice
1 red bell pepper, seeded and diced
$^1/_2$ cup yellow raisins
$^1/_2$ cup pitted dried apricots, chopped
$2^1/_2$ cups vegetable broth
1 tbsp light soy sauce
1 tbsp dry sherry (optional)
salt and freshly ground black pepper
$^1/_2$ cup unsalted cashew nuts or almonds
fresh herb sprigs, to garnish

1 Heat the oil in a large saucepan. Add the garlic, onion, and chili and cook for 2 minutes, stirring. Add the spices and rice and cook for 1 minute, stirring.

2 Add the bell pepper, yellow raisins, apricots, and broth, and mix well. Cover, bring to the boil, and simmer gently for about 25 minutes, until almost all the liquid has been absorbed and the rice is tender, stirring occasionally.

3 Add the seasoning, soy sauce, sherry, if using, and nuts, and stir to mix. Garnish with fresh herb sprigs.

VARIATIONS
● Use white long-grain rice in place of the brown rice.
● Use 1 cup mushrooms or broccoli in place of the bell pepper.
● Use your own mixture of ground spices such as curry powder, Mexican chili powder, and cardamom.

NUTRITIONAL ANALYSIS

(figures are per serving)

Calories = 362
Fat = 3.8g
of which saturates = 0.4g
monounsaturates = 1.1g
polyunsaturates = 0.6g
Protein = 11.1g
Carbohydrate = 72.7g
Dietary fiber = 2.3g
Sodium = 0.02g

Percentage of total calories from fat = 9%
of which saturates = 1%
Percentage of total calories from carbohydrate = 75%
of which sugars = 5%

NUTRITIONAL ANALYSIS

(figures are per serving)

Calories = 559	Protein = 12.5g
Fat = 17.9g	Carbohydrate = 91.7g
of which saturates = 3.4g	Dietary fiber = 5.7g
monounsaturates = 9.5g	Sodium = 0.5g
polyunsaturates = 3.4g	

Percentage of total calories from fat = 29%
of which saturates = 6%
Percentage of total calories from carbohydrate = 61%
of which sugars = 25%

STUFFED PEPPERS WITH TOMATO & CHILI

*A tomato and chili salsa complements the flavor of
the stuffed peppers perfectly in this light meal. Use different
colored peppers to make the dish even more appealing.*

Preparation time: 35 minutes
Cooking time: 35-40 minutes
Serves 4 (makes 4 peppers)

FOR THE SALSA
1 tsp olive oil
4 shallots, finely chopped
1 clove garlic, crushed
1 small red chili, seeded and finely chopped
*2 cups tomatoes, skinned, seeded,
and finely chopped*
*6 sun-dried tomatoes, soaked in warm water,
drained and finely chopped*
1 tsp dried herbs
salt and freshly ground black pepper

FOR THE STUFFED PEPPERS
4 large bell peppers
1 tsp olive oil
1 onion, minced
1 clove garlic, crushed
1 cup cooked brown rice
1 large tomato, skinned and finely chopped
1 cup corn kernels, drained
*6 tbsp reduced-fat mature Cheddar cheese,
finely grated*
1 egg, beaten
2 tbsp minced fresh parsley
1 tbsp minced fresh thyme
salt and freshly ground black pepper

1 To make the salsa, heat the oil in a
saucepan, add the shallots, garlic, and
chili and cook gently for 10 minutes,
stirring occasionally.

2 Add the remaining salsa ingredients,
mix well, and cook for 5 minutes,
stirring occasionally. Allow to cool. The
salsa may be served warm or cold.

3 Make the stuffed peppers. Slice the
tops off the peppers, and remove and
discard the cores and seeds. Blanch the
peppers in boiling water for 4 minutes,
then drain thoroughly.

4 Heat the oil in a saucepan. Add the
onion and garlic and cook for 5 minutes,
stirring occasionally. Add the rice, 1 tbsp
water, and the remaining
ingredients, and mix well.

5 Fill each pepper with
some filling and top with
the lids. Place in a
shallow ovenproof dish
and pour a little water
around the bases of
the peppers.

6 Cover with foil and
bake in a preheated
oven at 350° for
35-40 minutes, until
the peppers feel
tender when pierced
with a skewer.

7 Serve the stuffed
peppers with the tomato
and chili salsa, and some
crusty whole-wheat bread for a
more substantial meal.

VARIATIONS
● Use frozen peas in place of the corn.
● Use other chopped fresh herbs of your
choice such as basil and oregano.

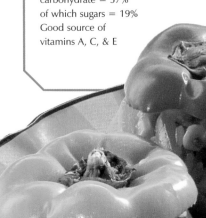

SPICY VEGETABLE
COUSCOUS

A spicy vegetable sauce and freshly steamed couscous make a satisfying dinner. Use packaged couscous, which needs little or no cooking.

Preparation time: 15 minutes, plus soaking time for the couscous

Cooking time: 45 minutes

Serves 4

1¹/₂ cups couscous
2 tsp olive oil
1 onion, minced
2 cloves garlic, crushed
1 small red chili, seeded and finely chopped
4 carrots, sliced
2 tsp ground cumin
2 tsp ground coriander (cilantro)
1 tsp ground allspice
4 zucchini, sliced
1¹/₂ cups mushrooms, sliced
1 red bell pepper, seeded and sliced
14-ounce can chick-peas (garbanzo beans), rinsed and drained
14-ounce can peeled, chopped tomatoes
1¹/₄ cups vegetable broth
salt and freshly ground black pepper
2 tbsp chopped fresh coriander (cilantro)

1 Soak the couscous according to the package instructions.

2 Meanwhile, heat the oil in a large saucepan over which a steamer, metal colander, or sieve will fit. Add the onion, garlic, chili, and carrots and cook gently for 10 minutes, stirring occasionally.

3 Add the spices and cook for 2 minutes, stirring. Add all the remaining ingredients, except the fresh coriander (cilantro), and mix well.

4 Bring to the boil and reduce the heat to simmer the vegetable mixture. Place the couscous in a steamer, colander, or sieve lined with cheesecloth (if the holes are large enough for the couscous to drop through), and place over the vegetables.

5 Cover with a lid and cook gently for 25-30 minutes, until the vegetables are tender and the couscous is hot, stirring both the vegetable mixture and couscous occasionally.

6 Stir the chopped fresh coriander (cilantro) into the couscous and serve the vegetables on a bed of couscous. Serve with warmed or toasted pita pockets.

The vegetable sauce is suitable for freezing.

VARIATIONS
● Serve the cooked vegetables on a bed of cooked cracked wheat or brown rice, in place of the couscous.
● Use 2 cups fresh tomatoes (skinned, seeded, and finely chopped) in place of the canned tomatoes.
● Use your own choice of ground spices such as chili powder, cinnamon, and allspice.

NUTRITIONAL ANALYSIS

(figures are per serving)

Calories = 384
Fat = 6.2g
of which saturates = 0.7g
     monounsaturates = 1.9g
     polyunsaturates = 1.8g
Protein = 15.4g
Carbohydrate = 71.9g
Dietary fiber = 7.5g
Sodium = 0.4g

Percentage of total calories from fat = 15%
of which saturates = 2%
Percentage of total calories from carbohydrate = 70%
of which sugars = 13%
Good source of vitamins A & C

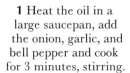

1 Heat the oil in a large saucepan, add the onion, garlic, and bell pepper and cook for 3 minutes, stirring.

2 Add the rice and mushrooms and cook for 1 minute, stirring. Add the broth, wine, and seasoning and mix well.

3 Bring to the boil and simmer, uncovered, for 25-30 minutes, until almost all the liquid has been absorbed, stirring occasionally.

4 Stir in the chicken, peas, lima beans, chick-peas (garbanzo beans), and yellow raisins, and cook gently for about 10 minutes, stirring occasionally.

5 Stir in the chopped herbs and serve the risotto immediately with fresh crusty bread and a mixed leaf side salad.

6 Garnish the risotto with Parmesan shavings just before serving, if liked.

VARIATIONS

● Use cooked, unsmoked chicken in place of the smoked chicken.
● Use frozen green beans in place of the peas.
● Use corn in place of the lima beans.

SMOKED CHICKEN & MUSHROOM
RISOTTO

Serve this tempting risotto for a substantial lunch, or dinner.

Preparation time: 10 minutes

Cooking time: 45 minutes

Serves 4

2 tsp olive oil
1 onion, chopped
2 cloves garlic, crushed
1 red bell pepper, seeded and diced
1 cup long-grain brown rice
1 cup mushrooms, sliced
2¹/₂ cups chicken or vegetable broth
1¹/₄ cups dry white wine
salt and freshly ground black pepper
1 cup diced cooked skinless, boneless smoked chicken
¹/₂ cup frozen peas
¹/₂ cup frozen lima beans
¹/₂ cup canned and drained chick-peas (garbanzo beans)
3 tbsp yellow raisins
2 tbsp chopped fresh mixed herbs
Parmesan shavings, to garnish (optional)

NUTRITIONAL ANALYSIS
(figures are per serving)

Calories = 519
Fat = 6.8g
of which saturates = 1.4g
   monounsaturates = 2.5g
   polyunsaturates = 1.9g

Protein = 25.8g
Carbohydrate = 81.6g
Dietary fiber = 7.8g
Sodium = 0.4g

Percentage of total calories from fat = 12%
of which saturates = 2%
Percentage of total calories from carbohydrate = 59%
of which sugars = 16%

TUNA & SHRIMP
RISOTTO

This tuna and shrimp risotto is quite similar to a paella. Serve on its own or with crusty bread and a side salad as an entrée.

Preparation time: 10 minutes

Cooking time: 45 minutes

Serves 4

1 1/4 cups long-grain brown rice
1 onion, chopped
1 clove garlic, crushed
1 1/4 cups mushrooms, sliced
2 1/2 cups fish or vegetable broth
2 cups dry white wine
pinch of ground saffron
salt and freshly ground black pepper
7-ounce can tuna in water, drained and flaked
8 cooked, peeled, and deveined jumbo shrimp
7-ounce can corn kernels, drained
3/4 cup frozen peas
2 tbsp minced fresh parsley
2 tbsp finely grated fresh Parmesan cheese
whole cooked jumbo shrimp and fresh herb sprigs, to garnish

1 Place the rice, onion, garlic, mushrooms, broth, wine, saffron, and seasoning in a saucepan and mix well.

2 Bring to the boil and simmer, uncovered, for 30-35 minutes, or until the rice is tender, stirring occasionally.

3 Add the tuna, shrimp, corn, and peas, and mix well. Cook over a higher heat for 5 minutes, stirring frequently, until most of the liquid has been absorbed. Add the parsley and stir to mix.

4 Serve immediately, sprinkled with Parmesan cheese and garnished with whole jumbo shrimp and fresh herb sprigs. Serve with warm, freshly-baked bread and a sweet pepper and tomato side salad.

NUTRITIONAL ANALYSIS

(figures are per serving)

Calories = 545
Fat = 5.9g
of which saturates = 2.0g
    monounsaturates = 1.3g
    polyunsaturates = 1.6g

Protein = 36.1g
Carbohydrate = 73.5g
Dietary fiber = 5.1g
Sodium = 1.5g

Percentage of total calories from fat = 10%
of which saturates = 3%
Percentage of total calories from carbohydrate = 51%, of which sugars = 6%

POTATOES

Potatoes are low in fat, contain some vitamin C, and are high in carbohydrates, making them a good source of energy. They are also a good source of fiber, especially when baked in their skins. The potato comes in many varieties, and is a versatile vegetable that can be cooked and eaten in many different ways. Often served as an accompanying vegetable, potatoes are also ideal for a wide variety of dishes such as vegetable bakes, baked potatoes with toppings, salads, casseroles, stews, pasties, turnovers, and soups.
Fat is often added to potatoes. For example, they are roasted in oil, creamed, or served as french fries. All of these cooking methods can increase the fat content of the potatoes considerably. Fortunately, there are healthy ways to enjoy your favorite kinds of potato. Delicious roasted potatoes can be made by using the minimum amount of shortening or by dry-roasting them. Instead of deep-frying French fries, try oven-baked fries which are lower in fat.

POTATO & CARROT
SOUP

A tempting, flavorful soup, this dish is ideal as an appetizer for cold winter nights or as a takeout lunchtime warmer.

Preparation time: 10 minutes
Cooking time: 30 minutes
Serves 4

1 onion, minced
1 pound potatoes, washed and cut into chunks
8 ounces carrots, sliced
3 sticks celery, sliced
3³/₄ cups vegetable broth
1 bay leaf
salt and freshly ground black pepper
2 tbsp minced fresh parsley

1 Place all the ingredients, except the parsley, in a large saucepan and mix well.

2 Cover, bring to the boil, and simmer for 20-25 minutes, until the vegetables are tender, stirring occasionally.

3 Remove from the heat and set aside to cool slightly. Remove and discard the bay leaf, then place the mixture in a blender or food processor and blend until smooth.

4 Return to the saucepan and add the parsley. Adjust the seasoning and reheat gently. Serve with some fresh crusty French bread or garlic bread croutons.

VARIATIONS
● Use ³/₄ cup sliced leeks (trimmed weight) in place of the onion.
● Use rutabaga or parsnips in place of the carrots.
● Use chopped fresh mixed herbs in place of the parsley.
● Use a bouquet garni in place of the bay leaf.

164

MOROCCAN POTATO
SALAD

This delicately spiced potato salad is delicious served as an appetizer or as an accompaniment to broiled fish or meat. Alternatively, serve it as a picnic treat.

Preparation time: 20 minutes

Cooking time: 20 minutes

Serves 6 as an appetizer or side salad

2 pounds small new potatoes, washed
3 tbsp tomato juice
$^1/_2$ tsp ground cumin
$^1/_2$ tsp ground paprika
$^1/_2$ tsp ground coriander (cilantro)
$2^1/_2$ tsp ground turmeric
$^1/_2$ tsp ground cinnamon
$^1/_2$ tsp ground ginger
1 clove garlic, crushed (optional)
2 bunches green onions (scallions), chopped
1 yellow bell pepper, seeded and diced
2-3 tbsp chopped fresh coriander (cilantro)
5 tbsp reduced-calorie mayonnaise
5 tbsp low-fat plain yogurt
salt and freshly ground black pepper

1 Cook the potatoes in a large saucepan of lightly salted, boiling water for 10-15 minutes, until cooked and tender. Drain thoroughly and allow to cool completely.

2 Place the tomato juice, spices, and garlic, if using, in a small saucepan and cook gently for 2 minutes, stirring. Allow to cool slightly.

3 Place the cold potatoes in a large bowl, add the green onions (scallions), yellow bell pepper, and coriander (cilantro), and stir to mix.

4 Place the mayonnaise, yogurt, spice mixture, and seasoning in a small bowl and mix together thoroughly. Pour the dressing over the potatoes and toss together to mix.

5 Cover and set aside for 30 minutes before serving. Alternatively, cover and chill in the refrigerator until ready to use.

6 As a side salad, serve with broiled fish such as sole or monkfish, or with lean meat such as chicken or lamb.

VARIATIONS

● Use 1 large minced red onion in place of the green onions (scallions).
● Use old potatoes, peeled and cut into small chunks, in place of the new potatoes.
● This salad may be served warm. Toss the warm cooked potatoes with the dressing and serve.

HERBED CHICKEN
& POTATO BAKE

Preparation time: 35 minutes

Cooking time: 1 hour

Serves 6 as an entrée

1 pound potatoes, washed and cut into thin slices
1 tbsp olive oil
3 tbsp low-fat spread
3 tbsp all-purpose flour
2¹/₂ cups chicken or vegetable broth, cooled
1¹/₄ cups low-fat or 2% milk
1 pound shallots
1¹/₄ cups mushrooms, sliced
1 cup diced cooked skinless, boneless chicken
1 cup frozen or canned corn kernels
14-ounce can black-eyed peas, rinsed and drained
2 tbsp minced fresh coriander (cilantro)
salt and freshly ground black pepper
fresh coriander (cilantro) leaves, to garnish

1 Parboil the potatoes in a saucepan of boiling water for 4 minutes, then drain thoroughly, and toss the potato slices in the oil. Set aside.

2 Place the low-fat spread, flour, broth, and milk in a saucepan. Heat gently, whisking continuously, until the sauce comes to the boil and thickens. Simmer gently for 3 minutes, stirring.

3 Peel the shallots, slice them thinly, and add to the sauce with the mushrooms, chicken, corn, black-eyed peas, coriander (cilantro), and seasoning, mixing well. Place the mixture in a shallow ovenproof casserole dish.

4 Arrange the potato slices over the chicken mixture, covering it completely.

5 Cover with foil and bake in a preheated oven at 400° for about 1 hour, until the potatoes are cooked, tender, and browned on top. Remove the foil for the final 20 minutes.

6 Garnish with fresh coriander leaves and serve with steamed vegetables and crusty bread.

VARIATIONS
● Use cooked turkey or lean ham in place of the chicken.
● Use 1 diced red or yellow bell pepper in place of the mushrooms.

NUTRITIONAL ANALYSIS

(figures are per serving)

Calories = 319
Fat = 8.2g
of which saturates = 2.0g
monounsaturates = 2.3g
polyunsaturates = 1.9g
Protein = 21.8g
Carbohydrate = 42.3g
Dietary fiber = 6.0g
Sodium = 0.5g

Percentage of total calories from fat = 23%
of which saturates = 6%
Percentage of total calories from
carbohydrate = 50%
of which sugars = 13%

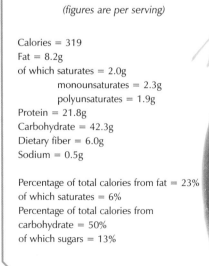

POTATO, CARROT, & PARSNIP
BAKE

*Root vegetables such as potatoes, carrots, and parsnips
are a tasty trio when cooked together in this simple but flavorful dish.
Serve with oven-baked fish or chicken and fresh vegetables.*

Preparation time: 35 minutes

Cooking time: 30 minutes

Serves 4 as an accompanying vegetable dish

4 medium potatoes, peeled and diced
2 carrots, thinly sliced
2 parsnips, peeled and sliced
$^1/_2$ cup finely grated reduced-fat mature Cheddar
cheese
2 tbsp chopped fresh chives
salt and freshly ground black pepper
fresh herb sprigs, to garnish

1 Cook the vegetables in a large saucepan of lightly salted, boiling water for about 20 minutes, until tender.

2 Drain and mash thoroughly. Add the cheese, chives, and seasoning and mix well.

3 Place the mixture in a lightly greased ovenproof dish and level the surface.

4 Bake in a preheated oven at 350° for about 30 minutes, until the top is lightly browned.

5 Garnish with fresh herb sprigs. Serve with oven-baked fish, such as trout or salmon, and steamed fresh seasonal vegetables, such as snow-peas and baby corn.

VARIATIONS

● Use rutabaga or jicama in place of the parsnips.

● Use other reduced-fat hard cheese such as Monterey jack in place of the Cheddar cheese.

● Use sweet potatoes or a mixture of sweet and white potatoes.

● Reserve a little of the cheese and sprinkle it over the bake before cooking.

NUTRITIONAL ANALYSIS

(figures are per serving)

Calories = 196
Fat = 4.2g
of which saturates = 2.2g
monounsaturates = 1.2g
polyunsaturates = 0.4g
Protein = 10.4g
Carbohydrate = 30.8g
Dietary fiber = 5.4g
Sodium = 0.2g

Percentage of total calories from fat = 19%
of which saturates = 10%
Percentage of total calories from
carbohydrate = 59%, of which sugars = 15%
Good source of vitamin A

BAKED POTATO
TOPPINGS

Baked potatoes are always a popular choice, especially when topped with flavorful savory mixtures such as these. Serve the baked potatoes with a topping of your choice and enjoy a nutritious light meal. Each topping is enough for 4 large baked potatoes.

Preparation time: 5 minutes, plus preparing the filling

Cooking time: 1-1½ hours

Serves 4 (makes 4 potatoes)

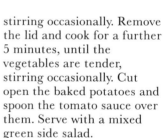

4 large baking potatoes, washed and dried

Pierce the potatoes with a fork. Bake near the top of a preheated oven at 400° for 1-1½ hours, until tender throughout. Cut a cross in the top of the potato or cut the potato in half to serve, and top with one of the following tasty toppings.

SMOKED BACON, EGG, & CORN
4 slices lean smoked bacon
4 medium eggs, hard-boiled and cooled
7-ounce can corn kernels, drained
4 tbsp reduced-calorie mayonnaise
2 tbsp minced chives
salt and freshly ground black pepper

Broil the bacon slices for 3-5 minutes, turning once, until cooked and crispy. Meanwhile, peel the eggs. Mash or finely chop the eggs and mix with the corn, mayonnaise, chives, and seasoning. Dice the cooked bacon. Cut open the baked potatoes and spoon the egg mixture over them. Sprinkle with the bacon and serve with a mixed tomato, bell pepper, and onion salad.

PINK SALMON & SOUR CREAM
7-ounce can salmon in water, drained and flaked
2 bunches green onions (scallions), chopped
1 beefsteak tomato, chopped
⅔ cup sour cream
salt and freshly ground black pepper

Mix together the salmon, green onions (scallions), tomato, sour cream, and seasoning. Cut open the baked potatoes and spoon the salmon mixture over them. Serve with a mixed green side salad.

SPICY TOMATO & MUSHROOM
1 pound tomatoes, skinned and chopped
1 small onion, minced
1 cup mushrooms, finely chopped
1 clove garlic, crushed
1 tsp chili powder
1 tsp ground cumin
salt and freshly ground black pepper

Place all the ingredients in a saucepan and mix well. Cover, bring to the boil, and simmer gently for 10 minutes, stirring occasionally. Remove the lid and cook for a further 5 minutes, until the vegetables are tender, stirring occasionally. Cut open the baked potatoes and spoon the tomato sauce over them. Serve with a mixed green side salad.

NUTRITIONAL ANALYSIS

(figures are per serving of Smoked Bacon, Egg, & Corn Baked Potatoes)

Calories = 515
Fat = 13.2g
of which saturates = 2.5g
    monounsaturates = 3.6g
    polyunsaturates = 1.3g

Protein = 22.1g
Carbohydrate = 82.2g
Dietary fiber = 6.5g
Sodium = 0.8g

Percentage of total calories from fat = 23%, of which saturates = 4%
Percentage of total calories from carbohydrate = 60%
of which sugars = 5%
Good source of vitamin C

HERBED POTATO
CAKES

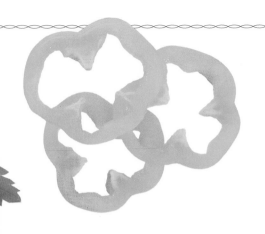

*A delicious accompaniment to broiled lean meat or fish,
these herbed potato cakes are simple to prepare and cook. The mixture
can also be made in advance and refrigerated until required.*

Preparation time: 30 minutes, plus cooling time

Cooking time: 10-15 minutes

Makes 8 potato cakes

8 medium potatoes
2 tbsp vegetable broth
4 leeks, trimmed and finely chopped
1 clove garlic, crushed
4 tbsp finely grated reduced-fat mature
Cheddar cheese
1 egg, beaten
1 tbsp chopped fresh parsley
1 tbsp chopped fresh chives
salt and freshly ground black pepper
1 tsp olive oil

1 Cook the potatoes in a saucepan
of lightly salted, boiling water for
about 20 minutes, until cooked and
tender. Drain and mash thoroughly.

2 Meanwhile, place the broth, leeks, and
garlic in a saucepan, cover and cook
gently for 10-15 minutes until tender,
stirring occasionally. Drain thoroughly.

3 Add the mashed potatoes, cheese, egg,
herbs, and seasoning and mix well. Set
aside to cool completely.

4 On a lightly floured surface, divide the
mixture into 8 portions and shape each
portion into a patty, and flatten slightly.

5 Heat the oil in a large nonstick skillet.
Fry the potato cakes until golden brown
on both sides, turning once.

6 Serve with broiled lean meat such as
chicken, steak, lamb, or pork and
seasonal fresh vegetables such as baby
carrots and green beans.

VARIATIONS
● Use sweet potatoes or a mixture of
sweet and white potatoes.
● Use 1 minced onion in place of the leeks.
● Use other reduced-fat hard cheese
such as Monterey jack.

NUTRITIONAL ANALYSIS

(figures are per potato cake)

Calories = 90
Fat = 2.4g
of which   saturates = 0.9g
    monounsaturates = 0.9g
    polyunsaturates = 0.3g

Protein = 5.0g
Carbohydrate = 12.6g
Dietary fiber = 1.5g
Sodium = 0.06g

Percentage of total calories from fat = 25%, of which saturates = 9%
Percentage of total calories from carbohydrate = 53%
of which sugars = 4%

LAMB & VEGETABLE CURRY

Preparation time: 25 minutes

Cooking time: 1 hour

Serves 4

2 tsp sunflower oil
12 ounces lean lamb fillet, cut into small dice
1 onion, sliced
2 cloves garlic, crushed
1 small red chili, seeded and finely chopped
1-inch piece fresh root ginger, peeled and minced
1 tbsp ground coriander (cilantro)
2 tsp ground cumin
1 tsp ground cinnamon
1 tsp ground turmeric
pinch of ground cloves (optional)
14-ounce can peeled, chopped tomatoes
1¹/₄ cups vegetable broth
1 pound small new potatoes, washed and dried
1 medium rutabaga, diced
2 leeks, trimmed and sliced
1 cup sliced mushrooms
2 medium carrots, sliced
salt and freshly ground black pepper
¹/₂ cup yellow raisins
2 tbsp chopped fresh coriander (cilantro)
fresh coriander (cilantro) sprigs, to garnish

1 Heat the oil in a large nonstick saucepan. Add the lamb and cook for 5 minutes, stirring occasionally. Remove from the pan using a slotted spoon and keep warm.

2 Add the onion, garlic, chili, and ginger to the pan and cook gently for 3 minutes, stirring. Add the spices and cook for 1 minute, stirring.

3 Add the lamb and all the remaining ingredients, except the yellow raisins and fresh coriander (cilantro), and mix well.

4 Cover, bring to the boil, and simmer for 45-60 minutes, until the lamb is cooked and tender,

NUTRITIONAL ANALYSIS

(figures are per serving)

Calories = 392
Fat = 10.8g
of which   saturates = 3.8g
    monounsaturates = 4.1g
    polyunsaturates = 1.4g

Protein = 24.9g
Carbohydrate = 53.4g
Dietary fiber = 7.1g
Sodium = 0.3g

Percentage of total calories from fat = 25%, of which saturates = 9%
Percentage of total calories from carbohydrate = 51%
of which sugars = 33%
Good source of vitamins A & C

stirring occasionally. Add the yellow raisins 10 minutes before the end of the cooking time.

5 Add the chopped fresh coriander (cilantro) and stir to mix. Garnish with fresh coriander (cilantro) sprigs and serve with warm crusty bread or pita pockets, or on a bed of boiled rice.

VARIATIONS
● Use lean beef or chicken in place of the lamb.
● Use parsnips, turnips, or jicama in place of the rutabaga.
● Use 2 cups skinned and chopped fresh tomatoes in place of the canned tomatoes.

 # BRAISED BEEF

& MUSHROOMS WITH NEW POTATOES & BASIL

Preparation time: 20 minutes

Cooking time: 2 ½ hours

Serves 4

12 ounces lean stewing or braising steak, diced
2 tbsp all-purpose flour, seasoned
2 tsp sunflower oil
4 cups pearl onions, peeled
1 clove garlic, crushed
2 carrots, sliced
1 ¼ cups button mushrooms
2 sticks celery, chopped
1 ¼ cups beef broth
⅔ cup red wine
1 tbsp tomato paste
salt and freshly ground black pepper
1 bouquet garni (thyme, bay leaf, and parsley tied in a bunch)
1 cup frozen lima beans
3 cups small new potatoes, washed
1 tbsp minced fresh basil
1 tbsp minced fresh parsley

1 Toss the beef in the seasoned flour. Heat the oil in a large nonstick saucepan, add the onions and garlic, and cook gently for 5 minutes, stirring occasionally.

2 Add the beef and flour, and cook gently for 5 minutes, stirring occasionally. Add the carrots, mushrooms, celery, broth, wine, tomato paste, seasoning, and bouquet garni, and mix well.

3 Bring to the boil, stirring, then cover and simmer gently for 2 hours, stirring occasionally.

4 Add the lima beans, bring back to the boil, and simmer gently for a further 30 minutes, until the beef is tender. Remove the bouquet garni.

5 Meanwhile, cook the potatoes in a saucepan of lightly salted, boiling water for 10-15 minutes, until cooked and tender. Drain thoroughly and toss with the fresh herbs.

6 Serve the braised beef with the boiled new potatoes and steamed seasonal fresh vegetables such as green beans and shredded cabbage.

VARIATION
● Use lean lamb in place of the beef.

NUTRITIONAL ANALYSIS

(figures are per serving)

Calories = 423
Fat = 7.7g
of which saturates = 2.5g
        monounsaturates = 3.1g
        polyunsaturates = 1.2g
Protein = 31.0g
Carbohydrate = 54.9g
Dietary fiber = 9.4g
Sodium = 0.2g

Percentage of total calories from fat = 16%
of which saturates = 5%
Percentage of total calories from carbohydrate = 49%
of which sugars = 13%

BEANS & LENTILS

*B*eans and lentils are the edible seeds of pod-bearing plants of the legume family, and are available in many varieties. Some, such as lima beans and peas, are eaten fresh, but many, such as chick-peas (garbanzo beans) and kidney beans, are used in dried or canned forms. Frozen beans are also widely available while other beans are fermented or processed to produce products such as flour, oil, or fresh and dried bean curd. Beans and lentils are naturally low in fat and high in carbohydrates, protein, and fiber, and contain a variety of essential vitamins and minerals.
Because generally they do not have a strong taste of their own, beans and lentils are ideal for mixing with more strongly flavored, richer foods. Once they have been cooked, they keep well in the refrigerator and also reheat well. Canned beans and lentils are ready to eat, so they may be added to cooked dishes such as chili con carne, or served cold in dishes such as salads.

CORN & PEA
SOUP

*This nutritious soup makes an excellent appetizer
for a meal or a quick snack.*

Preparation time: 20 minutes
Cooking time: 30 minutes
Serves 4

2 tsp sunflower oil
1 onion, minced
2 sticks celery, finely chopped
1 pound shelled fresh or frozen peas
1 bunch watercress, washed and chopped
3 cups vegetable broth
¹/₂ tsp sugar
salt and freshly ground black pepper
1 cup canned corn kernels

1 Heat the oil in a large saucepan. Add the onion and celery, and cook gently for 5 minutes, stirring occasionally.

2 Add the peas, watercress, broth, sugar, and seasoning and mix well. Cover, bring to the boil, and simmer gently for 25-30 minutes, until the vegetables are tender, stirring occasionally.

3 Remove the pan from the heat and allow to cool slightly. Place the mixture in a blender or food processor and blend until smooth.

4 Return the mixture to the saucepan and add the corn. Reheat the soup until piping hot, stirring, then serve with some warm, freshly baked bread.

VARIATIONS
● Use lima beans in place of the peas.
● Use 1 red onion or 4 leeks, trimmed and finely chopped, in place of the onion.
● Use half milk and half broth.

ROASTED PEPPER
& BROWN LENTIL DIP

*This delicious dip can also be served as a pâté
with fresh crusty bread or toast.*

Preparation time: 30 minutes

Cooking time: 10 minutes

Serves 6

1 cup brown lentils
vegetable broth
1 bay leaf
2 large mild sweet red peppers (such as chipotle)
1 onion, minced
1 clove garlic, crushed
³/₄ cup mushrooms, minced
*6 tbsp reduced-fat mature Cheddar cheese, finely
grated*
2 tbsp chopped fresh coriander (cilantro)
salt and freshly ground black pepper
2 tbsp low-fat plain yogurt (optional)
fresh herb sprigs, to garnish

1 Place the lentils in a saucepan and cover with plenty of vegetable broth. Add the bay leaf and stir to mix. Cover, bring to the boil, then simmer gently for 30-40 minutes, until the lentils are tender, stirring occasionally. Drain thoroughly and discard the bay leaf.

2 Meanwhile, broil the peppers until they are charred and blistered all over.

3 Remove from the heat, cover with a clean, damp cloth, allow to cool slightly, then peel off the skins. Core, seed, and dice the flesh.

4 Put the onion, garlic, mushrooms, and peppers in a saucepan with 2 tbsp broth. Cover and cook gently for 10 minutes, until the vegetables are tender, stirring occasionally.

5 Add the cooked lentils, cheese, coriander (cilantro), and seasoning, and mix well. Place the mixture in a blender or food processor and blend until smooth.

6 Transfer to a serving dish and allow to cool. Once cool, stir in the yogurt, if using. Cover and chill in the refrigerator before serving.

7 Garnish with herbs and serve with sliced vegetables and breadsticks (grissini).

NUTRITIONAL ANALYSIS

(figures are per serving)

Calories = 186
Fat = 3.8g
of which saturates = 0.6g
    monounsaturates = 1.3g
    polyunsaturates = 1.1g
Protein = 9.6g
Carbohydrate = 30.0g
Dietary fiber = 7.4g
Sodium = 0.6g

Percentage of total calories from fat = 19%
of which saturates = 3%
Percentage of total calories from
carbohydrate = 61%, of which sugars = 23%

NUTRITIONAL ANALYSIS

(figures are per serving)

Calories = 183
Fat = 3.4g
of which saturates = 1.5g
    monounsaturates = 0.7g
    polyunsaturates = 0.6g

Protein = 15.2g
Carbohydrate = 24.5g
Dietary fiber = 4.8g
Sodium = 0.3g

Percentage of total calories from fat = 17%, of which saturates = 7%
Percentage of total calories from carbohydrate = 50%, of which sugars = 12%
Good source of vitamin C

SWEET-&-SOUR
MIXED-BEAN SALAD

Preparation time: 20 minutes

Cooking time: 10 minutes

Serves 4

1³/₄ cups green beans, trimmed and halved
1 small red onion, sliced
1 small red bell pepper, seeded and diced
1 small yellow bell pepper, seeded and diced
¹/₂ cup raisins
7-ounce can corn kernels, drained
14-ounce can red kidney beans, rinsed and drained
14-ounce can chick-peas (garbanzo beans), rinsed and drained
2-3 tbsp minced fresh parsley

FOR THE DRESSING
3 tbsp olive oil
3 tbsp unsweetened apple juice
2 tbsp red wine vinegar
2 tbsp clear honey
2 tbsp light soy sauce
2 tbsp tomato ketchup
2 tbsp medium sherry
1 clove garlic, crushed
1 tsp ground ginger
salt and freshly ground black pepper

1 Steam the green beans over a pan of simmering water for about 10 minutes, until just tender. Drain and rinse under cold water to cool them. Drain well.

2 Place the cooled green beans, onion, bell peppers, raisins, corn, kidney beans, chick-peas (garbanzo beans), and parsley in a large bowl and mix together.

3 Place all the dressing ingredients in a small bowl and whisk together until thoroughly mixed. Pour over the mixed beans and toss together to mix.

4 Serve the mixed-bean salad with crusty French bread or toasted pita pockets.

VARIATIONS
● Use your own selection of canned beans.
● Use chopped fresh mixed herbs in place of the parsley.

● When making the dressing, place all the ingredients in a clean screw-top jar. Screw the top on the jar and shake well until the ingredients are thoroughly mixed.

NUTRITIONAL ANALYSIS

(figures are per serving)

Calories = 444
Fat = 11.7g
of which saturates = 1.6g
    monounsaturates = 6.5g
    polyunsaturates = 2.4g
Protein = 13.5g
Carbohydrate = 74.1g
Dietary fiber = 11.0g
Sodium = 1.2g

Percentage of total calories from fat = 24%
of which saturates = 3%
Percentage of total calories from
carbohydrate = 63%
of which sugars = 38%
Good source of fiber
& vitamin C

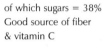

RED BEAN

& THREE-MUSHROOM SALAD

A colorful combination of beans and mushrooms tossed together in a light dressing, this recipe is ideal as an entrée salad served with warm bread or as a nutritious packed lunch.

Preparation time: 20 minutes

Serves 4 as an entrée

*two 14-ounce cans red kidney beans,
rinsed and drained
2 bunches green onions (scallions), chopped
1 bunch radishes, sliced
1/2 cup yellow raisins
3/4 cup brown cap or chestnut mushrooms, sliced
3/4 cup button mushrooms, halved
1 cup oyster mushrooms
3 tbsp olive oil
3 tbsp cider vinegar
1 tbsp whole-grain mustard
1 clove garlic, crushed
1 tbsp minced fresh parsley
1 tbsp minced chives
salt and freshly ground black pepper*

1 Place the kidney beans, green onions (scallions), radishes, yellow raisins, and mushrooms in a bowl and stir to mix.

2 Place the oil, vinegar, mustard, garlic, herbs, and seasoning in a small bowl and whisk together until thoroughly mixed.

3 Drizzle the dressing over the bean and mushroom salad, and toss together to mix. Serve with warm freshly baked bread.

VARIATIONS
● Use raisins or chopped, pitted dried apricots in place of the yellow raisins.
● Use 1 minced red onion in place of the green onions (scallions).

NUTRITIONAL ANALYSIS

(figures are per serving)

Calories = 304
Fat = 10.1g
of which saturates = 1.4g
    monounsaturates = 6.2g
    polyunsaturates = 1.7g

Protein = 12.0g
Carbohydrate = 43.9g
Dietary fiber = 9.7g
Sodium = 0.6g

Percentage of total calories from fat = 30%, of which saturates = 4%
Percentage of total calories from carbohydrate = 54%
of which sugars = 33%

SMOKED TOFU & VEGETABLE
KABOBS

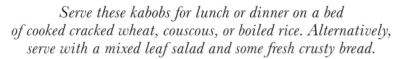

*Serve these kabobs for lunch or dinner on a bed
of cooked cracked wheat, couscous, or boiled rice. Alternatively,
serve with a mixed leaf salad and some fresh crusty bread.*

Preparation time: 25 minutes

Cooking time: 10-15 minutes

Makes 8 kabobs

FOR THE TOMATO SAUCE
1 cup canned peeled, chopped tomatoes
²/₃ cup tomato juice
1 tbsp tomato paste
1 clove garlic, crushed
2 shallots, minced
salt and freshly ground black pepper
1 tbsp chopped fresh basil

FOR THE KABOBS
³/₄ cup smoked tofu, cut into 8 cubes
1 red bell pepper, seeded and cut into 8 pieces
*1 small yellow bell pepper, seeded
and cut into 8 pieces*
2 small zucchini, each cut into 6 slices
8 cherry tomatoes
8 button mushrooms
8 pearl or button onions, peeled
8 boiled small potatoes
1 tbsp olive oil
1 tbsp lemon juice
1 tsp dried mixed herbs
salt and freshly ground black pepper
fresh basil sprigs, to garnish

1 To make the tomato sauce, place all
the ingredients, except the basil, in a
saucepan and stir to mix. Bring to the
boil and simmer gently, uncovered, for
about 15 minutes, stirring occasionally.
Add the basil and mix well. This sauce
may be served hot or cold and it can
be puréed in a liquidizer before serving,
if preferred.

2 To make the kabobs, thread the tofu
and vegetables onto 8 skewers, dividing
the ingredients equally.

3 Mix together the oil, lemon juice,
herbs, and seasoning, and brush the
mixture over the kabobs.

4 Broil the kabobs over a barbecue or
under a preheated broiler for about
10-15 minutes, until the tofu and
vegetables are cooked to your liking,
turning frequently. Brush the kabobs
with any remaining oil mixture while
they are cooking, to prevent them
from drying out.

5 Garnish with fresh basil sprigs and
serve with the tomato sauce.

VARIATIONS
● Use other flavored tofu such as
original or marinated in place of the
smoked tofu.
● Use your own selection of vegetables
and use cubes of lean meat such as
chicken or beef in place of the tofu.

NUTRITIONAL ANALYSIS
(figures are per serving)

Calories = 165
Fat = 5.5g
of which saturates = 0.8g
    monounsaturates = 2.4g
    polyunsaturates = 1.5g

Protein = 8.0g
Carbohydrate = 22.3g
Dietary fiber = 4.3g
Sodium = 0.01g

Percentage of total calories from fat = 30%, of which saturates = 4%
Percentage of total calories from carbohydrate = 51%, of which sugars = 27%
Good source of vitamin C

BEEF & BEAN
BURGERS

*The delicious combination of ground beef, beans, and spices ensures that
these extra-large burgers are a popular choice for brunch, lunch, or dinner.*

Preparation time: 25 minutes

Cooking time: 10-15 minutes

Serves 4 (makes 4 large burgers)

*9 ounces extra-lean ground beef
1 onion, minced
1 clove garlic, crushed
14-ounce can red kidney beans, rinsed, drained,
and mashed
4 tbsp wheatgerm
2 small carrots, coarsely shredded
1 egg, beaten
1 tsp ground cumin
1 tsp ground coriander (cilantro)
1 tsp chili powder
3 tbsp minced parsley
salt and freshly ground black pepper
1 tbsp sunflower oil
4 large whole-wheat or white hamburger rolls,
tomato slices and shredded lettuce, to serve*

1 Place the ground beef, onion, garlic,
kidney beans, wheatgerm, carrots, egg,
spices, parsley, and seasoning in a bowl and
mix thoroughly. On a lightly floured
surface, shape the mixture into 4 large
round patties and flatten them slightly.

2 Heat the oil in a good quality nonstick
skillet and cook the burgers for about 10-
15 minutes, turning once, until browned
on the outside and cooked to your liking.

3 Serve each burger in a hamburger
roll and top with tomato slices and
shredded lettuce. Serve with homemade
low-calorie coleslaw.

*These burgers are suitable for freezing before
they have been cooked.*

VARIATIONS

● The hamburgers can be brushed lightly
with oil and broiled instead of fried.
● Use the mixture to make 6 or 8
smaller burgers, if you prefer.
● Use other lean ground meats such as
pork, lamb, or turkey in place of the beef.
● Use 2 small leeks (trimmed weight),
minced, in place of the onion.
● Use other canned beans such as black-
eyed peas or chick-peas (garbanzo
beans) in place of the kidney beans.

NUTRITIONAL ANALYSIS

(figures are per burger including roll & salad)

Calories = 543
Fat = 14.3g
of which saturates = 4.2g
          monounsaturates = 5.8g
          polyunsaturates = 2.2g

Protein = 33.2g
Carbohydrate = 75.6g
Dietary fiber = 9.2g
Sodium = 0.8g

Percentage of total calories from fat = 24%, of which saturates = 7%
Percentage of total calories from carbohydrate = 52%, of which sugars = 8%
Good source of B vitamins & vitamin E

VEGETARIAN
CHILI

An appetizing and colorful meat-free dish, which is ideal served on its own or with boiled rice for lunch or a main meal.

Preparation time: 20 minutes

Cooking time: 50 minutes

Serves 4

1 tsp olive oil
1 onion, sliced
2 cloves garlic, crushed
3 leeks, sliced
1 tbsp all-purpose flour
1 1/4 cups vegetable broth
4 sticks celery, chopped
1 red bell pepper, seeded and diced
1 yellow bell pepper, seeded and diced
1 cup thinly sliced carrots
14-ounce can peeled, chopped tomatoes
2 tbsp tomato paste
1 tsp hot chili powder
1 tsp ground cumin
1/2 tsp sugar
salt and freshly ground black pepper
14-ounce can red kidney beans, rinsed and drained
14-ounce can chick-peas (garbanzo beans), rinsed and drained
minced fresh parsley, to garnish

1 Heat the oil in a large saucepan. Add the onion, garlic, and leeks and cook gently for 5 minutes, stirring occasionally. Add the flour and cook gently for 1 minute, stirring.

2 Gradually add the broth, stirring, then add all the remaining ingredients except the kidney beans, chick-peas (garbanzo beans), and parsley, and mix well.

3 Bring to the boil, stirring, then cover and simmer for about 30 minutes, until the vegetables are tender, stirring occasionally.

4 Add the beans and chick-peas (garbanzo beans), and stir to mix. Return to the boil and simmer, uncovered, for a further 10 minutes, stirring occasionally.

5 Garnish with chopped parsley and serve on a bed of boiled mixed brown and wild rice.

VARIATIONS
● Use other vegetables of your choice such as mushrooms, parsnips, corn, or succotash.
● Use other canned beans such as black-eyed peas and lima beans in place of the kidney beans and chick-peas (garbanzo beans).
● Use other spices such as curry powder in place of the chili powder.

NUTRITIONAL ANALYSIS
(figures are per serving)

Calories = 256
Fat = 4.3g
of which saturates = 0.5g
        monounsaturates = 1.1g
        polyunsaturates = 1.6g
Protein = 13.8g
Carbohydrate = 43.6g
Dietary fiber = 12.3g
Sodium = 0.6g

Percentage of total calories from fat = 15%
of which saturates = 2%
Percentage of total calories from carbohydrate = 64%
of which sugars = 28%
Good source of fiber & vitamins A, C, & E

LAMB & LENTIL
CASEROLE

This is a filling and nutritious casserole — ideal for warming up those cold winter evenings. Serve it with warmed pita or Armenian bread (lavash) or on a bed of cooked rice or cracked wheat.

Preparation time: 15 minutes

Cooking time: 1 hour

Serves 6

8 ounces lean lamb fillet,
cut into small cubes
2 tbsp all-purpose flour, seasoned
1 tsp olive oil
1 onion, sliced
1 clove garlic, crushed
3³/₄ cups beef or vegetable broth
1 cup whole brown or green lentils
1 cup sliced carrots
1¹/₄ cups button mushrooms
8 ounces baby new potatoes, washed
2 sticks celery, chopped
¹/₂ cup peeled, diced rutabaga
¹/₂ cup peeled, diced parsnip
14-ounce can peeled, chopped tomatoes
2 tsp mixed dried herbs
salt and freshly ground black pepper
fresh herb sprigs, to garnish

1 Toss the lamb in the flour. Heat the oil in a large nonstick saucepan and add the lamb, onion, and garlic. Cook for 5 minutes, stirring. Add the remaining flour and cook for 1 minute, stirring.

2 Gradually add the broth, stirring, then add all the remaining ingredients, except the fresh herb sprigs, and mix.

3 Bring to the boil, stirring, then cover and simmer for about 50 minutes, until the lamb, lentils, and vegetables are tender, stirring occasionally.

4 Garnish with fresh herb sprigs and serve with warmed pita or Armenian bread and a chef's salad.

VARIATIONS

● Use other lean meats such as beef, pork, or chicken in place of the lamb.
● Use 1 cup trimmed, sliced leeks in place of the onion.
● Use turnip in place of the rutabaga, and sweet potato or yam, cut in pieces, in place of the new potatoes.

NUTRITIONAL ANALYSIS

(figures are per serving)

Calories = 273
Fat = 5.4g
of which saturates = 1.7g
      monounsaturates = 1.8g
      polyunsaturates = 0.9g

Protein = 20.5g
Carbohydrate = 38.8g
Dietary fiber = 7.4g
Sodium = 0.4g

Percentage of total calories from fat = 18%, of which saturates = 6%
Percentage of total calories from carbohydrate = 53%, of which sugars = 13%
Good source of B vitamins

PORK & LIMA BEAN BAKE

Serve this layered pork-and-bean bake as a substantial midday or evening meal with some steamed fresh vegetables.

Preparation time: 35 minutes

Cooking time: 1 hour

Serves 6

1 pound potatoes, peeled and thinly sliced
1 tsp sunflower oil
1¼ cups lean ground pork
1 large onion, sliced
1 clove garlic, crushed
1 red chili, seeded and finely chopped
2 tbsp all-purpose flour
2 cups chicken or vegetable broth
14-ounce can peeled, chopped tomatoes
1 green bell pepper, seeded and diced
4 celery sticks, chopped
1 cup carrots, thinly sliced
2 leeks, sliced
2 cups canned lima beans, rinsed and drained
14-ounce can pinto beans, rinsed and drained
1 tbsp whole-grain mustard
2 tsp dried sage
2 tsp dried thyme
salt and freshly ground black pepper

1 Parboil the potatoes in a saucepan of lightly salted, boiling water for about 4 minutes. Drain thoroughly and set aside.

2 Heat the oil in a large nonstick saucepan, add the pork, onion, garlic, and chili, and cook for 5 minutes, stirring occasionally. Add the flour and cook for 1 minute, stirring.

3 Gradually add the broth and tomatoes and bring to the boil, stirring. Add all the remaining ingredients and mix together thoroughly.

4 Place half the pork mixture in a lightly greased ovenproof casserole dish and top with an even layer of half the potato slices. Spoon the remaining pork mixture over the potatoes and top with the remaining potato slices to cover the pork completely.

5 Cover with foil and bake in a preheated oven at 400° for 40 minutes. Remove the foil and cook for a further 20 minutes, until the potatoes are lightly browned.

NUTRITIONAL ANALYSIS

(figures are per serving)

Calories = 268
Fat = 4.0g
of which saturates = 0.9g
monounsaturates = 1.3g
polyunsaturates = 1.1g
Protein = 20.3g
Carbohydrate = 40.0g
Dietary fiber = 9.1g
Sodium = 0.6g

Percentage of total calories from fat = 14%
of which saturates = 3%
Percentage of total calories from
carbohydrate = 56%, of which sugars = 16%
Good source of B vitamins & vitamins A & C

CHICKEN MEDLEY

A delicious combination of chicken, fresh vegetables, and beans in a light cheese sauce, topped with crispy potatoes — a family favorite every time.

Preparation time: 35 minutes

Cooking time: 30-45 minutes

Serves 6

2 pounds potatoes, peeled and cut into chunks
2-3 tbsp skim milk
salt and freshly ground black pepper
3 tbsp low-fat spread
3 tbsp all-purpose flour
2 cups low-fat or 2% milk
2 cups chicken broth, cooled
½ cup finely grated, reduced-fat Cheddar cheese
1 cup diced cooked, skinless chicken breast
1 onion, minced and blanched
1 clove garlic, crushed
1¼ cups mushrooms, sliced
1 cup green beans, halved and blanched
¾ cup frozen baby lima beans
14-ounce can red kidney beans, rinsed and drained
14-ounce can black-eyed peas, rinsed and drained
¾ cup canned corn kernels, drained
2-3 tbsp chopped fresh mixed herbs or 2-3 tsp dried mixed herbs
fresh parsley sprigs, to garnish

1 Cook the potatoes in a saucepan of lightly salted, boiling water for 15-20 minutes, until cooked and tender. Drain thoroughly, then mash, and mix with the skim milk and seasoning. Set aside.

2 Meanwhile, place the low-fat spread, flour, milk, and broth in a saucepan and heat gently, whisking continuously, until the sauce comes to the boil and thickens. Simmer gently for

3 minutes, stirring. Remove the pan from the heat.

3 Add the cheese and stir until melted. Add all the remaining ingredients, except the parsley sprigs, adjust the seasoning, and mix well.

4 Spoon the chicken mixture into an ovenproof casserole dish and cover with the creamed potato topping. Make grooves in the top with the tines of a fork.

5 Bake in a preheated oven at 375° for 30-45 minutes, until the potato topping is crisp and browned.

6 Garnish with fresh parsley sprigs and serve with steamed fresh seasonal vegetables such as broccoli flowerets and broiled tomatoes.

VARIATIONS

● Use cooked turkey or lean smoked ham in place of the chicken.
● Use garden peas in place of the fava beans.
● Use chick-peas (garbanzo beans) in place of the black-eyed peas.

NUTRITIONAL ANALYSIS
(figures are per serving)

Calories = 473
Fat = 10.1g
of which saturates = 3.9g
monounsaturates = 2.0g
polyunsaturates = 1.9g
Protein = 35.0g
Carbohydrate = 64.6g
Dietary fiber = 9.3g
Sodium = 0.6g

Percentage of total calories from fat = 19%
of which saturates = 8%
Percentage of total calories from carbohydrate = 51%, of which sugars = 10%
Good source of calcium & B vitamins

FRUIT & VEGETABLES

*F*ruit and vegetables are available in many shapes, sizes, colors, and textures.
The range to choose from is vast and most varieties, including exotic items, are
available to be eaten and enjoyed all year round.
Fruit and vegetables are usually served as part of a meal.
They are low in fat and are packed full of a whole range of vitamins and minerals,
such as vitamins A, C, and E, as well as iron and dietary fiber.
Many, such as citrus fruit, salad vegetables, and green vegetables, have a low energy value
and are therefore low in calories and fat. Others, such as dried fruit, root vegetables, peas,
and corn, have a slightly higher energy value, mainly from carbohydrates, which means they
contain slightly more calories, but are still low in fat.
Besides eating them raw, most fruit and vegetables can be cooked in a variety of ways,

CRUNCHY MIXED VEGETABLE
STIR-FRY

*A colorful combination of vegetables quickly stir-fried so that
they remain crunchy, this dish can be served on its own,
or with boiled egg noodles or rice.*

Preparation time: 20 minutes

Cooking time: 15 minutes

Serves 4

1 tsp cornstarch
2 tbsp soy sauce
2 tbsp dry sherry
1 tbsp tomato ketchup
salt and freshly ground black pepper
2 tsp sesame oil
1 clove garlic, crushed
2 leeks trimmed and thinly sliced
1 red bell pepper, seeded and sliced
2 carrots, cut into matchstick strips
2 zucchini, cut into matchstick strips
¹/₂ cup bean sprouts
¹/₂ cup shredded collard greens
¹/₂ cup snow-peas, trimmed

1 Blend the cornstarch with the soy
sauce, sherry, tomato ketchup, and
seasoning. Set aside.

2 Heat the oil in a large nonstick skillet
or wok. Add the garlic, leeks, bell pepper,
carrots, and zucchini and stir-fry over a
high heat for 3-4 minutes.

3 Add the bean sprouts, collard greens,
and snow-peas and stir-fry for 1-2 minutes.

4 Add the cornstarch mixture and stir-fry
for 1-2 minutes. Serve immediately.

VARIATION
● Use a mixture of vegetables of your
choice such as mushrooms, green
peppers, baby corn, onion, cabbage, or
Chinese (Napa) cabbage, and broccoli.

OVEN-ROASTED ROOT
VEGETABLES

Root vegetables, lightly tossed in flavored oil and oven-roasted until tender and crisp, make an ideal accompaniment to broiled fish or lean meat. Alternatively, they can be served on their own as a lunch or dinnertime snack.

Preparation time: 15 minutes

Cooking time: 1 hour

Serves 4

1¹/₂ cups sweet potatoes,
peeled and cut into chunks
1¹/₂ cups potatoes, peeled and cut into chunks
1 cup parsnips, peeled and cut into chunks
1 cup rutabaga, peeled and cut into chunks
1 cup celery root, peeled and cut into chunks
3 tbsp olive oil
1 clove garlic, crushed
2 tsp chopped fresh rosemary
salt and freshly ground black pepper
fresh rosemary sprigs, to garnish

1 Parboil all the vegetables in a large saucepan of lightly salted, boiling water for 3 minutes, then drain thoroughly.

2 In a large bowl, mix together the oil, garlic, rosemary, and seasoning. Toss the vegetables in the oil to coat them lightly all over.

3 Place the vegetables in a roasting pan. Bake in a preheated oven at 425° for 45-60 minutes, until the vegetables are crisp and tender, turning over occasionally.

4 Garnish with fresh rosemary sprigs and serve with broiled fish such as sole or salmon and steamed seasonal fresh vegetables such as garden peas and baby carrots.

VARIATIONS
● Use turnip in place of the rutabaga.
● Use carrots in place of the parsnips.
● Use other herbs such as mixed herbs or thyme in place of the rosemary.
● Use flavored oil such as chili oil or herb oil in place of the olive oil.

NUTRITIONAL ANALYSIS

(figures are per serving)

Calories = 114
Fat = 2.8g
of which saturates = 0.5g
monounsaturates = 0.6g
polyunsaturates = 1.3g
Protein = 5.5g
Carbohydrate = 15.6g
Dietary fiber = 5.6g
Sodium = 0.6g

Percentage of total calories from fat = 22%
of which saturates = 4%
Percentage of total calories from
carbohydrate = 51%
of which sugars = 42%
Good source of vitamins A & C

NUTRITIONAL ANALYSIS

(figures are per serving)

Calories = 279
Fat = 9.9g
of which saturates = 1.5g
monounsaturates = 6.3g
polyunsaturates = 1.2g

Protein = 5.0g
Carbohydrate = 45.0g
Dietary fiber = 6.9g
Sodium = 0.09g

Percentage of total calories from fat = 32%, of which saturates = 5%
Percentage of total calories from carbohydrate = 60%, of which sugars = 21%
Good source of vitamin C

183

STEAMED CHOCOLATE & CHERRY
PUDDING

A wickedly tempting, light chocolate sponge pudding, topped with a layer of succulent cherries and served with a light chocolate sauce.

Preparation time: 25 minutes

Cooking time: 1¹/₂ hours

FOR THE CHOCOLATE PUDDING
14-ounce can pitted cherries in syrup
3 tbsp cocoa powder, sifted
¹/₂ cup soft margarine
¹/₂ cup sugar
2 eggs, beaten
1¹/₂ cups self-rising flour, sifted
¹/₂ cup raisins
skim milk, to mix

FOR THE CHOCOLATE SAUCE
5 tsp cornstarch
1 tbsp cocoa powder
300 ml (¹/₂ pint) low-fat or 2% milk
2 tbsp sugar

1 To make the pudding, drain the cherries, reserving 2 tbsp juice. Place the cherries and the reserved juice in a lightly greased 2¹/₂-pint heatproof bowl. Set aside.

2 In a mixing bowl, blend the cocoa powder with 3 tbsp hot water. Set aside.

3 Cream the fat and sugar together until pale and fluffy. Add the cocoa mixture and mix well. Gradually add the eggs, beating well after each addition.

4 Fold in half the flour, then fold in the remaining flour with the raisins and enough milk to make a soft dropping consistency.

5 Spoon the chocolate mixture over the cherries and level the surface. Cover with a double layer of greased parchment paper or nonstick baking paper, folded to fit securely over the top of the heatproof bowl, and secure

6 Place the bowl in the top half of a steamer over a saucepan of boiling water. Cover with the lid and steam for about 1¹/₂ hours, until the pudding is risen and cooked, topping up the boiling water regularly.

7 Meanwhile, make the chocolate sauce to accompany the pudding. Place the cornstarch and cocoa powder in a saucepan and blend with 3 tbsp milk, to form a smooth paste. Gradually blend in the remaining milk.

8 Heat gently, whisking continuously, until the sauce comes to the boil and thickens. Simmer gently for 2 minutes, stirring. Add the sugar to taste and stir well.

9 Turn the pudding out on a serving plate and serve immediately with the chocolate sauce.

VARIATIONS
● Use yellow raisins or chopped ready-to-eat dried apricots in place of the raisins.
● Use other canned fruits such as peaches or apricots in place of the cherries.
● Serve the pudding with low-fat topping or sauce, or reduced-fat cream, in place of the chocolate sauce.

NUTRITIONAL ANALYSIS

(figures are per serving   serving 6)

Calories = 524
Fat = 20.4g
of which saturates = 5.1g
      monounsaturates = 5.6g
      polyunsaturates = 8.3g
Protein = 8.7g
Carbohydrate = 81.4g
Dietary fiber = 2.5g
Sodium = 0.4g
Percentage of total calories from fat = 35%
of which saturates = 9%
Percentage of total calories from
carbohydrate = 58%
of which sugars = 41%

CARROT & RAISIN
CAKE

*A delicious moist cake, ideal for slicing and packing up
for a mid-morning snack or an afternoon treat.*

Preparation time: 20 minutes
Cooking time: 1-1½ hours
Serves 12

FOR THE CAKE
³/₄ cup low-fat spread
1 cup light soft brown sugar
3 eggs
³/₄ cup all-purpose flour, sifted
³/₄ cup whole-wheat flour, sifted
1 tsp double-acting baking powder
1 tsp baking soda
1 tsp ground mixed spice
1 cup coarsely grated carrots
³/₄ cup yellow raisins
skim milk, to mix

FOR THE FROSTING
1 cup confectioner's (powdered) sugar
1 tsp finely grated lemon rind
1-2 tbsp freshly squeezed lemon juice
pared lemon rind, to decorate

1 Place the low-fat spread, brown sugar, eggs, flours, baking powder, baking soda, and spice in a bowl and beat together until thoroughly mixed.

2 Add the carrots and beat until well mixed. Fold in the yellow raisins and enough milk to make a soft dropping consistency.

3 Turn the mixture into a lightly greased, deep 7-inch round cake pan and level the surface.

4 Bake in a preheated oven at 350° for 1-1½ hours, until firm to the touch and lightly browned.

5 Allow to cool slightly in the pan, then turn out onto a wire rack to cool completely.

6 To make the frosting, sift the sugar into a bowl. Add the lemon rind and gradually add some lemon juice, mixing

well — the frosting should be thick enough to coat the back of a spoon.

7 Spread the frosting over the top of the cold cake and decorate with pared lemon rind. Serve in slices.

VARIATIONS
● Use other dried fruits such as chopped, ready-to-eat dried apricots, pears, or peaches in place of the yellow raisins.
● Use white sugar in place of the light soft brown sugar.
● Omit the spice, if preferred.

NUTRITIONAL ANALYSIS

(figures are per slice)

Calories = 261
Fat = 7.7g
of which saturates = 2.0g
      monounsaturates = 0.7g
      polyunsaturates = 1.9g
Protein = 4.8g
Carbohydrate = 46.5g
Dietary fiber = 1.6g
Sodium = 0.06g

Percentage of total calories from fat = 27%
of which saturates = 7%
Percentage of total calories from
carbohydrate = 67%
of which sugars = 53%

SPICY FRUIT
COMPOTE

Serve this dish of dried fruit steeped in a fruity sauce flavored with a hint of spice for breakfast, or as a brunch or dessert.

Preparation time: 10 minutes
Serves 4

²/₃ *cup unsweetened orange juice*
²/₃ *cup unsweetened apple juice*
²/₃ *cup dry white wine*
1 tsp ground mixed spice
1¹/₂ cups mixed dried fruits, such as apple rings, peaches, prunes, pears, and apricots
2 tbsp toasted flaked almonds, to decorate

1 In a bowl, mix together the orange juice, apple juice, white wine, and mixed spice.

2 Add the dried fruit and mix well. Cover, chill, and leave to soak in the refrigerator overnight, stirring a couple of times.

3 Serve the fruit compote either chilled or at room temperature, decorated with toasted almonds. Serve on its own or with low-fat ice cream or reduced-fat cream.

VARIATIONS
● The fruit juices, wine, and spice may be heated until boiling and poured over the fruit while hot. The fruit can then be cooled and chilled as above, before serving, or alternatively the compote may be served warm.
● Use a selection of fresh fruits such as peaches, apricots, dates, and oranges, in place of the dried fruits.
● Use other mixtures of fruit juices and wine, such as pineapple juice, grapefruit juice, and rosé wine.

NUTRITIONAL ANALYSIS
(figures are per serving)

Calories = 255
Fat = 4.0g
of which saturates = 0.3g
      monounsaturates = 2.2g
      polyunsaturates = 1.0g

Protein = 3.9g
Carbohydrate = 48.0g
Dietary fiber = 7.1g
Sodium = 0.02g

Percentage of total calories from fat = 14%
of which saturates = 1%
Percentage of total calories from carbohydrate = 71%
of which sugars = 70%
Good source of vitamin C

QUICK IDEAS FOR FRUIT COMPOTES

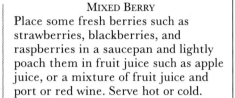

PEACH & PEAR
Mix together some canned or fresh sliced peaches and pears with fruit juices such as apple and orange juice. Add 1 tsp ground mixed spice or nutmeg to taste, and serve warm or cold.

MIXED BERRY
Place some fresh berries such as strawberries, blackberries, and raspberries in a saucepan and lightly poach them in fruit juice such as apple juice, or a mixture of fruit juice and port or red wine. Serve hot or cold.

APRICOT & GRAPE
Slice some fresh or canned apricots and place them in a bowl with some halved red and green seedless grapes. Mix together some pineapple or orange juice, add some light dry or rosé wine (optional), and pour over the fruit. Leave to stand at room temperature or chill for an hour or so before serving.

NUTRITIONAL ANALYSIS

(figures are per serving)

Calories = 234
Fat = 5.3g
of which saturates = 1.5g
  monounsaturates = 2.5g
  polyunsaturates = 0.4g
Protein = 6.2g
Carbohydrate = 42.4g
Dietary fiber = 3.2g
Sodium = 0.04g

Percentage of total calories from fat = 20%
of which saturates = 6%
Percentage of total calories from carbohydrate = 68%
of which sugars = 60%

BANANA APRICOT FOOL

This dessert made with puréed fruit is quick and easy to make and full of flavor. Serve it on its own, or with some fresh fruit or vanilla wafers.

Preparation time: 15 minutes
Cooking time: 10 minutes
Serves 6

1 cup ready-to-eat dried apricots
2 tbsp sugar
juice of 1 large orange
3 medium bananas
1 package low-fat vanilla dessert, made according to package instructions
²/₃ cup low-fat yogurt
2 tbsp toasted chopped hazelnuts, to decorate

1 Place the apricots, sugar, and orange juice in a saucepan. Cover, bring to the boil, and simmer gently for 10 minutes, stirring occasionally. Remove the pan from the heat and set aside to cool completely.

2 Peel and slice the bananas. Place the bananas and cooled apricot mixture in a blender or food processor and blend until smooth. Add the vanilla dessert and low-fat yogurt and blend until well mixed.

3 Transfer to a serving dish, cover, and chill until ready to serve.

4 Decorate with the hazelnuts and serve with some fresh fruit or wafer biscuits.

VARIATIONS
● Use other dried fruits such as prunes, pears, or peaches in place of the apricots.
● Add 1 tsp ground mixed spice or ginger to the apricots, if liked.
● Use reduced-fat sour cream or sour cream substitute in place of the yogurt.

INDEX

Apple & Cinnamon Coffeecake 24
Apple Pudding 67
Apricot & Cinnamon Raisin Squares 65
Apricot & Date Breakfast Loaf 25
Apricot & Grape Compote 187
Avocado & Shrimp Cocktail 31

Baked Bananas with Lime Cream 128
Baked Cod with Watercress Sauce 42
Banana Apricot Fool 187
Beef & Bean Burgers 177
Beef & Mushroom Phyllo Parcels 92
Beef & Vegetable Kabobs 49
Beets & Greens with Coriander
    Sauce 89
Bell Pepper, Tomato, & Spinach
    Pasta Salad 157
Braided Cheese & Poppyseed
    Bread 134
Braised Beef & Mushrooms with New
    Potatoes & Basil 171
Braised Spring Vegetables 88
Bran Fruit Cereal 21
Breakfast Bulgur Wheat with Dried
    Fruit 112
Broiled Calamari with Tomato &
    Lentil Salsa 107
Broiled Fruit Kabobs 20
Broiled Peppered Pineapple 129
Broiled Poussins 99
Bulgur Wheat, Mushroom, &
    Garlic Salad 158
Buttermilk & Red Fruit Soup 122
Buttermilk Pancakes 113

Caper Sauce 45
Carrot & Raisin Cake 185
Carrot, Tomato, & Pepper Soup 78
Ceviche of Sole 105
Cheddar & Leek Pasta Sauce 153
Cheese & Chive Sauce 45
Cheese & Date Bread 137

Cheese & Pear Scones 141
Cheese, Herb, & Onion Bread 135
Cheese-topped Vegetables
    Provençal 41
Chicken Breasts with Vermouth &
    Watercress Sauce 98
Chicken & Mustard Sauce 45
Chicken & Vegetable Stir-fry 96
Chicken Medley 180
Chicken Teriyaki 97
Chick-pea & Mixed-bean
    Casserole 119
Chili & Macaroni Bake 154
Chili Con Carne 34
Chilled Cucumber & Mint Soup 27
Citrus Dressing 77
Club Sandwich 137
Cod, Corn, & Broccoli Crêpes 140
Coq au Vin 48
Coriander & Chili Polenta with Spicy
    Sauce 118
Corn & Pea Soup 172
Corn, Leek, & Mushroom Pizza 144
Country Vegetable & Barley
    Casserole 55
Crunchy Mixed Vegetable Stir-fry 182
Curried Chick-pea & Brown Rice
    Salad 57

Eastern Mediterranean Casserole 90
Eggplant & Tomato Crostini 81
Eggplant, Tomato, & Zucchini Pasta
    Bake 51

Farmhouse Vegetable Stew 53
Fat-free Chicken Broth 76
Fettuccine with Spinach & Blue
    Cheese Sauce 152
Flounder Fillets with Mushroom, Dill,
    & Lemon 109
Fresh Figs with Berries & Orange
    Cream 124

Fresh Tomato & Basil Soup 26
Fruit & Nut Pilaf 159
Fruit & Spice Coffeecake 139
Fruit Bars 143
Fusilli Salad 156
Fusilli with Zucchini & Lemon 117

Green Bean & Kohlrabi Salad 82
Green Pepper & Avocado Dip 80

Halibut Steaks Provençal 108
Herbed Chicken & Potato Bake 166
Herbed Mushroom Pâté 28
Herbed Potato Cakes 169
Honey-baked Fruit 67

Lamb & Lentil Casserole 179
Lamb & Vegetable Curry 170
Lamb & Vegetable Stir-fry 46
Lamb, Eggplant, & Chick-pea
    Casserole 100
Lemon & Mint Turkey Burgers 95
Light Vegetable Broth 76

Mediterranean Pasta Medley with
    Tuna & Corn 151
Mediterranean Vegetable Lasagna 50
Minted Zucchini & Pea Soup 79
Mixed Berry Compote 187
Mixed Root Vegetables 85
Mixed Tomato & Pepper Salad with
    Parsley Dressing 56
Moroccan Potato Salad 165
Multi-colored Mixed-bean Salad 59
Mushroom & Zucchini Pasta
    Sauce 153
Mushroom Risotto 54
Mushroom Sauce 45
Mussel & Potato Soup 102
Mustard Yogurt Dressing 77

Nectarine Choux Ring 68

Orange & Cinnamon Crêpes 147
Orange & Date Salad 125
Oriental Dressing 77
Oriental Noodle Salad with
    Chicken 115
Oriental Salad 82
Oriental Seafood Soup 103
Oriental Vegetable Stir-fry 40
Oven-roasted Root Vegetables 183

Papaya & Bean Sprout Salad 83
Parsley or Tarragon Sauce 45
Pasta Shells with Smoked Fish,
    Shrimp, & Garden Peas 150
Pasta Twists with Smoked Ham &
    Tomato Sauce 148
Peach & Lemon Cheesecake 146
Peach & Mint Soup 123
Peach & Pear Compote 187
Pears with Blue Cheese 31
Pineapple Bran Muffins 143
Pineapple Upside-down Cake 66
Pink Salmon & Sour Cream Baked
    Potato 168
Pizza Dough 37
Pork & Lima Bean Bake 180
Pork Pita Pockets 93
Potato & Carrot Soup 164
Potato, Carrot, & Parsnip Bake 167
Profiteroles 69

Quick Cherry Brulée 63
Quinoa Salad with Grapes & Snow-
    peas 114

Raisin & Lemon Cookies 142
Raspberry Meringue Nests 70
Ratatouille 86
Ratatouille Ring 52
Red Bean & Three-mushroom
    Salad 175

Red Onion Marmalade 94
Red Snapper Parcels 110
Red Summer Fruit Roulade 62
Rhubarb, Strawberry, & Anise Phyllo
    Pie 127
Roasted Paprika Potatoes 85
Roasted Pepper & Brown Lentil
    Dip 173
Roasted Vegetables 60
Roast Pepper & Mushroom Pizza 38

Sage & Onion Sauce 45
Sautéed Potatoes with Bacon &
    Herbs 23
Sautéed Root Vegetables 61
Savory Rice 22
Seafood Cocktail 30
Seafood Ragout 110
Seared Cod with Green Chili
    Sauce 111
Shrimp & Monkfish Kabobs 106
Smoked Bacon, Egg, & Corn Baked
    Potato 168
Smoked Chicken & Mushroom
    Risotto 162
Smoked Ham, Tomato, & Basil
    Pizza 39
Smoked Salmon Salad 104
Smoked Tofu & Vegetable Kabobs 176
Spaghetti with Mixed Vegetables 153
Spiced Apple Strudel 71
Spiced Chicken & Pepper Rolls 33
Spicy Fruit Compote 186
Spicy Roast Chicken 44
Spicy Seafood Pizza 36
Spicy Shrimp & Mushroom Phyllo
    Clusters 43
Spicy Tomato & Mushroom Baked
    Potato 168
Spicy Vegetable Couscous 161

Spinach & Bell Pepper Frittata 87
Steamed Broccoli with Lemon &
    Parmesan 84
Steamed Chocolate & Cherry
    Pudding 184
Stir-fried Julienne of Vegetables 61
Stir-fried Turkey with Spring
    Vegetables 47
Strawberry Chocolate Flan 126
Strong Vegetable Broth 76
Stuffed Bell Peppers 90
Stuffed Peppers with Tomato & Chili
    Salsa 160
Sun-dried Tomato & Olive Soda
    Bread 136
Sweet-&-sour Mixed-bean Salad 174

Tomato Sauce 37
Tortellini Primavera 155
Tropical Tapioca 128
Tuna & Shrimp Risotto 163
Tuna & Watercress Dip 29
Tuna & Zucchini Omelet 32
Tunisian Couscous 121
Turkey Stir-fry with Bok Choy &
    Noodles 94

Vegetarian Chili 178
Venison Chili 101
Vermicelli with Tomato & Basil 116

Warm Pasta Salad 58
Whole-wheat Raisin & Orange Muffins 138
Whole-wheat Spaghetti with Country-
    style Chicken Sauce 149
Wild & Basmati Rice Pilaf with Dried
    Cranberries 120

Zucchini, Cheese, & Onion Potato
    Bake 35